Greg Perry

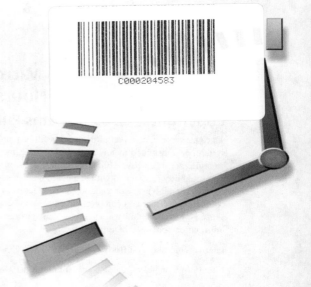

SAMS Teach Yourself
Microsoft®
Windows® Me
Millennium
Edition
in 24 Hours

SAMS

A Division of Macmillan USA
201 West 103rd St., Indianapolis, Indiana, 46290 USA

Sams Teach Yourself Microsoft® Windows® Me in 24 Hours

Copyright © 2000 by Sams Publishing

International Standard Book Number: 0-672-31953-5

Library of Congress Catalog Card Number: 00-104813

Printed in the United States of America

First Printing: July 2000

02   01   00   4   3   2

Trademarks

Warning and Disclaimer

ACQUISITIONS EDITOR
Betsy Brown

DEVELOPMENT EDITOR
Laura N. Williams

MANAGING EDITOR
Charlotte Clapp

PROJECT EDITOR
Elizabeth Roberts Finney

COPY EDITOR
Rhonda Tinch-Mize

INDEXER
Eric Schroeder

PROOFREADERS
Kimberly Campanello
Jason Hicks

TECHNICAL EDITORS
Bill Bruns
Natasha Knight
Dallas Releford

TEAM COORDINATOR
Amy Patton

INTERIOR DESIGNER
Gary Adair

COVER DESIGNER
Aren Howell

PRODUCTION
Jeannette McKay

Contents at a Glance

Contents

About the Author

GREG PERRY is a speaker and writer on both the programming and the applications sides of computing. He is known for his skills at bringing advanced computer topics down to the novice's level. Perry has been a programmer and trainer since the early 1980s. He received his first degree in computer science and then a master's degree in corporate finance. Perry's books have sold more than two million copies worldwide, with most of his titles being translated into several foreign languages. His works include *Absolute Beginner's Guide to Programming*, *Absolute Beginner's Guide to C*, *Sams Teach Yourself Office 2000 in 24 Hours*, and *Sams Teach Yourself Visual Basic 6 in 21 Days*. He also writes about rental-property management, designs and produces Web pages, and travels as a hobby.

Dedication

One family stands out from all others. I dedicate this book to my friends,
the Sutton family in Skiatook. Knowing all of you is a blessing.

Acknowledgments

I have the opportunity to work with the best people in the publishing business. My sincere thanks go to the editors and staff at Sams Publishing who strive to produce computer books that teach all levels of computer users from beginners to experts. The people at Sams Publishing take their jobs seriously because they want readers to have only the best books possible.

During the production of this book, Laura Williams had patience with me and that says tons. We exchanged current events as well as manuscript chapters, and I know that Laura's thinking is right.

To correct my problems, Elizabeth Roberts Finney worked hard but then went and got married during the production of this text; I suppose her priorities are exactly where they should be!

In addition to Laura and Elizabeth, Dawn Pearson and Rhonda Tinch-Mize made my writing acceptable and I'm grateful. The Technical Editors, Bill Bruns and Dallas Releford, had quite a job to do given my writing, but the job got done well.

I alone am responsible for any problems if there are any.

My lovely and gracious bride, Jayne, stands by my side day in and day out. Thank you, my dear Jayne. Thanks also to my Dad and Mom, Glen and Bettye Perry, who are my biggest fans. I love you all.

Tell Us What You Think!

As the reader of this book, *you* are our most important critic and commentator. We value your opinion and want to know what we're doing right, what we could do better, what areas you'd like to see us publish in, and any other words of wisdom you're willing to pass our way.

You can fax, email, or write me directly to let me know what you did or didn't like about this book—as well as what we can do to make our books stronger.

Please note that I cannot help you with technical problems related to the topic of this book, and that due to the high volume of mail I receive, I might not be able to reply to every message.

When you write, please be sure to include this book's title and author as well as your name and phone or fax number. I will carefully review your comments and share them with the author and editors who worked on the book.

Fax: 317-581-4770

Email: windows_sams@macmillanusa.com

Mail: Mark Taber
         Associate Publisher
         Sams Publishing
         201 West 103rd Street
         Indianapolis, IN 46290 USA

Introduction

You probably are anxious to get started with your 24-hour Windows Me tutorial. Windows Me is an exciting operating system by Microsoft, the third Windows 9*x* operating system version since the original release of Windows 98 back in 1998; the wait was more than worth it.

This book's goal is to get you up to speed as quickly as possible. Take just a few preliminary moments to acquaint yourself with the design of this book described in the next few sections.

What's New with Windows

Different, better, and still the same best describes how Windows Me compares to previous versions of Windows. Despite the similarities, there are major differences in Windows Me that you should know about ahead of time so that you can use Windows Me the way it is supposed to be used. Microsoft designed Windows Me so that you can concentrate on using your software and hardware rather than concentrate on using Windows Me.

Windows Me improves upon the Windows 95 and Windows 98 interfaces that have become the standard. If you are new to the Windows environments—perhaps because you upgraded from Windows 3.1 or from an Apple operating system—consider yourself fortunate! You are about to be impressed. Some of the Windows Me key features are

- The Internet's online environment is more closely associated with the Windows desktop.

- The new Windows Media Player plays all your favorite multimedia content with ease.

- The Start menu is more operational and hides little-used programs until you're ready to access them. In addition, you can make menu changes on-the-fly without messy dialog boxes.

- Advanced system tools, such as the automatic update of Windows system files when they get damaged, now help protect your computer files and monitor your hardware.

- Improved hardware support features enable you to attach new devices into your computer without having to set hardware switches or determine appropriate interrupt settings.

- One of the benefits that current Windows users will appreciate is that Windows Me does not require as many mouse clicks and double-clicks as previous versions of Windows did.

- Windows Me does most of the setup work for you when you want to network another computer to yours.
- Monitor newsgroups and make postings from Outlook Express's common interface.
- Your desktop now becomes an online access tool that lets you access Internet Web pages as easily as you access your own PC's files.

What This Book Will Do for You

Although this is not a reference book, you'll learn almost every aspect of Windows Me from the user's point of view. There are many advanced technical details that most users will never need, and this book does not take up your time with those. I know that you want to get up to speed with Windows Me in 24 hours, and this book fulfills its goal.

Both the background and the theory that a new Windows Me user needs is presented. In addition to the background discussions, this book is practical and provides more than 75 useful step-by-step To Do tasks that you can work through to gain hands-on experience. The To Do tasks guide you through all the common Windows Me actions you'll need to make Windows Me work for you, instead of you working to use Windows Me.

Can This Book Really Teach Windows Me in 24 Hours?

Yes. You can master each chapter in one hour or less (by the way, chapters are referred to as "hours" in the rest of the book). Although some chapters are longer than others, the material is balanced. The longer chapters contain several tasks, and the shorter chapters contain background material. The balance provided by the tasks, background, and insightful explanations and tips make learning Windows Me using this book fresh at every page.

Conventions Used in This Book

There is generally a question-and-answer section at the end of the chapter to reinforce ideas. This book also uses several common conventions to help teach the Windows Me topics. Here is a summary of the typographical conventions:

- The first time a new term appears, the term is *italicized*.
- Commands and computer output appear in a special `monospaced` computer font.
- Words you type appear in a **boldfaced** computer font.
- If a task requires you to select from a menu, the commands are separated with a comma. For example, this book uses File, Save As to select the Save As command from the File menu.

In addition to typographical conventions, the following special elements are included to set off different types of information to make them easily recognizable:

Special notes augment the material you are reading in each hour. They clarify concepts and procedures.

You'll find numerous tips that offer shortcuts and solutions to common problems.

The Caution sections warn you about pitfalls. Reading them will save you time and trouble.

Who Should Read This Book

Although this book is geared toward beginning computer and Windows users, advanced users will find it handy as well. Readers rarely believe that lofty claim for good reason, but the design of this book and the nature of Windows Me make it possible for this book to address such a wide audience. Here is why: Windows Me is a major improvement over the previous versions of Windows because of its ease of integration into the networking, multimedia, and Internet's online technology. If you do not yet use the Internet, you'll still appreciate the new features and improvements that Microsoft put into Windows Me.

Readers unfamiliar with windowed environments will find plenty of introductory help to bring them up to speed quickly. This book teaches you how to start Windows Me, how to exit Windows Me, and how to manage almost every aspect of Windows Me. This book talks to beginners but does not talk down to beginners.

For readers who presently use Windows 98, this book also addresses you. Here is how: There are several sidebars that explain how a specific Windows Me feature improves upon or replaces a Windows 98 feature. With your fundamental base of Windows 98 understanding, you'll appreciate the new Windows Me features. Windows Me is similar to Windows 98 and Windows 95, so you will feel comfortable learning Windows Me. But there are more than enough new features to keep Windows 95 and Windows 98 users interested and happy for a long time.

What To Do Now

Turn the page and get started on your 24-hour tutorial!

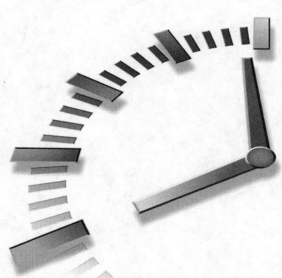

PART I

Wake Up with Windows Millennium Edition (Me)

Hour

HOUR 1

What Windows Me Is All About

Who says that a productive computer user cannot have fun being productive? Windows Millennium Edition, also called Windows Me and often just Windows, from the Microsoft Corporation is fun, friendly, and powerful. This hour introduces you to Windows Me. You will learn some of the goals that the Microsoft programmers had in mind when they designed Windows Me. Also, you will learn how Windows Me improves upon previous versions of Windows and other operating environments by fully integrating an online environment into the operating system.

In this hour, you will

- Discover how Microsoft designed Windows Me to be as easy and intuitive as possible
- Learn what makes Windows Me more powerful than many other operating environments

- Start Windows Me

- Log on to Windows Me

- Access and manipulate common Windows Me controls, such as command buttons and check boxes

- Learn when you need to perform a shutdown of Windows Me

Getting a Feel for Windows Me

Most users like the look and feel of Windows Me, and they appreciate the fact that Windows Me is also enjoyable to use. Although Windows Me is both fun and easy to master, it is also a computer interface system that offers tremendous power for anyone who uses PCs. With Windows Me you can access your computer's hardware, data files, and online content easily, even if you are new to computers.

Windows Millennium is actually the third edition of the operating system that began as Windows 98. Windows Millennium includes the latest support for hardware, online interaction, and networked-usability of any version of Windows 98 or Windows 95 that came before Windows Me. Throughout this and the next 23 hours, you'll not only learn the fundamentals of Windows in general, but you'll also master the specific new features that make Windows Millennium so powerful and easy to use.

Windows Me contains a computer interface that attempts to please all groups of people, including novice computer users and advanced computer programmers. To achieve the lofty goal of pleasing a broad spectrum of users, Microsoft designed an interface that is intuitive without being intrusive. In addition to the usable interface, Windows Me blurs the distinction between your home or office PC and other computers around the world. The Windows Me operating environment incorporates the online world because the information you want is not always on your hard disk. Windows Me helps you access the Internet as easily as you access the files on your own PC.

Figure 1.1 shows a typical Windows Me screen that Windows Me users might see. The Windows Me screen is often called a *desktop*, which you will learn to manage just as you manage the desk at which you sit. Your screen might show a different set of *icons*, pictures and text, and perhaps your desktop's background is different, but you'll surely see many of the same elements on your screen.

The artwork that forms the background for a Windows Me screen is called *wallpaper*, which comes from a graphics file you can supply. In Hour 4, "Understanding the My Computer Window," you will see how you can change or remove the wallpaper if you don't like the artwork on your desktop.

FIGURE 1.1

The Windows Me screen, like a clean desktop, is normally free of clutter.

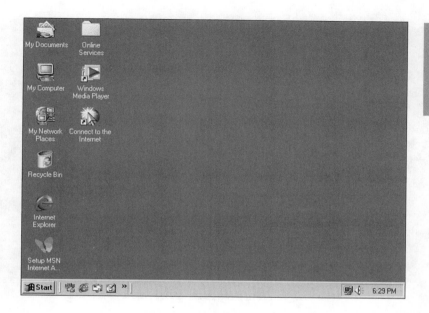

If you've upgraded from Windows 95, you will appreciate that Microsoft did not dramatically change the Windows Me interface. Nevertheless, Microsoft did add considerable customization tools to Windows so that you can change the way the Windows Me interface operates and looks, even making your desktop look much like a Web page.

Figure 1.2 shows the same Windows Me desktop as before, except that the desktop contains a graphical wallpaper file to make things more interesting. In addition, notice a column of buttons at the right of the screen that gives you one-button access to popular Internet sites by using the *Internet Explorer Channel Bar*. The channel bar enables you to switch from Internet site to site by using a television's channel-button analogy.

Throughout this entire 24-hour tutorial, references will be made to *online services*, the *Internet*, *Web integration*, *remote computers*, and other terms that refer to you using your PC within the framework of an Internet connected environment. That Internet environment might come from a dedicated Internet connection at work, a modem at home, or another way you interact with the Internet community. If you don't use the Internet, that's okay. Windows Me will not force you to do so. Windows Me stands on its own as the best PC graphical environment on the market, and you don't have to be online to enjoy its benefits.

FIGURE 1.2

Wallpaper and online services can make your desktop less boring.

The Windows Me screen acts like a desktop from which to work on your computer. If you want to write letters with a word processor, start the word processor program from the Windows Me environment. Windows Me is always there to help you interact with your programs and with the computer hardware.

Computers controlled by graphical user interfaces (GUIs), such as Windows Me, no longer require the tedium of typed commands required by older computer environments. Windows Me is extremely graphical in nature. Instead of typing a command that directs the computer to start a program, you use the mouse or keyboard to point to an icon on the screen to activate the matching program.

If you are fairly new to computers, you might not understand why you would want to use Windows Me. Perhaps you've used a word processor or a spreadsheet but never have taken the time to find out what this Windows stuff is all about. Other newcomers to Windows Me might have migrated to the PC world from a Mac, from Windows 3.1, or from a big, mainframe computer. In a nutshell, Windows Me is all of the following:

- An operating system that manages your hardware and software interactions. Windows Me provides uniform access to your system so that programs can more accurately use your system's resources (such as disks and printers).

- A graphical user interface that enables you to start programs, go online, and control hardware graphically.

- Total Web integration that blurs the distinction between the PC on your desk and the Internet.

- A Web-based desktop environment that complements or replaces your standard Windows Me desktop. You can place Web pages right on your desktop instead of accessing the Internet solely from an Internet browser program. If you want help, you can search Windows Me help files or access the Internet to locate a help topic—all from within your desktop environment (see Figure 1.3).

FIGURE 1.3

The Windows help area searches both your PC and, optionally, the Internet to give you answers when you need assistance.

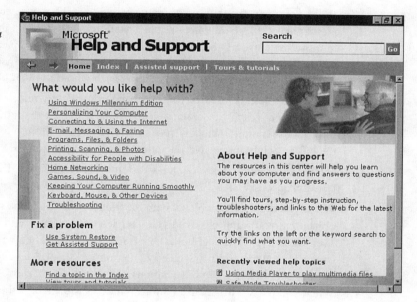

- A more efficient disk storage system called *FAT32* that makes your hard disks capable of holding almost twice as much as before.

- A safer system security that helps protect against possible *virus programs* (programs that can destroy disk contents) and also keeps your system fine-tuned and running properly. With Internet access, you will be able to download the latest Windows updates as Microsoft releases future enhancements.

- A network management system that helps seamlessly integrate a *network* (a wired connection to other computers) and the Internet into your work environment.

Possibly the single greatest reason to use Windows Me is this: Microsoft designed Windows Me so that you can concentrate on using your software and hardware—not so that you have to concentrate on using Windows Me commands. As you'll see throughout this book, the keyboard and mouse complement each other to give you easy control over every aspect of Windows Me.

Mouse Around

The odds are good that you've used a mouse if you've used a computer before. Using the mouse involves following the mouse cursor around the screen. The *mouse cursor* is the pointing arrow that moves as you move your mouse. In Hour 4, you learn how to change the mouse cursor shape from the arrow to something else.

Here's a quick review of the possible mouse actions you can perform:

- When you *move* the mouse, you physically move the mouse across your desk. (You might have a trackball, which remains stationary as you spin the trackball's sphere to move the cursor. Other mouse alternatives include touch pads that you point to and run your finger over to simulate mouse clicks and movements.) When you point to an object on the screen, you are moving the mouse to that object.

- When you click the mouse, you press and immediately release the left mouse button. To select graphical screen objects, you often click the left button. You use your right mouse button to display special pop-up menus. Hour 4 explains how to swap the left and right mouse button actions if you are left-handed.

- When you double-click, you press and immediately release the left mouse button twice in succession.

- When you drag screen objects with the mouse, you move the mouse cursor over an object that you want to move to another screen location. With the mouse cursor over the object, press and hold the left mouse button. The item under the mouse cursor is now temporarily welded to the mouse cursor. As you move the mouse (while still holding the mouse button), the screen object moves with the cursor. When you release the mouse button, Windows Me anchors the object in the mouse cursor's new position. In Windows terminology, *drag and drop* refers to the action of moving a screen object (such as an icon) to a different location.

Later hours will teach you additional ways to use the mouse. For example, the mouse can help you create special links, called *shortcuts*, to programs you use often. In addition, you can use the mouse to copy objects, such as files, from one location to another.

You can almost always use the keyboard instead of the mouse to perform many Windows Me operations. For many users, using the mouse is often easier than using the keyboard. If you are uncomfortable using a mouse, don't fret—mouse actions soon become second nature.

1

If you've used Windows 95 or an earlier Windows version, you'll appreciate how Windows Me enables you to use a single-click to select screen objects instead of the double-click so common in previous versions. Depending on your setup, you can even launch programs by resting the mouse over an icon without clicking at all! You learn how to add this one-click selection to Windows Me objects in Hour 12, "How Windows Ties into the Web."

First Things First

Windows Me automatically loads when you turn on your computer.

> To issue the Ctrl+Alt+Delete key combination, press and hold down the keys sequentially: Press and hold down the Ctrl key, press and hold down the Alt key, and then press the Delete key (you'll actually hold down all three keys). Release all three keys at once to begin the reboot process. A window appears, asking if you're sure and you must issue the reboot key sequence once more to activate the reboot. Unless your PC freezes completely, reboot sparingly. This lesson's final section explains how to shut down your PC properly.

Logging On

If you are not connected to a network, nothing in this section applies to you. Even if you access the Internet, you do not need to know this section's material if your computer is not part of a networking system. You can skip ahead to the next section, "Sampling Windows Me."

If your PC is connected to a network, you must log on to the network when you start Windows Me.

You will have to ask the person responsible for installing the networked Windows Me on your PC for your username and password. After you receive the logon information, you can log on to the computer and access Windows Me. The following To Do item explains how to log on.

To Do: Logging into Windows Me

1. When you see the logon screen, type your username exactly as the system administrator set it up. Often, your username is your full name or your first initial and last name.

▼ 2. Press the Tab key.

To Do

▼   3. Type your password exactly as the system administrator set it up. Asterisks appear
        in place of the actual password you type so that no one looking over your shoulder
        can read your password.

▲   4. Press Enter to start Windows Me.

If you receive an error message, you must check with the system administrator to make
sure that you are properly authorized to use the networked Windows Me. If this is the
first time you or anyone else has logged on with your username, the initial password you
enter will be the permanent password, unless you change the password later. Windows
Me requests the first password twice to be sure that you type the initial password exactly
as it should be.

> By design, networks enable more than one user access to the same files. In
> other words, assuming that you have the proper electronic authorization,
> you can access files stored on any person's PC that is connected to your PC.
> The extra benefits that a network provides also require extra security pre-
> cautions so that unauthorized users do not have access to other people's
> files.

You can change your password by double-clicking the Windows Me Control Panel's
Password icon and entering your current and new password. Click the Change Windows
Password button to change the password. If you need further help with the Control Panel,
turn to Hour 4.

Command Controls

As you work with Windows Me, you'll see all kinds of windows appear and disappear. A
window such as the one shown in Figure 1.4 is sometimes called a *dialog box*. Dialog
boxes contain various *controls* with which to manage Windows Me. These controls can
be *command buttons* that you click with your mouse to start or cancel a task; *check boxes*
with a check mark, indicating an item you selected by clicking the mouse over the box;
and *option buttons* that you select from a choice of options. Some dialog boxes contain
multiple tabbed pages so that you can read and select from two or more pages of controls
within the same dialog box.

Page tabs

FIGURE 1.4

Dialog box windows often contain several controls that select options and determine behavior.

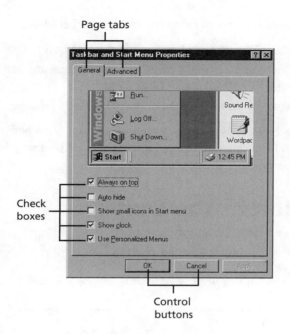

Check boxes

Control buttons

Figure 1.4 shows a dialog box called the Taskbar and Start Menu Properties dialog box. You learn all about the taskbar in the next section. For now, concentrate on the various controls you see in the dialog box. Although you can use your keyboard to select any control, pointing and clicking your mouse is often much easier.

There are three ways to select an onscreen command button:

1. Click the button with the mouse.
2. Press Tab to highlight the buttons in succession. Shift+Tab moves backward. You will know that a button is highlighted when a dotted outline appears around the button's caption. Moving the highlight between onscreen controls is called *changing the focus*. As soon as the focus (the dotted highlight) appears on the button you want to select, press Enter to activate that button.
3. Press Alt plus the underlined letter on the button's caption. This combined keystroke is called a *hotkey*. Figure 1.4 contains only one command button with such a hotkey—the Apply key. You can select the Apply command button by pressing Alt+A.

Figure 1.4 contains five check boxes at the left of the dialog box. Certain windows need check boxes to indicate a yes or no possibility.

There are three ways to check (or uncheck) a check box:

1. Click either the check box or the message next to the check box with the mouse.
2. Move the focus to the check box text (by pressing Tab or Shift+Tab) and press Enter.
3. Press Alt plus the hotkey of the check box's message.

In Hour 2, "How to Manage Windows," you will learn how to leave a window without completely closing the window; it will be out of your way, but you will be able to return to it whenever you want.

Save Before You Quit

You are probably anxious to get started, but before you learn more about using Windows Me, you must learn how to quit Windows Me properly. Because of the integration of Windows Me and your computer's hardware and software, you must take a few extra steps when quitting your Windows Me session and turning off your computer.

> If you do not properly shut down Windows Me, you can lose work that you just completed. At the worst, you can damage a Windows Me configuration file and cause problems for Windows Me the next time you start your PC.

Surely you've noticed the button in the lower-left corner of the Windows Me screen labeled Start. This area of the screen is known as the *taskbar*, and this button is called the *Start button*. The taskbar is perhaps the most important element in Windows Me because you'll use it to launch and switch between running programs. Windows Me *multitasks*, which means that you can run more than one program at the same time. In other words, you can download a file from another computer, print a spreadsheet, listen to an opera on an audio CD, and type with a word processor, all at the same time. The taskbar lists each program currently running. Figure 1.5 shows a taskbar that lists two programs and the My Computer window in memory at the same time.

> Think of the taskbar as a television channel changer. On a television, there are several channels with programs going at the same time; you can switch between the channels by using the remote control. When you run more than one Windows Me program, you can switch among the programs by clicking the program buttons in the taskbar.

FIGURE 1.5

The taskbar lists every program running.

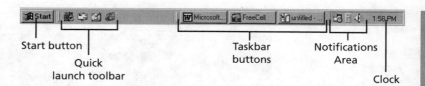

Start button

Quick
launch toolbar

Taskbar
buttons

Notifications
Area

Clock

The taskbar does more than list and manage running programs—it is the starting point for just about everything you do in Windows Me. If you want to rearrange files, start programs, change screen colors, modify the mouse, or view the contents of files, the taskbar contains the power to do all those things. The taskbar is the launch pad for just about everything you'll want to do in Windows Me.

The taskbar also contains the commands you need to shut down Windows Me and your computer. In Hour 3, "Take Windows Me to Task," you'll delve much more deeply into the operations of the taskbar. At this point though, you will learn just enough to master the Windows Me shutdown process because without the proper shutdown, you face the risky consequences of data loss, as you learned at the start of this section.

Place the mouse cursor over the Start button, but do not click the mouse button. After a brief pause, Windows Me displays a small ToolTip caption box next to the mouse cursor that reads Click here to begin. If you are unsure of what a Windows Me button does, move the mouse cursor over the button and wait a moment.

When you click the Start button on the taskbar, the Start menu pops up, as shown in Figure 1.6. The Start menu gives you access to every part of your computer. Table 1.1 describes what each option of the Start menu does. From the Start menu, you can start programs, check disk space, manage files, and properly shut down the computer. You might also add additional programs at the top of the taskbar to launch those programs more quickly. For now, you should master how to shut down your PC.

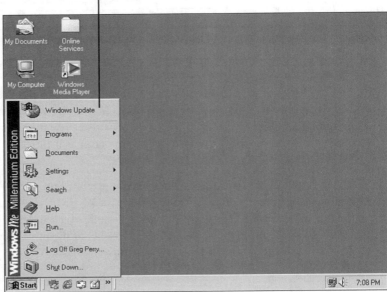

You can add programs here

FIGURE 1.6

The Start menu is the command center for the rest of Windows Me.

TABLE 1.1 Common Start Menu Commands

Command	Description
Programs	Displays lists of program groups and names that you can run.
Documents	Displays a list of documents, or data files, that you've recently opened and might want to return to. Windows Me works from a data-driven viewpoint and enables you to work on your data without worrying about tedious program-starting details. Selecting a document, no matter which program created that document, launches the program and loads that data document into the program.
Settings	Enables you to change the configuration of Windows Me.
Search	Enables you to search your PC's and other computer's files for specific data.
Help	Provides online help for the various tasks you can perform in Windows Me.
Run	Gives you the ability to execute programs or open program group folders if you know the proper commands.
Log Off	If you work in a multiuser environment, you and others can log on to Windows Me, and Windows Me behaves the way you set it up in your personal profile. Some Windows Me Start menus do not contain a Log Off option.
Shut Down	Enables you to safely shut down your computer without losing data that you might otherwise lose if you did not shut down properly.

1

Although you can select the various Start menu commands, please understand that the most important command on the Start menu is the Shut Down command. Before you do too much, even before you really master the ins and outs of the Start menu, you should read the rest of this section to learn how to shut down your computer safely. You don't want to write the first chapter of a best-selling novel only to find that Windows Me sent the chapter into oblivion because you did not shut down the computer properly before turning off the power.

Activating Menu Commands

Windows Me menus list various options and commands available to you at the time. When confronted with a menu, such as the Start menu, there are several ways you can select the item you want.

You can point to an item on the menu with the mouse. As you move the mouse cursor over the menu items, a highlight follows the mouse cursor through the menu, clearly showing you which menu item the mouse cursor is over. If your hands are on the keyboard when you display a menu, you can press the up and down arrow keys to move the highlight through the menu's commands.

Some menu commands, such as the Shut Down command, contain ellipses (...) to the right of the command name. The ellipsis indicates that if you choose this command, a dialog box appears, requiring additional information.

Windows Me does not always display a complete menu's list of options. Windows attempts to display only those menu options you use frequently and hides the rest. You can display the entire menu by clicking the arrows at the bottom of a menu. You can control whether Windows displays the full menu or only the *Personalized menus* as they are known and as you'll learn in Hour 3.

Some menu commands, such as the Start menu's Programs and Documents commands, display arrows to the right of the command names. The arrows indicate that other command menus appear if you select from those commands. Sometimes Windows Me menu commands *cascade* (trigger additional menus, often called *submenus*) several levels deep, such as the one shown in Figure 1.7. You can decrease the cascade, removing one or more of the extra cascaded menu levels, by moving the mouse one menu to the left or by pressing the Esc key. (Esc always removes the current menu.)

Some menu commands, such as Help, do not contain anything to the right of the command name. These commands perform an immediate service, such as displaying a Help screen, displaying a menu, or starting a program from your disk drive.

If a menu command contains an underlined letter, such as Help, you can select that menu command by pressing Alt plus the letter. Alt+H is the hotkey that activates the Help menu command.

FIGURE 1.7

Some menus trigger other menus, producing a cascaded menu look.

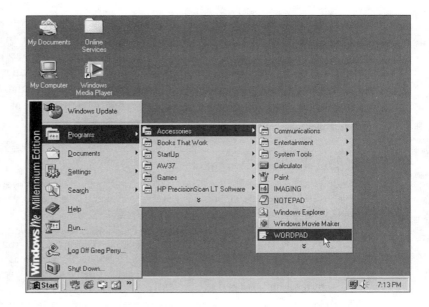

If you explore a bit and display a cascaded menu or select another command from the Start menu, press Esc until the Start menu disappears, and the Start button returns to normal. As mentioned earlier, this is an important time to learn about the Shut Down command.

Press the Start button once again and select the Shut Down command by clicking on the down arrow to display the option. The ellipsis after the words Shut Down indicates that a dialog box window will appear. Figure 1.8 shows the resulting Shut Down window. There is more than one way to shut down your computer, however, depending on your current need. In addition, your Shut Down menu might contain more or fewer options depending on your PC's configuration.

FIGURE 1.8

You must decide how you want to shut down the computer.

Here are three ways to select an option from a drop-down list of choices:

- Point to one of the options with the mouse and click the mouse button.
- Use the keyboard's up and down arrow keys to move the focus (the focus's dotted line surrounds the selected option button) among the selections.
- Press Alt plus the underlined letter of the option you want to select. For example, Alt+R is the hotkey sequence for Restart.

Simply selecting an option does not trigger any action. After you select the desired option, you must activate the OK command button to execute that option's command. If you choose Cancel, Windows Me removes the Shut Down window and returns you to the Windows Me environment. If you push the Help command button, Windows Me displays online help that describes the options in more detail.

Table 1.2 describes the three most common shut down options. (You might have more depending on your computer's configuration.) Most of the time, you will select the Shutdown option because you are turning off the computer. When you select the first option, Windows Me pauses briefly and then displays a message telling you that you can turn off the computer's power. Select the Shutdown option now and click the Yes button to initiate the shut down.

> When you see command buttons, Windows Me highlights one of them by darkening the button's edges, as shown on the OK button in Figure 1.8. If you press Enter, Windows Me activates the OK button for you. As a shortcut to using Windows Me and command buttons, you can always press Enter to trigger the activation of the highlighted button instead of using the mouse or keyboard to find and press that same button.

TABLE 1.2 The Shut Down Commands and Their Descriptions

Command	Description
Shut Down	Writes all unsaved information to disk and prepares Windows Me so that you can turn off your PC. If your hardware supports the feature, your PC can power down automatically when you select the Shut Down option.
Restart	Performs a shut down but then reboots the computer for you. Sometimes, you will be instructed to restart Windows Me after installing a new program or after changing a Windows Me option.
Stand By	Sends your PC into a low-power state with all your programs and data awaiting you, but it shuts down the spinning of the hard drive and turns your monitor to a power-saving blank state.

You might have to develop the habit of shutting down Windows Me properly before turning off the computer. Perhaps you can stick a note to the computer's on/off switch until you get used to running the Shut Down command. Again, the Shut Down command is cheap insurance against data loss, and the Shut Down habit is a good one to develop.

Summary

You are off to a great start! It's time to push your own Start button, gear up your mind's memory chips, and begin exploring Windows Me to learn what it can do for you. Over the next 23 hours of study and tutorial, you will master the Windows Me environment and learn many shortcuts.

Keep in mind that Windows Me is not an end in itself. The application programs that you want to run are the most important parts of using your computer. It is Windows Me's job to help you work with your applications as painlessly as possible.

Q&A

Q When will I have to log on to Windows Me?

A If your computer is connected to a network, chances are good that you will have to log on before you can use Windows Me. In a network environment, computers have connections to each other so users have physical access to other people's files. By delegating usernames and passwords, the system administrator assigns protection and privileges to all users on the system.

Q Why do asterisks appear when I enter my network password?

A Asterisks appear in place of the actual characters that you type so that someone looking over your shoulder cannot steal your password.

Q What happens if I do not use the Shut Down procedures for my computer?

A If you do not shut down your computer before turning off the power, you can lose data files or even system configuration files. Most of the time, you probably will be okay if you do not shut down the computer properly, but your data is worth too much not to get into the habit of properly shutting down the system and safely storing all data.

Workshop

The quiz and exercise questions are designed to test your knowledge of the material covered in this hour. The answers are in Appendix C, "Answers to Quizzes."

Quiz

1. Why is the Windows screen called the *desktop*?

2. *True or false*: Windows Me helps you locate files on the Internet.

3. What is the difference between moving and dragging your mouse?

4. What is the artwork called on your Windows desktop?

5. Describe why your Windows Start menu cascades.

Exercises

1. Start your computer and open your Windows Start menu. Look through the options and programs there.

2. Shut down your computer to a powered-off state. Turn the computer back on again. As your computer starts, notice all the messages that go by and the sounds your disk makes. Windows Millennium requires quite a lot of overhead and Windows gathers that overhead and tests your computer's memory and hardware every time you turn on your machine.

HOUR 2

How to Manage Windows

In this hour, you are going to learn a lot about the Windows Me interface and become comfortable with managing windows and icons.

To help you learn the Windows Me interface, you will follow along with several practice examples in this hour. The coverage is so complete that some people who have used Windows for years might not know more than you'll learn in these pages. This hour's techniques will help you manage almost every aspect of Windows Me that you will work with in the future. In other words, after you master the basics of the window and screen management tools, you'll use those capabilities in all your Windows Me applications work.

In this hour, you will

- Discover why windows management is important
- Learn what the parts of a window are called
- Resize and move windows
- Learn when the System menu is useful
- Change the appearance and behavior of windows and toolbars

Windows appear all over the place when you work with Windows Me—
that's why it's called Windows! Therefore, learning proper windows management now will reap big-time savings and reduce confusion in the future.

I Do Windows!

The first window that you will work with is called the My Computer window. This lesson focuses on managing the window, whereas Hour 4, "Understanding the My Computer
Window," explains how to use the contents of the My Computer window. First, locate the
My Computer icon on your Windows Me desktop. Double-click the icon to open the My
Computer window. Most icons on the desktop open to windows when you double-click
them, as you'll see throughout this book. Some icons produce program windows, whereas
others produce windows from which you select additional items.

Figure 2.1 shows the My Computer window with all its control buttons and window components labeled. You will find this same window structure in almost every window that
you open, as well as in applications that you run, such as a database program. Although
you saw simpler windows (dialog boxes) in the previous hour, the window in Figure 2.1 is
more typical of the windows with which you will work. Your My Computer window, and
your other windows, might differ slightly from the look of Figure 2.1's window. Perhaps
the text is underlined or perhaps the large buttons toward the top of the window do not
appear on you're My Computer window. Your My Computer window might not show a
graphic image to the left of the items listed in the window's right side. As you progress in
this 24-hour tutorial, you will learn what these differences mean and how to change them.

ToolTips that pop up to describe elements appear throughout Windows Me.
For example, if you rest the mouse over a window's Close button (the X in
the upper-right window corner), the Close ToolTip description appears.

Familiarize yourself with the buttons and window sections pointed out in Figure 2.1
because almost every window contains these window controls or a subset of them. Here
are some of the more general things you can do with such a window on the screen:

- *Minimize* the window down to an icon on the taskbar, eliminating the window from the screen, while keeping it active.

- *Maximize* a minimized window to partial- or full-screen size.

- Move a window from one location to another on the screen.

- Bring a window to the top of a stack of windows so that you can work within that window. (Because of the Windows Me multitasking capability, hidden windows can still perform data processing, such as calculating and printing.)

- Display different contents in the window by selecting a new address from the toolbar's Address field. If you display new window contents, you can click the back toolbar button to return to the window's previous contents. You even can display the contents of an online Web page by preceding the address with `http://`, such as `http://www.mcp.com/`.

- Drag items, with the mouse, from one window to another or to a different location within the same window.

- Close a window completely, removing its icon from the taskbar and stopping the application that is running inside the window.

FIGURE 2.1

Use a window's controls and menus to manage the window.

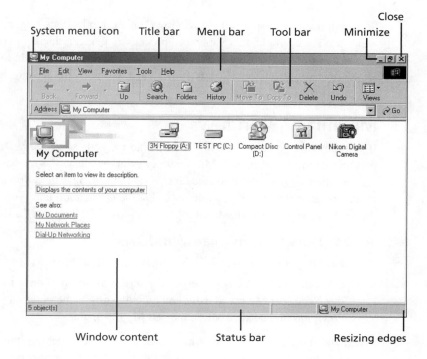

You can have one or more windows on your screen, some overlapping other windows, some completely covering others, and you will sometimes see windows side by side or above others. The taskbar indicates the contents of all your open windows, In a typical Windows Me user's day, the user might have two or more applications running at the same time. Each of those applications might display one or more windows of its own.

You must learn how to manage windows if you want to be as productive as possible. Don't jump to the conclusion, though, that multiple windows result in confusion. On a typical desk, even the desks of the most organized people (the author not being one of them!), you'll find all sorts of paper stacks, and those stacks don't imply disorganization. The desk's user simply has to know how to organize the stacks and bring the most important stacks to the forefront when he wants to work on them. It is the same with Windows Me.

> When you start a program or open a window, the taskbar gets a new button with the name of that program or window appearing on the taskbar button.

Some applications display single windows. Other applications might display multiple windows. For example, there are word processors that can display two documents side by side in two different windows. Almost all windows in Windows Me look and act just as all the others look and act. Consistency means that you only have to master one set of windows management tools.

Minimizing Windows

If you temporarily finish working with a window, you can minimize the window by pressing its Minimize button. Minimizing a window clears the window from your desktop, but the program is still loaded, active, and out of sight until you are ready to return to the program. The taskbar continues to list the application until you completely close the application. Open your My Computer window to follow this To Do item.

To Do: How to Minimize Windows

1. Find the Minimize button on your My Computer window.
2. Click the button. Look closely at the screen as you minimize the window. Notice that Windows Me graphically and quickly shrinks the outer edges of the window down into the taskbar button labeled My Computer.

When you minimize a window, whatever window or icon behind it appears. Remember that a window is active when its icon and description still appear on the taskbar, as shown in Figure 2.2.

FIGURE 2.2
The window's taskbar button still appears after you minimize a window.

Show desktop   A window entitled
My Computer is running
but is minimized

The taskbar button in Figure 2.2 contains the caption My Computer because the minimized window's title bar contained the title My Computer. The taskbar button usually contains the same title listed in the application's title bar.

> Click the taskbar's Show Desktop icon to minimize *all* open windows at once and return to the Windows Me desktop screen.

Enlarging Windows

Windows Me supplies several ways to enlarge a window. You can enlarge a minimized window from its taskbar status to the window's regular size. You can also maximize a window that's already showing to take up the entire screen space. You can alter the size of a window by doing one of the following:

- Click the window's taskbar button when the window is minimized.
- Click the window's Maximize button to enlarge the window to full screen. (The Maximize button changes to a Restore button as soon as you maximize a window.)
- To manually expand or shrink a window, drag one of the window's corners outward or inward.

Try using the taskbar buttons to display minimized windows. In other words, if you have one or more minimized windows and want to work with one of those window's programs, click the matching taskbar button, and the window reappears at its original size. You can practice minimizing windows by following the next To Do item.

To Do: More Minimizing of Windows

1. Click the My Computer taskbar button. The My Computer window reappears.

2. Notice how the window quickly and visually grows from the taskbar back to its original size? Perhaps you want to see that again. Minimize the now enlarged My Computer window once again to shrink the window down into the taskbar.

3. Click the My Computer taskbar button and watch the window return to its original and enlarged state.

As long as a window contains a Maximize button, you can maximize that window to the screen's full size. (Some windows are designed to be no larger or smaller than a preset size; these windows have Maximize or Minimize buttons that are disabled, indicated by grayed-out buttons.) When you want to dedicate the entire screen to a window, you can usually maximize the window by clicking the window's Maximize button.

> You also can maximize a window by double-clicking the window's title bar. Double-click once again, and the window returns to its previous size.

To Do: Maximizing Windows

1. Click the My Computer window's Maximize button. The window grows to consume the entire screen. Figure 2.3 shows what you will see when you click the My Computer window's Maximize button. The My Computer window does not contain many items, so maximizing it is not very beneficial other than for this practice. The more a window contains, the larger you will want to make it so that you can see contents which might not fit in a non-maximized window.

There is no need for Windows to keep a Maximize button on a window that's already maximized; thus, the Restore button takes the Maximize button's place when maximized. The Restore button always restores the window to the size it measured before you maximized it.

A Restoration button replaces the Maximize button

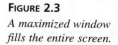

FIGURE 2.3

A maximized window fills the entire screen.

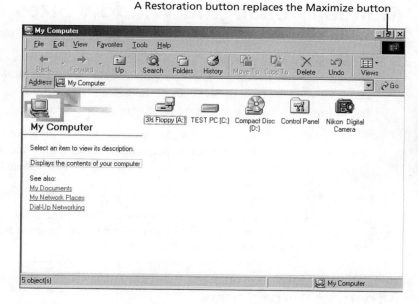

2. Click the My Computer window's Restore button. The window resizes (down) to its original size. As soon as you restore the window's size, you will see that the Restore button switches back to a Maximize button once again.

3. This time, double-click the My Computer window's title bar (point the mouse anywhere over the title in the window's title bar before double-clicking). Double-clicking the title bar maximizes a window just as pressing the Maximize button does.

4. Restore the My Computer window's original size again by clicking the Restore button.

You will often want to maximize a window if you are doing a lot of work within that window's program. For example, most word-processor users maximize the word-processing window while typing a document so that more screen real estate goes to that document and, therefore, more of it appears on the screen at one time.

> If you have loaded several programs and one program's window is covering up another program, you can click the taskbar button that matches the hidden program to bring that covered window to the top of the window stack and into view.

Manually Changing Window Sizes

This section shows how you can resize a window by dragging the mouse.

When you point to any window's edge or corner, the mouse cursor changes from its default shape (the pointing arrow) to a bidirectional arrow. The bidirectional arrow indicates that you are at one of the edges of the window and that you can drag the edge or corner inward or outward to change the size of the window.

When you drag one of the four straight edges, the window grows or shrinks left, right, up, or down. When you drag one of the four window corners, the window grows or shrinks in both height and width in the direction of the cursor's bidirectional diagonal shape.

Some windows enlarge or shrink only to dimensions preset by the window's programmers. Therefore you will not be able to resize every window that appears on your monitor.

Moving Windows

The windows that appear on your Windows Me desktop don't always appear in the location you want. That's okay. By using the mouse, you can easily drag a window to another location on the screen. The title bar acts like a handle for the window—to move the window, you drag the window's title bar.

Sometimes, you need to rearrange the windows on your screen so that they form a more logical appearance as you work. To move a window, drag its title bar. As you move the window by dragging the title bar, an outline of the window follows the mouse. When you release the mouse button, the window appears in the new location as the following To Do item shows.

When you run multiple programs at the same time, monitors measuring 17 inches diagonally and larger make window management easier. The bigger size enables you to read the text in multiple windows more easily. Although you can work in high-resolution graphics comfortably from a 15-inch monitor, a 17-inch monitor gives you more viewing room and enables Windows to display more text at one time inside a window.

To Do

To Do: Moving a Window

1. Move the My Computer window by dragging the title bar and moving the mouse. The window moves with the mouse.

2. Release the mouse button to end the dragging session and anchor the window in its new location.

3. Move the window once again. Move the window off the edge of the screen. As you can see, when you move a window over the screen's edge, Windows Me clips (chops off) a portion of the window. When you move the window back into full view, it reappears in its entirety.

Any time your screen's window arrangement is inappropriate, move one or more open windows to different locations.

2

Closing a Window

Windows is obviously full of windows that contain executing programs which work with data values of all kinds. When you run several programs at once, you open many windows that do not relate to each other. This multiwindowed operating system concept provides a flexible and manageable way to run and control several programs at once.

When you're finished with an open window, you must close the window. Closing a window eliminates the window from view, and if that window contained a running program (as most do), it will cease executing. The window's taskbar button will no longer appear on the taskbar.

Remember that closing a window differs from minimizing the window. Closing a window stops a program; minimizing a window keeps it running in the background and on the taskbar, so you can quickly return to using the program once again.

If you open a window from an icon, as you did when you first opened the My Computer window, closing the window eliminates it from your desktop area, but the icon remains on the screen in its original place. Unless you take some advanced steps to erase the icon and its contents, it remains on your Windows desktop area whether the corresponding window is open or closed.

You can rearrange icons on your screen by dragging them with the mouse just as you rearrange windows. In addition, if you right-click over your desktop and select Arrange Icons, a pop-up menu appears that enables you to select the order of your desktop icons (alphabetically, by type, size, date, or automatic arrangement). When checked, the Auto Arrange option always orders your icons for you when you move one out of alignment but offers less flexibility than not selecting this option.

Keep in mind that some windows contain running programs (such as the window you see when typing in a word processor program), whereas other windows contain icons and even more windows (such as the My Computer window). You can close both types of windows by clicking the Close button. When running a program, you also can close its primary window and terminate the entire program by double-clicking the program's icon in the upper-left corner of the window or by selecting File, Exit (for programs) or File, Close (for windows) from the program's menu.

Using the System Menu

All windows contain icons in the upper-left corner. The icon is the same one you see when the window is closed. For example, you clicked a large PC icon on the Windows Me desktop to open the My Computer window. When open, the My Computer window contains a small icon that matches the startup icon you double-click to start the program.

Earlier (in the section "Closing a Window") you learned to double-click this icon to close a window. The icon also represents a System menu with which you can control the window's size and placement. Figure 2.4 shows the My Computer window's System menu that appears when you click a window's System menu icon. Almost every Windows Me program contains this menu.

What's on the System Menu?

The System menu is a typical Windows Me menu. Many menus operate as the System menu operates—the list of menu choices stays out of the way until you are ready to choose from it. You learned about another kind of menu in Hour 1, "What Windows Millenium Edition Is All About": the Start menu. After you display a menu, you can move through the selections by using the keyboard's up and down arrow keys, as well as by using the mouse.

You can quickly display the System menu by pressing Alt+Spacebar. The first thing you will notice about Figure 2.4 is that the top choice, Restore, is grayed out. Often one or more menu items are grayed out, meaning that the choice is unavailable at this time but, depending on circumstances, might be available from this menu at a later time.

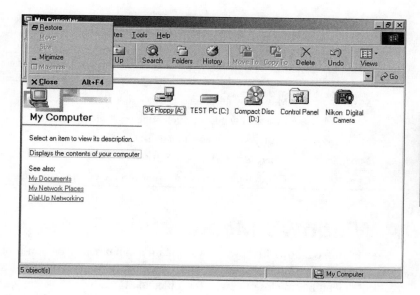

FIGURE 2.4
You can control a window's size and placement through the System menu.

Just like the Start menu, the System menu offers a list of shortcut keys with which you can quickly select a menu item. For example, N selects the System menu's Minimize command as long as the System menu is shown at the time you press N.

There's another kind of shortcut key on the System menu. Alt+F4 selects the System menu's Close command. The Alt+F4 key, unlike a hotkey, is an *accelerator key*, which means that the System menu does not have to be visible when you press Alt+F4 to close the window. Accelerator keys generally involve Alt or Ctrl keys and appear to the right of their associated menu choices.

As with the Start menu, you also can select from the System menu by clicking the mouse. Remember that the Esc key closes an open menu and so does another Alt keypress. You now know everything there is to know about using and choosing Windows Me menus!

When you use a window's menu bar (shown previously in Figure 2.1), you select commands and shortcut keys from the menu bar just as you do from the System menu. The only difference is that the commands on the menu bar always appear at the top of the window, whereas the System menu appears only when you click the System menu icon.

Table 2.1 explains what each System menu command does.

TABLE 2.1   The System Menu Commands

Command	Description
Restore	Restores a window that you've maximized. The Restore command is available only when the window is maximized or completely minimized.
Move	Moves a window on the screen to a different location.
Size	Resizes a window by enlarging or shrinking the window.
Minimize	Shrinks the window to the taskbar icon.
Maximize	Enlarges the window to full-screen size.
Close	Closes the window and terminates the window's running program.

A Window's Menu

Most of Windows Me's windows contain a menu bar. Even non-program windows that display information such as the My Computer window display a menu bar. You can use the menu bar to close the window, open additional windows, copy, cut, and paste information from one window to another, get help, and even access the Internet for related information. (The Internet's never far away in Windows.)

As you progress over the next 22 lessons, you'll learn ways to use the window menu bar options to traverse windows and to find the information you need. When you select an option from a menu bar, that option's menu pulls down to display a list of actions. For example, Figure 2.5 shows an open View menu. Throughout the remaining lessons, when asked to select View, Details, for example, you will click the View menu bar option and select Details with your mouse or arrow keys.

FIGURE 2.5

Windows contains menus that enable you to control operations on and within the window.

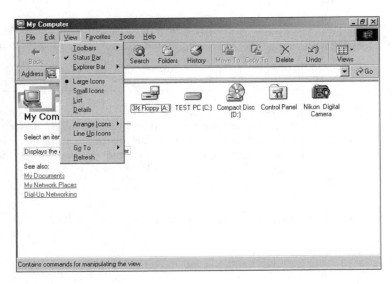

The menu bar enables you to control the way that the window looks and behaves. If the window's icons are too large to hold all of a window's contents, you can select smaller icons or change the window to a list view format as the following To Do item demonstrates.

To Do: Managing the Window Contents

1. From the open My Computer window, select View, Small Icons. The window's icons become smaller so that they can display in a smaller space.

2. Select View, Details to see the window's contents compacted even further. The list view shows extra information about the window's contents such as the size, date created, free disk space, and other statistics relative to the item in the window.

▲ Use a window's menu bar to change the window's appearance and behavior. More of the menu bar options will come in handy as you learn more about Windows Me.

A Window's Toolbar

A *toolbar* is a ribbon of buttons across the top of a window. Some programs have multiple toolbars. The toolbar you see atop the My Computer window is fairly common and appears throughout most windows that appear in Windows Me. Toolbar buttons give you push-button access to common actions you perform with the window.

As you work within a window, the toolbar changes to reflect actions that become available. For example, if you open a folder icon located in a window, not only does the clicked folder's contents replace the window's original contents, but the toolbar changes, as well.

All of the window toolbars in Windows Me are known as *Explorer toolbars* because they mimic the actions of Internet Explorer, a Web browser that comes with Windows Me. Many toolbar buttons are standard across applications and windows, so you will learn to recognize them quickly.

Toolbars change as you work within the window. In addition, you might want to modify a toolbar's behavior to access its benefits more efficiently. Although total toolbar management is a lengthy topic, simple toolbar management is easy, as you will learn in the next To Do item.

To Do: Managing the Toolbar

▼ To Do

1. Maximize the My Computer window. Notice that the Back toolbar button (the button with the left-pointing arrow) is grayed out.

2. Double-click Control Panel and then the Scanners and Cameras folder found in the Control Panel's window. The folder contains an icon, enabling you to set up a new scanner or digital camera that you might add to your system, as well as icons for existing scanners or cameras you've already designated. Notice that the Back toolbar button is now available, enabling you to return to the previous window contents.

3. Click the Back button and the original My Computer contents return. (Forward takes you to the Scanners and Cameras folder.) No matter how many windows and subfolders you open within a window, you always can retrace your steps backward and forward with the Back and Forward buttons.

4. Modify the way the toolbar looks. Right-click over the right-end of the toolbar (an area where no buttons appear) and click Customize. Click the down arrow next to Text Options and click on No text labels to select that option (assuming that it was not already selected). Click Close. As Figure 2.6 shows, the window's toolbar buttons now display in less space without the textual descriptions. (You also can control the toolbar's appearance from the View, Toolbar menu bar option.) If your toolbar already displayed the text labels, the labels will now be gone. Select Show text labels from this same dialog box to show the labels once again.

5. The text labels make the toolbar grow to accommodate the labels. Many of the toolbar areas have *Toolbar handle controls* (refer to Figure 2.6) that enable you to slide that portion of the toolbar left or right to make room for something else. Drag one of the sliders left or right to see how the toolbar adjusts to the Toolbar handle control. If you double-click a toolbar's slider, the tools on the slider come into view (and cover up other items) or hide to bring hidden items into focus once again.

6. A window's contents don't dictate what you view in the window. The area of the toolbar labeled Address is not a button but instead describes the white box to the right of Address. The box is a *drop-down list box* that can display choices you might want to use. Click the list box's down arrow (at the right of the list box) to see a list of areas you can go to from the window. Whether you choose a disk drive or the Internet (by dragging the mouse or using the keyboard), the contents you pick will appear inside the window and replace the window's original My Computer contents. As always, the Back button returns you to where you started.

▲

Tool bar handle control

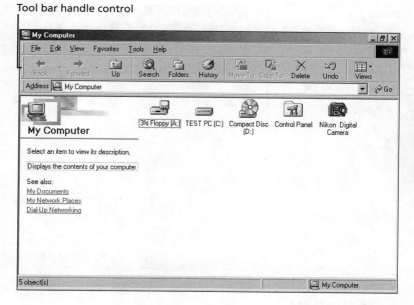

FIGURE 2.6

By hiding the text labels, you save toolbar room.

2

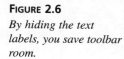

The Address list box, as well as the other traversal features of the toolbar such as the Back and Forward buttons, means that Windows Me doesn't limit you; just because you open a window doesn't mean that you want to stay with that window. The toolbar enables you to move from one window's contents to a totally unrelated window and even to an Internet site (that will display in the window) if you've got a connection.

One Last Note About Windows

You can completely change the way the My Computer window looks by selecting Tools, Folder Options and clicking Use Windows classic folders from the menu. When you click OK, the window changes to the view shown in Figure 2.7. In Classic view, the descriptive pane that appears on the left in Web view disappears. Classic view gives you more room to display files, but it doesn't provide you with the detailed information about each file that you'll find in Web view. You'll learn more about the Web-based window view in the next hour's lesson.

FIGURE 2.7

You might prefer to view your windows in a Classic windows format.

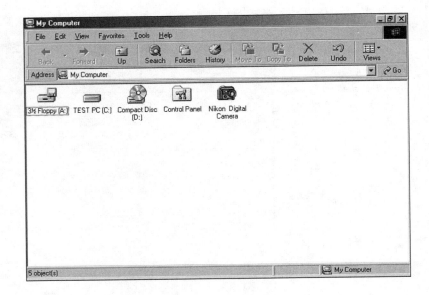

Summary

This hour taught you the ins and outs of windows management. Learning how to manage windows is a fundamental skill that Windows Me users must understand. Windows Me enables you to open, resize, move, and close windows. The windows on your desktop contain the running applications, and part of running Windows Me programs requires being able to position those windows where you want them.

Mastering fundamental windows management, as you've done so far this hour, is like learning to drive a car. You have to learn the basics before getting into traffic. Now you are ready to begin racing down the road by seeing what Windows Me can really do.

Q&A

Q What's the difference between a shortcut key and an accelerator key?

A Both shortcut (or hot) keys and accelerator keys involve selecting commands from Windows Me menus. The shortcut keystrokes appear as underlined letters in menu commands. When you use the hotkey (such as R to select Restore), the matching menu item executes.

Accelerator keys have the added distinction of enabling the user to select menu commands by pressing keystrokes without first having to display a menu. For example, you can often press Ctrl+O instead of selecting File, Open from most menus. Accelerator keys appear at the right of their corresponding menu commands.

Q Don't the pop-up ToolTips replace the need for text labels?

A When you hide a toolbar's text labels, you make room for more buttons and you get more screen real estate for the window's contents. If you forget what a button is for, rest your mouse cursor on the button without clicking the button, and the ToolTip shows the button's description. The ToolTips don't appear when you display the buttons' text labels. As you grow more familiar with Windows Me toolbars, you won't need the text labels and you'll want to make more room for the rest of your window elements. You can rely on the ToolTips when you need to know what a button does.

2

Workshop

The quiz and exercise questions are designed to test your knowledge of the material covered in this hour. The answers are in Appendix C, "Answers to Quizzes."

Quiz

1. Why can you manipulate the My Computer window as you do most other windows?

2. What is the difference between closing and minimizing a window?

3. *True or false*: When you minimize a window, its taskbar button goes away.

4. How does a toolbar differ from a window menu?

5. How do you change the size of a toolbar?

Exercises

1. Open the Control Panel by opening the Windows Start menu, selecting Settings, and then clicking Control Panel. Minimize, maximize, and resize the Control Panel window. Close the window.

2. Open several windows at once, such as the My Computer, Control Panel, and the Help window from the Start menu. Notice how Windows Me arranges them. Click on the title bar of any window to bring that window into view and to make it the active window. The other windows remain open, but the active window shows completely. The next hour, "Take Windows Me to Task," shows you more ways to manage several windows that you open at once.

HOUR 3

Take Windows Me to Task

The taskbar and the Start button are closely related. Most Windows Me users use the Start button to display the Start menu and then execute a program. When the program begins running, the taskbar displays a button with an icon, along with a description that represents the running program.

The taskbar, the Start button, and the Start menu are the most fundamental components in Windows Me. The taskbar is the cornerstone of Windows Me. This hour explains how to customize the taskbar to best suit your computing style. Along the way, you also learn how to make your desktop items mimic the one-click operation of the taskbar.

In this hour, you will

- Learn where the Start menu comes from
- Move, resize, and change the appearance of the taskbar
- Learn why the Start menu's Programs command might not execute all programs
- Simplify icon selection

A Quick Taskbar and Start Button Review

In Hour 1, "What Windows Millennium Edition Is All About," you used the Start menu to shut down your computer properly. Clicking the taskbar's Start button produces the Start menu. The Start menu does all these things and more:

- It makes itself available to you no matter what else you are doing in Windows Me.
- It displays a list of programs on your system using the Start menu's cascading system.
- It provides easy access to recently opened data documents that you can look at or edit.
- It provides a search engine that navigates through all your files looking for the one you need.
- It activates the Windows Me help engine, which provides online help for working within Windows Me.

The next few sections explain how you can customize the taskbar and its associated Start menu so that the Start menu acts and looks the way you expect.

Sometimes the Start button temporarily disappears (when you're working in a full-screen MS-DOS session, for example). Press Ctrl+Esc to display the Start menu when you cannot see it. If your keyboard contains a key with the Windows logo, that key also displays the Start menu.

Moving the Taskbar

The taskbar does not have to stay at the bottom of your screen. You can move the taskbar to either side of your monitor or even to the top of your screen. The taskbar placement is easy to change.

Figure 3.1 shows that a side taskbar does not have the width necessary to display lengthy descriptions. When you place the taskbar at the bottom or top of the screen, the taskbar has more room for longer descriptions.

If you place the taskbar at the top of the screen, the Start menu falls down from the Start button, whereas the Start menu pops up from the Start button when you place the taskbar at the bottom of the screen.

FIGURE 3.1
You can place the taskbar on any edge of your screen.

The newly placed taskbar

When working on a wide spreadsheet or document, you might want as much screen width as you can get. You then want the taskbar at the bottom or top of your screen. When working with graphics, you usually need more vertical screen space, so you can move the taskbar to either side of the screen.

Moving the taskbar to any of the four edges of your screen is easy. Simply drag the taskbar to the new location as the following To Do item demonstrates.

To Do: Relocating the Taskbar

1. Find a blank spot on your taskbar and point to the spot with the mouse cursor. Be sure that you are pointing within the taskbar and not over a button.

2. Drag the taskbar to another edge of the screen. As you drag the mouse, the taskbar moves with the mouse and appears at the edge of the screen where you release the mouse.

3. Release the mouse button to anchor the taskbar at its new position.

The Taskbar Properties Menu

A right mouse button click often displays a *context-sensitive menu* of options available to you. Windows Me looks at what you are doing when you right-click. Depending on the context, Windows displays commands appropriate to that task. The taskbar is one such location where the right mouse button brings up a helpful menu, called the *taskbar properties menu*. You can use it to change the appearance and performance of the taskbar and the windows controlled by the taskbar. After finding a blank spot on your taskbar, right-clicking brings up the context-sensitive taskbar properties menu shown in Figure 3.2.

FIGURE 3.2

A right-click on a blank space of the taskbar displays a context-sensitive menu.

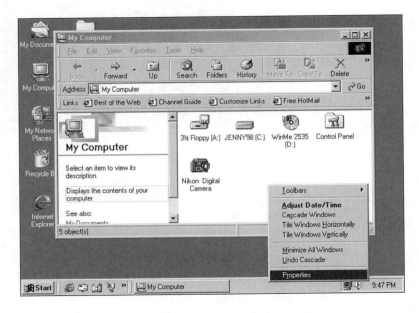

The taskbar properties menu is not necessarily a menu you want to display often. Most users play around with different taskbar and window settings for a while until they find preferences that suit them best. Thereafter, those users might rarely use the taskbar properties menu.

The taskbar actually displays several menus depending on where you right-click. If you right-click over the quick launch area, the area with the Show Desktop and Internet Explorer icon, one of the most helpful taskbar menus appears. The first option, View, enables you to select large or small icons on the taskbar. If you use a small monitor or just want extra help seeing the icons, select View, Large to change the taskbar icons to a larger size. You can change the icons back to small ones by selecting View, Small.

Show Text adds a textual description to the taskbar icons. Until you familiarize yourself with the icons, you might want to display the text that describes them. Although the text description takes room on your taskbar, the description can help tell you what each icon means. On many monitors, some icons no longer fit on the screen with the text description. Simply click the arrow to the right of the icon to display a list of other taskbar items from which you can select, as Figure 3.3 shows.

FIGURE 3.3

Although the icons don't all fit on the taskbar at once, you can easily display the remaining icons and their descriptions.

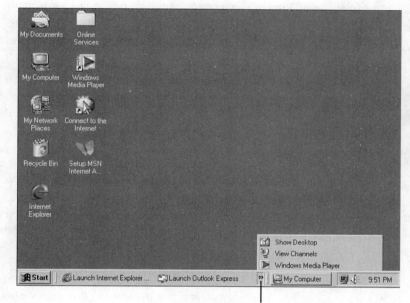

3

Point here and click to show list

Refresh displays your taskbar once again. Although it's rare, you can place icons on the taskbar that do not appear right away. The Refresh option shows the taskbar in its current state.

If the icons are too difficult to manage, select Open from the taskbar's right-click menu. A window opens with all the icons from which you can choose more easily visible. The window will remain open until you close it.

Like Show Text, the Show Title option adds text to the taskbar. Instead of adding text to each icon, the text labels each toolbar set that your taskbar displays.

All the taskbar right-click menu options described so far are new with Windows Me and did not appear on the taskbar for previous editions of Windows.

Right-click over the toolbar and select Toolbars to see a array of choices. Table 3.1 explains each kind of element you can place on the taskbar from this menu.

TABLE 3.1   You Can Add These Toolbar Elements to Your Windows Me Taskbar

Toolbar Element	Description
Links	Displays popular Web links that you can quickly return to with the click of a button. You can modify the list of links.
Address	Displays a drop-down list box on your taskbar that you can click to return to recent Web and file locations.
Desktop	Displays a ribbon of icons that match those on your Windows Me desktop. You can click on one of the icons to start that icon's program or open that icon's window instead of having to return to your desktop to locate the icon.
Quick Launch	Adds Internet access control buttons so that you can quickly get on the Web. In addition, the Show Desktop icon appears in the Quick Launch section so that you can minimize all open windows with a single taskbar click.
New Toolbar	Enables you to select a disk drive, folder, or Web location whose contents appear as a secondary toolbar slider control on the taskbar. Subsequently, the taskbar's right-click menu contains the new toolbar that you can deselect to hide once again.

You can change your computer's date and time by selecting Adjust Date/Time. Select Adjust Date/Time to display the Date/Time Properties dialog box shown in Figure 3.4.

More quickly display the Date/Time Properties dialog box by double-clicking the time on the right side of the taskbar.

The next three menu options are important when you want to work with more than one open window. These menu options offer three ways of arranging your open windows so that they are more manageable. If you open two or more windows at once, all those windows can be difficult to manage individually. You could maximize each window and display only one window at a time. There are many reasons, however, to keep more than one window open and displayed at the same time, such as when you want to copy data from one window to another. (Hour 5, "Using Explorer to Navigate," explains how to copy between windows.)

FIGURE 3.4

You can change your PC's date and time.

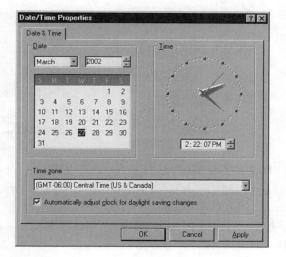

Tiling Windows

When you want to see more than one open window at a time, the taskbar properties menu gives you tools that provide quick management of those windows so that you do not have to size and place each window individually. Figure 3.5 shows how too many windows open at the same time can be confusing.

Three ways exist to organize several windows that are open at once: You can cascade them, horizontally tile them, or vertically tile them. The following To Do item demonstrates the cascade option.

FIGURE 3.5

Too many open windows can quickly cause disorganization.

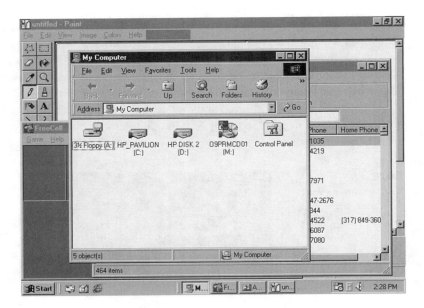

To Do: Working with Cascading Windows

1. Double-click the My Computer icon to open the My Computer window.

2. Double-click the Recycle Bin icon to open that window as well. Although you might not understand the Recycle Bin until Hour 5, the open window helps show the effects of the taskbar's properties menu.

3. Display the Start menu and select the Programs, Accessories, Word Pad option. Shortly, you'll see the Word Pad program appear. You'll learn how to use Word Pad in Hour 10, "Using the Desktop Accessories." Again, this window is just to put more on your desktop to work with for this task.

4. Now that you've opened three windows, ask Windows Me to organize those windows for you. Display the taskbar's properties menu by right-clicking after pointing to a blank spot on the taskbar.

5. Select the menu item labeled Cascade Windows. Windows Me instantly organizes your windows into the cascaded series of windows shown in Figure 3.6.

   Notice that the title bars of *all* open windows appear on the Windows desktop area. When you want to bring any of the hidden windows into focus, click that window's title bar, and the window will rise to the top of the window stack. The cascading effect always gives you the ability to switch between windows. As long as any part of a hidden window is peeking out from under another, you can click the title bar to bring that hidden window into focus.

FIGURE 3.6

The windows are now more manageable.

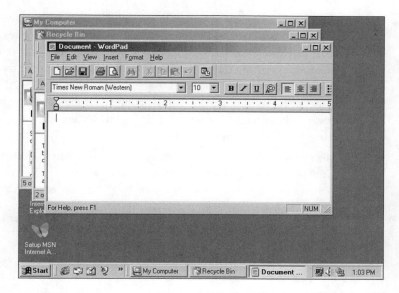

3

6. Sometimes, you need to see the contents of two or more windows at the same time. Windows enables you to *tile* the open windows so that you can see the actual body of each open window. Windows supports two kinds of tiling methods: horizontal tiling and vertical tiling. Display the taskbar's properties menu and select Tile Windows Horizontally. Windows will properly resize each of the three open windows, as shown in Figure 3.7. (If a window's title bar is hidden but another part of the window is visible, you can bring that window into focus by clicking over the part of the window that is visible.)

FIGURE 3.7

The windows are now tiled horizontally.

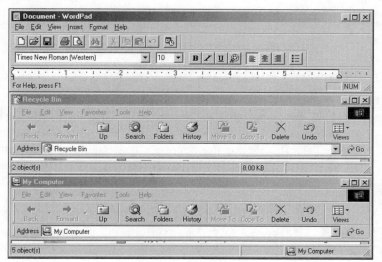

▼

At first glance, the tiling might seem too limiting to you. After all, to fit those three open windows on the screen at the same time, Windows cannot show you a lot of any one of the windows. Keep in mind that all the window resizing and moving tools that you learned about in Hour 2 work even after you've tiled windows. Therefore, you can move the Word Pad window toward the top of the screen, after tiling the windows, if you want to see more of that window. (Scrollbars automatically appear in tiled windows if the contents of the window consume more space than can be displayed at once. Click the arrows at each end of the scrollbar to move window contents into view.)

7. The vertical tiling method produces side-by-side windows that are fairly thin but offer yet another kind of open window display. Select Tile Windows Vertically and Windows reformats the screen again. Now that you've vertically tiled the open windows, you can restore the original placement of the windows by selecting Undo Tile. (The Undo option appears only after you've selected the Cascade, Tile, or Minimize option.)

8. The Minimize All Windows taskbar properties menu option attempts to minimize all open windows at the same time. The problem with the Minimize All Windows option is that not all windows can be minimized. Therefore, the option minimizes only those windows that have a minimize button (most do). The Show Desktop icon minimizes all open windows in one step. The Show Desktop icon appears on the Quick Launch taskbar toolbar, so you must display that toolbar before you see the Show Desktop icon. Don't minimize any windows now, however, because you need them open for the next set of steps.

▲

No matter how you tile or cascade the windows, each window's Minimize, Maximize, and Restore buttons work as usual. Therefore, you can maximize any cascaded window at any time by clicking that window's Maximize button.

Working with Taskbar Properties

The taskbar properties menu not only controls the appearance and performance of open windows, but also controls the appearance and performance of the taskbar. The Properties menu option displays the Taskbar and Start Menu Properties tabbed dialog box shown in Figure 3.8. (This same dialog appears when you select Start, Settings, Taskbar & Start Menu.) With the Taskbar Properties dialog box, you can change the way the taskbar appears and performs, and you also can change the contents of the Start menu.

In Hour 7, "Desktop Management," you'll learn how to use the Taskbar and Start Menu Properties dialog box to change the contents of the Start menu.

FIGURE 3.8

You can change the taskbar's appearance and performance by using the Taskbar and Start Menu Properties dialog box.

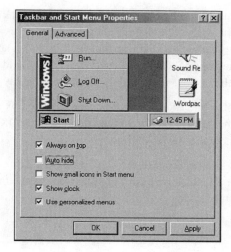

Using Dialog Boxes

When Windows displays a tabbed dialog box, it is offering you more than one dialog box at the same time. (Each box, or page, is called a *property sheet*.) Instead of displaying two or more dialog boxes on the screen at the same time, the tabs give you a way to select which dialog box you want to respond to. You can even respond to one dialog box and then click another tab, and that tab's dialog box then appears so that you can respond to it. Windows often puts an OK command button on a dialog box that you can press when you are finished responding to the dialog box's controls.

In addition to the OK button, some dialog boxes have an Apply button. Generally, these dialog boxes change a Windows setting, such as the font size. If you click Apply, Windows puts your dialog box settings into effect but does not close the dialog box. Therefore, you can see the results of your dialog box settings without getting rid of the dialog box. Press Cancel if you want Windows to ignore your changes.

The Taskbar and Start Menu Properties dialog box accepts information that controls the way the taskbar appears on the screen. You can allow (or disallow) windows to overlap the taskbar if those windows are large enough to do so, you can eliminate the clock from the taskbar, and you can even minimize the taskbar so that it does not appear until you need it.

The first check mark option, Always on Top, is normally checked because Windows Me, by default, displays the taskbar at all times. The taskbar is most helpful when it appears on the screen, right? The only problem with the taskbar's being on the screen at all times is that one complete row of the screen is consumed by the taskbar instead of by your own windows. Uncheck the option by clicking over the check mark or anywhere on the words beside it. The graphic inside the dialog box actually changes when you remove the check mark to show a window overlapping the clock in the taskbar. Click OK to see the results of the unchecked option. (If you clicked the Apply command button, Windows Me would have changed the taskbar immediately while still displaying the dialog box.)

Try this: Display the Taskbar and Start Menu Properties dialog box again. Check the Auto hide option, check the Always on Top option, and click the OK button. Click anywhere on the desktop. Where did the taskbar go?

The taskbar is now out of sight and out of the way except for a thin horizontal line across the bottom of your screen. The taskbar hasn't gone far—point the mouse cursor to the bottom of the screen and the taskbar will reappear. You can now have your taskbar and hide it, too!

> If you display the Taskbar and Start Menu Properties dialog box but decide that you don't want to make any changes after all, click the Cancel command button.

The third check mark option controls how the Start menu's icons are displayed. If you want to save some screen room when you display the Start menu, you can request small icons, and the Start menu will consume less screen space.

If you uncheck the next option, labeled Show Clock, the taskbar's clock goes away from the right edge of the taskbar after clicking the OK command button on the dialog box.

The final option, Use personalized menus, turns on and off the display of the Windows Me menus that show only your most recently-chosen options. If you'd rather see all Windows menu options every time you display a menu, uncheck the Use Personalized Menus option.

Display the Taskbar and Start Menu Properties tabbed dialog box once again and set options to your desired values. Before clicking the OK command button, click Apply to apply your changes and then click the tabbed page labeled Advanced (at the top of the dialog box). You see the second dialog box, which is shown in Figure 3.9.

The Advanced page enables you to change the appearance of the Start menu. Because you have yet to really learn what the default Start menu is all about, I will save the discussion of this dialog box until Hour 7.

Click the Cancel command button to close the dialog box and return to the regular Windows desktop. Close all windows that are now open by clicking the Close button in the window's upper-right corner.

FIGURE 3.9

The Advanced dialog box appearing from behind the taskbar options.

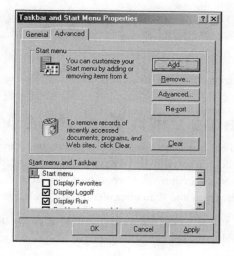

Sizing the Taskbar

What happens if you open a number of windows by starting several programs? The single-line taskbar fills up very quickly with buttons and icons and descriptions that represent those open windows. The taskbar can get extremely full if you display multiple toolbars on the taskbar. Figure 3.10 shows such a taskbar. If you're doing a lot of work, the taskbar gets squeezed for space. However, you can solve that problem rather easily.

FIGURE 3.10

The taskbar needs more room.

Just as you can resize a window, you also can resize the taskbar. Simply point to the top edge of the taskbar (or the inside edge if you've moved the taskbar to an edge or top of the screen) and drag the edge toward the center of the screen. The taskbar enlarges as you drag your mouse.

When you enlarge the taskbar, it can more comfortably hold several buttons for open windows, and the descriptions on those buttons can be longer. Use the pop-up ToolTips if you need a reminder of the purpose of the taskbar buttons, such as the Show Desktop button. Figure 3.11 shows the same taskbar as the one shown in Figure 3.10. This time, the taskbar is larger, and you can see what each program is more easily by the descriptions on the taskbar buttons.

FIGURE 3.11

The taskbar now has more breathing room.

Close all open windows to prepare for the next section.

Starting Programs with the Start Menu

The Start menu offers an extremely simple way for you to start the programs on your computer. Two or three clicks start virtually any program on your disk drive. The Programs command on the Start menu launches your programs. To start a program, you display the menu that contains the program and then click the program's name or icon.

Microsoft gives you the Solitaire card game. You can practice starting programs from the Start menu by starting Solitaire.

To Do: Playing Solitaire

1. Click the Start button to display the Start menu.

2. Select the Programs command. A cascaded menu will appear next to the Start menu. Your computer is unique, and a different set of commands might appear here.

   Each of these items in the second menu represents either a program or a folder of programs. When you buy a program such as a word processor, the word processor might come with several related programs that help you manage the word processor environment. The word processor folder opens to yet another window (you can tell by the presence of an arrow at the right of the word processor's folder) that then lists all the related programs in the folder.

3. Select the Games command to display the programs in the Games folder. If you don't see Games, first select Accessories and look there.

4. Click the Classic Solitaire game. You see the opening Solitaire card game screen.

5. There's no time to play right now! This hour's closing quickly. Therefore, terminate the Solitaire program by clicking the window's Close button (the button with the X, as you learned in Hour 2). Solitaire goes away and you are back to the regular Windows Me desktop.

Using the Run Command

In addition to the Start menu's Programs command, you can use another method to start programs that aren't set up on the Programs' cascade of menus. The Run command on the Start menu provides a way for you to execute specific programs.

Reaching Your Files

A pathname is the exact computer system location of a file. The document and folder concept in Windows makes working with paths much easier than before Windows. Most often, you specify pathnames visually by clicking folder icons instead of typing long pathnames, as you had to do before Windows.

The folders in Windows used to be called *directories*. A directory is just a collection of files and other directories. In file listings, Windows often displays a folder icon with a name to represent a directory that holds other files. Folders can hold subfolders, so the location of a file, the file's path, might be deep within several nested folders on a disk or CD-ROM drive.

A full pathname begins with a disk drive name followed by a colon (:) followed by a backslash (\). If the file resides in the disk drive's top folder (called the *root directory*), you then type the filename. If, however, the file resides in another folder, you must list the folder after the backslash. If the file resides in several nested folders, you must list each folder in order, from the outermost to the innermost, and separate each folder name with a backslash. Both of the following are full pathnames to specific files:

`c:\autoexec.bat`

`d:\Sherry\WordProc\Home\Insure\Fire and Casualty`

The first filename is `autoexec.bat` located in the root directory. The second filename is `Fire and Casualty` located within a series of nested directories.

3

The Start menu's Run command offers a tedious way to execute any program on your computer. If you want to run a program that would not properly set up in Windows (perhaps the program is an old MS-DOS–based program), you have to execute the program using Run.

To run a program from the Run menu option, display the Start menu and select the Run command. Windows displays the Run dialog box.

There might or might not be text next to the Open text prompt. Windows Me needs to know the exact name and path of the program you want to open (and run).

Almost all users install Windows Me on drive C. If your Windows Me system is installed on another drive, substitute your drive name for the `C:` and type the following exactly as you see it (using either uppercase or lowercase letters): `C:\WINDOWS\SOL` and press Enter.

The Solitaire game is normally installed on the Windows directory on drive C. The name of the program is `SOL.EXE`. To execute any program with an `.EXE` filename extension, you need to type only the first part of the filename, such as `SOL`. If Solitaire does not start, you might have typed the line incorrectly. Try again and be sure that you use backslashes and not forward slashes.

You might be one of the lucky few who never needs the Run command. Nevertheless, there are many programs on the market that Windows cannot execute in its environment. Using Run, you can execute any program on your computer as long as you know the program's pathname and filename.

> Windows supports a strong data document concept. It is data-driven more than program-driven. If you type a data file (such as a Microsoft Word document) instead of a program name with the Run command, Windows automatically starts the program needed to work with that data file and loads the data file for you. Therefore, you worry less about your programs, and you can concentrate more on your data. In addition, you can type an Internet address (often called a uniform resource locator, or, URL) at Run and Windows Me automatically starts your Internet browser and takes you to the Web site you entered.

Introduction to Your Active Desktop

Windows Me's Active Desktop not only changes the look of Windows Me, but also the way you work with Windows Me. Your Windows Me desktop can display icons, text, and windows, but also more active content. You can display *HTML-based* documents on the Windows Me background. (HTML is the language behind Web pages and stands for Hypertext Markup Language.)

> This section serves only as an introduction to the Active Desktop that's so important to Windows Me. Complete chapters of this book are devoted to exploring the Active Desktop concepts. If you are new to the Internet, and especially if you are new to Windows, you might not see the full purpose of the Active Desktop at this time. Before this 24-hour tutorial is over, you'll know all you need to know to use Windows Me efficiently and effectively.

You can place Web pages on the Windows Me background's wallpaper. If those Web pages contain the special ActiveX controls that some Web pages contain (ActiveX controls energize Web pages with sound, videos, and interactive features), that active content will appear as well. If you've set up special push content, your Internet provider will bring your requested Internet information directly to your Windows Me desktop. Hour 14, "Understanding the Internet's Push and Channel Content," explores the push content in more detail.

If you're not connected to the Web, you can still benefit from the Active Desktop features, such as the single-click selection described next.

If you've used a Web browser before, you know that you can select Web page items just by resting your mouse over the item, and you can open items with a single-click. Normally, you have to click once over a Windows item to select it and double-click the item to open it. You've already opened windows in these lessons by double-clicking them. By providing the same kind of select and open capabilities as the Web provides, Windows Me moves one step closer to integrating your desktop with the online world.

Using the Active Desktop means that you don't have to start a Web browser and request information, such as current stock prices, to see that data while you work in Windows Me. You can even set up the Web content to appear as a screen saver.

Hour 12, "How Windows Ties into the Web," explains how to integrate Windows Me and the Web to prepare you for the Active Desktop. In the meantime, you might want to convert your Windows Me desktop to the Web-like desktop that simplifies the way you select desktop items and open windows. By following the next To Do item, you can change your single- and double-mouse clicks to the Web-browser equivalents.

To Do: Changing the Mouse Clicks

1. Open your My Computer window to gain access to window options.

2. Select Tools, Folder Options. The first dialog box page, the one with the General tab, contains options that determine how your desktop items respond to your selections. Click the option, Enable Web Content on My Desktop, to enable your desktop to display Web pages as background. Click the option labeled Enable Web content in folders to make your open folder windows act and look like Web content. The final option, Click Items as Follows, determines whether Windows Me opens items when you single- or double-click them. Select the single-click option as well as the next option below, Underline Icon Titles Consistent with My Browser, to make your Windows desktop respond like a Web browser. (Your Web options may already be enabled.)

▼   3. Click OK to close the dialog box. Your Windows Me desktop changes immediately
             and the icons there now have underlined labels. (Resize the My Computer window
             so that you can see the left part of your Windows Me desktop.)

             Your My Computer window now changes to the Web style view to complement
▲   your desktop. Figure 3.12 shows the result.

FIGURE 3.12

*You can now select
items by pointing to
them and open items
with a single mouse
click.*

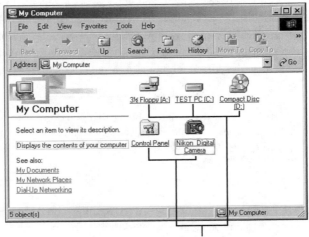

Examples of underlined

Summary

This hour concentrated mostly on the taskbar. The taskbar gives you a play-by-play status of the open windows on your system. As you open and close windows, the taskbar
updates with new buttons to show what's happening at all times. If you start more than
one program, you can switch between those programs as easily as you switch between
cable TV shows: Click a button on the taskbar.

The taskbar works along with the Start menu to start and control the programs running
on your system. Use the Programs command on the Start menu to start programs with a
total of two or three mouse clicks. Although you can use the Run command to start programs, the Programs menu is easier to use as long as the program is set up properly in
Windows Me.

To reduce your selection requirements, you can also change to the single-click option.
You are then able to open windows as easily as you select from the taskbar. The single-
click option makes integration of the Web into Windows Me more seamless.

Q&A

Q **Why would I use the taskbar properties menu to organize my open windows when I can do the same thing manually?**

A The taskbar properties menu gives you the ability to adjust the appearance of your screen's open windows with one mouse click. If you select a cascading window scheme, Windows Me ensures that all open window title bars appear on the screen, with the most recently opened window as the front window of focus. You can bring one of the hidden windows into focus by clicking the window's title bar. If, instead, you select the horizontal or vertical tiling options, Windows Me displays a little of all open windows on top of each other or side-by-side.

If you normally work in only one window at a time, you won't use the taskbar properties. However, you can use the taskbar properties menu to change the appearance of the taskbar itself.

Q **How can I use the taskbar properties menu to change the appearance or performance of the taskbar?**

A The taskbar is set by default to appear, no matter what else is on your screen. Microsoft thought it best to keep the taskbar on the screen so that you can switch between programs and adjust the Windows Me performance easily. However, to maximize the screen space and clear away as much as possible, you can change the taskbar's performance so that onscreen windows cover the taskbar, giving you an additional line for the open window. In addition, you can select that Windows Me always hide the taskbar completely, showing you the taskbar only when you point to the bottom of the screen with the mouse cursor. If you increase the size of the taskbar, you can still hide it through the properties' Auto hide feature. The increased size will appear when you show the taskbar, but the taskbar will not be in the way when hidden.

The taskbar properties menu also controls the size of the Start menu's icons, so you can decrease the width of the Start menu if you prefer. You also can eliminate (or add) the clock from the taskbar so that the taskbar has room for another window's button.

Q **Help! My taskbar has fallen and I can't get my Start menu up! What did I do and how can I fix it?**

A You've changed the options in the Taskbar Properties dialog box to hide the taskbar, or you've dragged the top of the taskbar to the bottom of your screen to shrink the taskbar. The taskbar is not gone for long, however. To see the taskbar again, all you need to do is point to the bottom of the screen with the mouse, and the taskbar appears once again.

3

Workshop

The quiz and exercise questions are designed to test your knowledge of the material covered in this hour. The answers are in Appendix C, "Answers to Quizzes."

Quiz

1. Which option enables you to keep the taskbar off the screen until you're ready to use the taskbar?

2. What happens when you right-click over a blank area of the taskbar?

3. What are the two ways to change your PC's date and time?

4. What does it mean to *tile* windows?

5. Name one way that Windows Me's single-click feature mimics Web browsing.

Exercises

1. Move your taskbar to each edge of the screen. Determine which is best for you. Remember that you can hide the taskbar with the Auto Hide option if the taskbar consumes too much screen real estate.

2. Reverse the Web-based folder and desktop views by checking the appropriate options in the My Computer window's Folder Options dialog box. Note the changes in the way your folders and desktop looks and responds. Throughout the rest of this 24-hour tutorial, you'll see both the Web-based folder view as well as the classic desktop view. The one you use is based on your preference. If you use the Internet a lot, you'll probably want to keep the Web view to keep your interface consistent.

HOUR 4

Understanding the My Computer Window

The My Computer icon opens to a window, as you learned in Hour 3, "Take Windows Me to Task," and contains information that relates to your computer's hardware and software. You will often open the My Computer window when you add or remove both hardware and software. The My Computer window provides access to many different areas of your computer.

Many computer beginners and advanced users ignore the My Computer window more than they should. The My Computer window, which always appears on your Windows Me desktop, enables you to access every hardware device on your system in a uniform fashion.

In this hour, you use the My Computer window to change the behavior of your mouse and also to modify the screen background that you see. You must look at the desktop often, so changing the graphics behind the desktop can break the monotony that you might otherwise face with a dull Windows Me desktop screen. People often spend the first few sessions with any new operating environment getting to know the environment and modifying the appearance to suit their preferences. In this hour, you learn about the My Computer window while you modify your work environment.

In this hour, you will

- Discover the contents of the My Computer window
- Learn where to go for mouse control changes
- Learn why a startup disk can help you locate system problems

Looking at My Computer

Your computer system is comprised of hardware (the system unit, monitor, keyboard, CD-ROM, networked components, and so on), firmware (the internal memory), and software (for example, Windows Me, MS-DOS, word processors, spreadsheets, and games). There are several ways to access your computer's hardware and software through different areas of Windows Me. The My Computer window contains one of the most helpful hardware and software management resources available in Windows Me.

If your My Computer window is not still open from Hour 3, open it now by double-clicking the icon. (Of course, if you changed your window-open command to a Web view that requires only a single-click, you need to click only once.) When you double-click the My Computer icon, Windows Me displays the My Computer window.

Introducing the My Computer Window

The My Computer icon is important or Microsoft would not have put it at the top of the opening Windows Me screen. Its importance will become apparent throughout this book and in your own work as you learn more about Windows Me.

People's needs for the My Computer window differ greatly, depending on which systems they use to run Windows Me. For example, a network user probably displays the My Computer window more often than a single user working primarily on a spreadsheet program. The network user might have more reason to check the properties of a shared printer or a shared disk drive.

If you have a computer that is compatible with Plug-and-Play and you add Plug-and-Play hardware to the computer, such as a new internal high-speed modem, Windows should be able to detect that you've installed that new modem the next time you start your PC. Some devices, such as USB (Universal Serial Bus) and the PC card devices that plug into most laptops and some desktop systems, automatically configure themselves when you insert the cards; they don't require that you first turn off your computer.

Before looking at a sample My Computer window work session, you should understand that there are three ways to view the My Computer window, as well as most other Windows Me windows:

- As a Web page, as you learned in Hour 3
- In the icon view (with large or small icons)
- In the list view (with or without detail)

The icon view is the default view that is set when you install Windows Me. The My Computer window figures in this hour show the icon view format. Newcomers prefer the familiarity that an icon view provides. Later, you will learn how to move files from one disk drive to another by dragging a file to the disk icon where you want to put that file instead of typing a disk drive name as computer users of older operating systems have to do.

As you progress, you might prefer to switch to a list view. A list view shows window contents down the screen in a list of items more like a table of contents. Although small icons still appear next to most of the items in a list view of the My Computer window, the icons are extremely small. The list view gives you the ability to see more items at once without the clutter of icons filling the screen.

When you first open the My Computer window, the difference between the views is not extremely important because the My Computer window shows a high-level overview of the system with rarely more than a few icons. Nevertheless, as you add hardware and as you traverse additional windows from within the My Computer window, your current view might no longer be adequate to display the data. For example, for only a few icons, the large icon view works well. If you open windows with additional icons, however, you might want to switch to the small icon view (by selecting View, Small Icons).

Often, the list views work better than the icons, depending on the information you've displayed inside the My Computer window. Figure 4.1 shows a detailed view. The detailed list view (available from the View menu) means that descriptions for the icons appear to the right and that the icons appear in a smaller format.

The detailed view becomes even more important if you display additional information in a window. The detailed list view shows the filename, size in bytes, file type, and the most recent date modified.

4

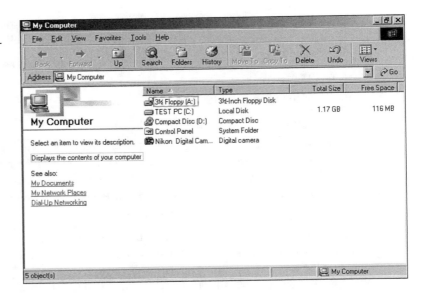

FIGURE 4.1

The My Computer window shown in a detailed list view.

Working with My Computer

The best way to begin learning about the My Computer window is to work within it. Follow the next To Do item to see some of the things that are possible with My Computer and, therefore, with all windows that you need to manage.

To Do: Working in the My Computer Window

1. Open the My Computer window if you don't have it open already.

2. From the menu bar, select View, List. The view instantly changes to the list view.

3. Select View, Details. The list view expands to tell you more about each item, such as free space and total space on the disk and CD-ROM drives.

4. Go back to the View, Large Icons display. (The View, Small Icons display provides extremely small icons on most systems that do not add any readability over the list view.)

5. Maximize the My Computer window by clicking the Maximize button or by double-clicking the title bar.

6. Double-click the C disk drive icon. At first, Windows Me hides the contents of drive C, while providing links to the most common items, such as the My Documents folder. However, there may be times when you need to view the complete contents of the hard drive. Click View the Entire Contents of the Drive. When you do, you should see a window of folders and other icons. Each folder represents a folder on your disk drive named C. A folder is a list of files (and subfolders)

stored together in one group. The folder name appears under each folder icon. If you also see a hand holding the folder, the folder is known as a *shared folder* available to others on the network you're working on.

The grayed-out icons you might see are hidden or system files and folders. Depending on your window options, you might or might not see these icons. Select Tools, Folder Options and click the View tab to designate whether you want to see all hidden files and folders (in which case Windows Me grays out the system and normally hidden files and folders), all files except the hidden ones, or all files except both the hidden and system files. You generally won't work with system or hidden files, and by turning off their display, you clean up your file listings considerably. Click OK to save your changes.

> Folders enable you to group similar files together so that you can work with the entire group at once instead of having to work with individual files. For example, you can keep all your personal correspondence in a single folder so that you can copy it more easily to a disk when you want to back up that set of files.

The icons that look like pieces of paper are document icons that represent individual files, including programs and text files, on your system's C drive. You find other kinds of icons as well. If you see the list view when you display the C disk drive, use View, Large Icons to see the icons.

The window you're now looking at is a completely different window from the My Computer window. The window contains your C drive's contents. Anytime you want to traverse your C drive, or any other drive, and look at its contents, you can do so from the My Computer window. Minimize the window to see the My Computer window, which was originally hidden, come back into view.

7. To look at the contents of a file folder, double-click the file folder. When you do, the current window will change to reflect the new file folder. In previous versions of Windows, a new window was opened each time you selected a different drive or folder in My Computer. Now, the contents of the new drive or folder replaces the old contents in the My Computer window. Return to old contents by clicking the Back button. If you want to display a new window each time you change to a different drive or folder, select Tools, Folder Options and click Open Each Folder in Its Own Window.

8. Click the Back button so that you return to the drive C window. If you have lots of files on drive C, and most people do, you might have to use the scrollbars to see all the window's contents. As you open new folders, you can always return to the previous folder window by clicking the toolbar's Back button.

9. Click the Back button to return to the My Computer window.

4

10. Every time you change the window contents from the My Computer window by clicking an icon such as the C drive icon, a new set of window contents appears. You can traverse right back through all the windows you visited and return to the My Computer window contents by pressing the Back button on the toolbar, just as you do to traverse back through Web pages you might have traveled.

Click the arrow next to the My Computer toolbar's Views button. A view list drops down from which you can quickly select large icons, small icons, a list, or a detailed list view without having to first open the Views menu. If you don't see the View button, click the down arrow at the far right side of your taskbar to select the View button.

Other My Computer Folders

You will master some folders residing inside My Computer as you learn more about Windows Me. The Control Panel folder, discussed later in this hour, describes the non-printer devices connected to your PC, such as your modem, as well as system-setting options and printers.

If you've displayed the Web view folder options from the My Computer window, you'll see these three options at the left of the folder icons:

- My Documents—Contains a list of data files for many of your application programs.
- My Network Places—Contains a list of computers that are networked to yours (although you might not see this option if you do not use a network).
- Dial-Up Networking—Enables you to change your modem connection settings if you use a dial-up service to connect to the Internet.

Fortunately, most Internet installations automatically make Dial-Up Networking setting changes for you because the Dial-Up Networking options can be tedious.

All the windows view commands you've learned so far work throughout the Windows Me environment. Therefore, you can now change views for all windows you work with.

Introducing the Control Panel

The Control Panel icon enables you to adjust and manage the way hardware devices are attached to and respond to your computer. From the My Computer window, open the Control Panel icon, and you see a window like the one in Figure 4.2. If your Control Panel looks different with fewer options, click the option labeled View All Control Panel options. The compact Control Panel is nice to view once you familiarize yourself with the contents. Until then, display the full Control Panel window with all its icons showing.

The Control Panel's toolbar and menus are similar to those of the My Computer window. When you master windows basics for one kind of window, you can apply that talent to all other windows. From the Control Panel, you can change or modify system and hardware settings.

FIGURE 4.2

Modify the system settings from within the Control Panel.

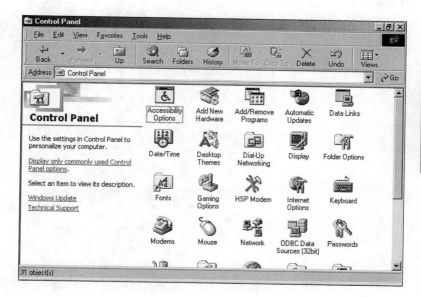

Be very sure that you know what to change before modifying values within the Control Panel. You could change a required setting that might be difficult to reverse later.

Modifying the Mouse Properties

Some operations inside the Control Panel are complex and could violate your system's setup. Many tasks are safe inside the Control Panel, however. Follow the next To Do item to learn how to modify the way your mouse behaves.

To Do: Modifying the Way the Mouse Behaves

1. Open the Control Panel window within the My Computer window if you have not yet done so.

2. Open the Mouse icon. The icon indicates that the mouse settings are found here. You see the Mouse Properties dialog box appear, as shown in Figure 4.3.

FIGURE 4.3

You can change the behavior of the mouse.

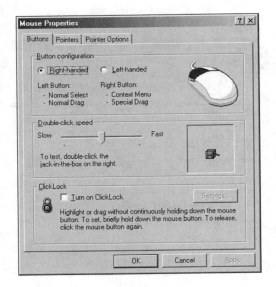

3. If you are left-handed but your mouse is set for a right-handed user, you can select the option button marked Left-Handed to change the mouse button functions. The buttons then change their functionality as described in the text beneath each button after the change. (The change will not take effect until you close the Mouse Properties dialog box or click the Apply button.) You can change the button back to its original state by clicking on the other hand.

4. Click the tab marked Pointers at the top of the Mouse Properties dialog box. From the Pointer portion of the dialog box, you can change the default appearance of the mouse. A scrolling list of mouse shapes indicates all the kinds of cursor shapes that appear when certain Windows Me events take place.

5. To change the normal mouse cursor (called the Normal Select shape), double-click the row with the Normal Select text. Windows Me displays another screen, shown in Figure 4.4. Different mouse cursors appear for different reasons. The Pointers dialog box enables you to select shapes for the various mouse cursors that can appear. The shapes that end with an .ani filename extension are animated cursors that move when they appear. If you see no animated cursors, you can add them at another time from the Control Panel's Add/Remove Programs option's Windows Setup tab. If you see no extra cursor sets, browse to the following folder to find them by clicking the Browse button: C:\Windows\Cursors.

FIGURE 4.4

Select a mouse cursor shape file.

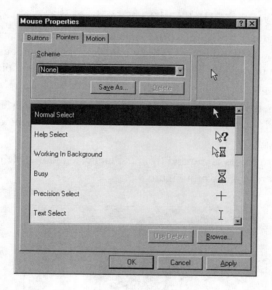

6. Windows Me needs to know the theme you want to use for your mouse cursors. Just for grins, click the down arrow next to (None) inside the Scheme area and point to 3D Pointers in the choices. Windows changes the cursors to three-dimensional shapes. (If 3D Pointers is not available, make another selection.)

7. Before leaving the Mouse Properties window, click the Use Default button to return the standard mouse cursor to its default pointer shape. If you've already returned to the Control Panel, you have to click the Mouse icon again to set the cursor back to its default shape.

8. Click OK and close the Control Panel. You can now close the My Computer window as well.

Using the Right Mouse Button

Windows Me uses the right mouse button to display context-sensitive menus with choices you can select at that time. You don't always need the My Computer window to make changes to your system as the following To Do item proves.

In Hour 1, "What Windows Millennium Edition Is All About," you learned that wallpaper is the name for the background you see on the screen when you start Windows Me and work within its windows. You can change that wallpaper to a different picture or eliminate the wallpaper altogether with a right mouse click.

To Do: Modifying Your Wallpaper

1. With all windows closed (click the toolbar's Show Desktop button, if the button appears, to quickly minimize all the windows), move the mouse cursor over the wallpaper in the middle of the screen. If your screen has no picture behind the icons but displays only a solid color, you do have wallpaper, but it's boring!

2. Point anywhere on your desktop and right-click. Windows Me looks to see that your mouse is pointing to the wallpaper and displays a menu of choices that are relevant to your position.

3. Select the Properties command from the menu. Windows Me opens the Display Properties screen, shown in Figure 4.5.

FIGURE 4.5

A right-click displays a wallpaper selection screen.

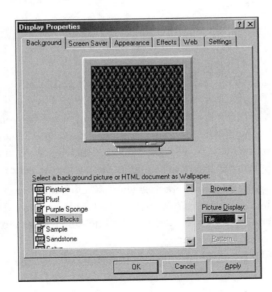

▼   4. Toward the bottom of the dialog box, you'll find a list of choices. These choices determine the wallpaper pattern or a Web page that you might want to use for your desktop's background. Scroll through the list of choices looking for an interesting name, such as Red Blocks, and click on that selection. Windows models the new wallpaper style in the small screen to give you a preview of it. You can go with that selection or choose another. (You may want to modify your selection by selecting an option such as Tile or Stretch from the Picture Display list box.)

   5. When you are happy with your selection, click the OK button, and presto, you've hung new wallpaper without messy cutting or gluing! Some wallpapers require that you change to the Active Desktop. Don't select any of these (marked with a
▲   painted window icon) for now.

You'll learn other uses of the right mouse button as you progress through this book. You learned here how to change the wallpaper pattern so that you don't get too bored by the same old look.

Startup in Emergencies

Now that you've familiarized yourself with Windows, its environment, and the Control Panel, this is a great time to ensure against a minor or major disaster. During the course of using Windows Me, you will add hardware and software. Windows Me makes adding such components relatively easy, but in some cases, problems might occur. Perhaps you receive a bad installation disk, or a hardware conflict arises that freezes up Windows Me.

By making a startup disk, you can safely get your computer started and access your hard disk when you otherwise cannot start your machine. The startup disk is little more than an MS-DOS boot disk, although the disk does contain several MS-DOS and Windows Me utility programs (such as the Scan Disk utility explained in Hour 21, "Using the Advanced System Tools") that can help you locate disk and memory troubles that can cause boot problems.

 If you use a laptop on the road, always carry a startup disk with you! The startup disk will help save you when you do not have Windows Me installation disks, MS-DOS disks, or utility programs readily available.

Before creating a startup disk, locate a high-density formatted disk. Make sure that the disk contains no data you need because the startup process overwrites all data on your disk. Follow the next To Do item to create a startup diskette.

4

To Do: Creating a Startup Diskette

1. Click the Start button.
2. Select Settings, Control Panel to display the Control Panel window.
3. Double-click the Add/Remove Programs icon.
4. Click the Startup Disk tab to display the Startup Disk page shown in Figure 4.6.

FIGURE 4.6

Create a startup disk for emergencies.

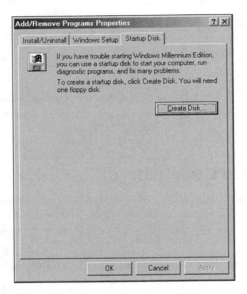

5. Click the Create Disk button. The dialog box will tell you when you need to insert the disk you use for the startup disk.
6. After the startup disk creation process ends, close the Control Panel and put the startup disk in a safe place.

After you create a startup disk, you have a disk in case of emergencies. If you find that you cannot access your hard disk or boot your computer because your system files are corrupt, you can regain hard disk access by inserting the startup disk and rebooting your computer. The startup disk will not be able to cure any problems, but you will have system access once again so that you can begin tracing the difficulties.

Summary

This hour taught you how to use the My Computer window. Don't be dismayed that this hour just skimmed the surface of what's available in the My Computer window because the My Computer icon provides a launching point for many powerful hardware and software interactions that sometimes take a while to master. The typical Windows Me user does not have to know all the details of the My Computer window to use Windows Me effectively.

Q&A

Q Will I use the My Computer icon a lot?

A This question's answer varies with different people. Some people use their computers primarily for one or two application programs. These people don't modify their computers very often and do not perform a lot of file interaction or system management, so they would rarely, if ever, need to open the My Computer window.

On the other hand, if you modify the hardware on your computer often, you might have to access the My Computer window often. As described in Hour 3, Windows Me is designed for use with Plug-and-Play hardware, which means that you don't have to configure Windows Me every time you change hardware on your computer. Not all hardware devices are compatible with Plug-and-Play, however, and you might have to modify some Windows Me system settings using the My Computer window when you install new computer hardware, such as a second printer.

Q I like the animated cursors, but will they slow down my computer?

A If you use a slow computer, you don't want to do anything that will drain more speed from the processor. Nevertheless, the animated cursors do not seem to cause much of a drain on the processor's resources. The animated cursor icons are small and efficient. Therefore, you should feel free to use whatever cursors you want to use.

Workshop

The quiz and exercise questions are designed to test your knowledge of the material covered in this hour. The answers are in Appendix C, "Answers to Quizzes."

Quiz

1. What are some of the items you can manage from the My Computer window?
2. Why does Windows Me offer multiple views of the same window?
3. How can you tell if a folder is shared?
4. If you need to modify the way your mouse behaves, where would you go?
5. Why do you need a startup disk?

Exercises

1. Change your mouse button's orientation to swap the left and right mouse buttons. Close the Mouse dialog box and use the mouse for a while. You'll see that the buttons are reversed. Change the buttons back. You'll learn many ways to adjust your computer's behavior as you explore the rest of this 24-hour tutorial.

2. Shut down your computer. Insert your startup diskette in the disk drive. Turn your computer on once again. The diskette takes over; you won't see Windows Me! From the prompt that appears, you or anyone else well-versed in diagnosing computer problems can often get your computer back and running if a failure keeps Windows Me from starting properly when you start your computer without the startup disk.

PART 2

Morning Windows Desktop Exploration

Hour

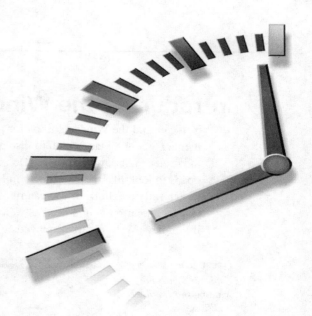

HOUR 5

Using Explorer to Navigate

Windows Me includes a comprehensive program that you might use every time you turn on your computer, the Windows *Explorer,* which graphically displays your entire computer system in a hierarchical tree structure. With Explorer, you have access to everything inside your computer (and outside if you are part of a network or on the Internet).

This hour demonstrates the Windows Explorer, a program that enables you to manipulate all of your computer's software and hardware. After you've learned about Explorer, the hour wraps up by showing you some time- and disk-saving features of Windows Me.

In this hour, you will

- Change the various displays of the Windows Explorer
- Learn why Explorer makes managing your computer almost painless
- Learn what shortcuts are all about
- Use the Recycle Bin

Introducing the Windows Explorer

You can find the Windows Explorer program listed on the Start menu's third cascaded menu. Click the Start button to display the Start menu. Select Programs, Accessories, and then select Windows Explorer. (Do not select Internet Explorer!) The Explorer window opens to look like the one shown in Figure 5.1. Although the figure shows the Explorer screen fully maximized, you can run Explorer in a smaller window if you want something else to appear on your screen as well. In addition, you might see additional information if you have Web folders displayed.

FIGURE 5.1

Explorer's opening window shows folders and files.

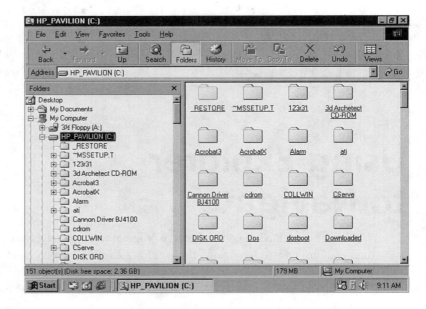

Your Explorer screen might look slightly different, depending on your Windows Me configuration. You can see how to change your Explorer's view later in this section.

You can quickly start Explorer by right-clicking over the Start menu and selecting Explore from the pop-up menu that appears. Explorer opens to the Windows\Start Menu folder. If you have a Windows keyboard, one with the flying Windows logo on a key (called the Windows key), you can start Explorer even faster by pressing Windows+E.

The left side of the Explorer screen contains a hierarchical overview of your computer system. You will recognize many of the icon entries from your My Computer window. If a vertical scrollbar appears on the left window, scroll to see the rest of the hierarchical system tree.

> If a folder icon appears with a plus sign to the left of it, as the Windows folder does, that folder contains additional folders. Folder icons without the plus sign contain only data files (called *documents* throughout Windows Me) but not additional folders. When you open a folder and display its contents, the plus sign changes to a minus sign, as you'll see in the To Do item a little later.

The right window contains a pictorial overview of the contents of whichever device or folder you select in the left window. The overview might contain large or small icons or a list view, depending on the view you select. Starting with Windows Me, you can display a thumbnail view that shows a small version, the *thumbnail* of any Web page or graphic image that appears in the Windows Explorer window. As you select different items in the left window, the right window changes to reflect your changes. The following To Do item guides you through an initial exploration of Explorer.

To Do: Working with Explorer

▼ To Do

1. Start Windows Explorer and scroll through the left window pane until you see the icon for the C: drive in the window. (Click the My Computer icon in the left window.)

2. If you see a plus sign next to your C: icon in the left window (you might have to scroll the window's scrollbar to see the C: icon), click the plus sign to display the contents of the C: drive. The plus becomes a minus sign, and the left window opens the C: icon showing the list of folders and documents on the C: drive. Click the drive's minus sign again to close the window. Click once more to turn the plus to a minus and watch the right window. As you change between these two views of the C: drive (detailed and overview), watch the right window.

5

> Notice that the right window does not change as you click the C: icon in the left window. The reason is that the right window always displays the contents of whatever you highlight in the left window. Whether the C: icon is open (with a minus sign) or closed (with a plus sign), the C: icon is highlighted. If you were to click one of those documents on the C: drive, the right window would then update to show the contents of that folder (don't click a folder just yet).

▼

▼   3. Click the highest level in the left window, labeled Desktop, and Windows Me displays the contents of your desktop in the right window.

4. Click the C: icon to display the contents of the C: drive. Depending on the contents and size of your C: drive, the right window can contain a few or many document files.

5. Press Alt+V to open the View menu on the menu bar. Select Toolbars to display a list of tools you can display on your toolbar. You will recognize the tools from the My Computer window. For example, you can add text labels to the toolbar icons if you right-click the toolbar and select Customize.

   Click the drop-down list box on the toolbar labeled Address Bar (display the Address Bar item from View, Toolbar if you don't see the list box) to see another access method for swapping between devices, folders, and files on your computer. If you ever display more information than can fit in the left window, the Address drop-down list box compacts the list so that detail does not appear in your viewing area.

6. Display the View menu once again. The Large Icons window (the default display view) consumes most of the right window. Therefore, select View, Small Icons to make more room available in the right window. The View, Small Icons command shrinks the size of the icons to show more items in the right window.

7. Select View, List. Windows Me Explorer retains the small icon sizes and displays the items by type of item (folders first and then documents).

8. Select View, Details. Windows Me Explorer displays the items in a detailed format that describes the name, type, and modified date of each item. Actually, given the detail that you normally have by using Explorer, you will almost always want to display the right window in this detailed list view. When you work with files, you will often need to know their size, type, or last modified date.

   Click Name, the title of the first detailed column in the right window. Watch the window's contents change as you then click Modified. Explorer sorts the display to appear in date order (oldest first). Click Modified again and Explorer displays the items in reverse date order from the most recent to the oldest. If you click any column twice in a row, Windows sorts the column in reverse order. You can always sort columns in order or reverse order by clicking the column's name when working in a columnar Windows window.

9. If you want to see more of one of Explorer's windows, you can drag the vertical dividing line that falls between the two windows to the left or right. For example, if you want the left window to be smaller to make room for more large icons, drag
▼   the center column to the left and release the mouse when the left window is as

▼   small as you want it. (Remember that the mouse cursor changes shape when you place it at the proper position on the dividing column.)

Explorer does not update the display every time you resize a window. Therefore, if you enlarge the right window while in an icon view, Explorer does not automatically rearrange the right window's icons to fill up the newly enlarged space. You will almost always want to select View, Refresh after modifying Explorer's window sizes. Perform Refresh when you open Explorer in a window and then add or delete files from another window.

> If you make the left or right window too small, Windows Me adds a horizontal scrollbar to the small window so that you can scroll its contents back and forth to see what's highlighted or to select another item.

10. The Explorer environment is always updating itself to reflect your current actions. Therefore, the right-click menu commands change, depending on whether you select a text document, folder, sound document, graphics document, disk drive, or network drive. Click a folder and right-click to see the menu that appears. Now, right-click over a document file to see a slightly different menu. The actions you might want to perform on a document are often different from the actions you might want to perform on a folder, and the menu reflects those differences. The right-click's pop-up menus are context-sensitive, so they contain only the options you can use at the time.

> Open a folder by double-clicking it, and then return to the previous (parent) folder by clicking the Up icon on the Explorer's taskbar. Use the Up toolbar button to return to your previously open Explorer window. You can return to the previous folder you opened (which is not necessarily the parent folder) by clicking the Back button.

11. Many Explorer users copy files to and from disk drives and other kinds of drives, such as networked drives.

You can use Explorer to copy and move individual files or multiple files at once. Often, you want to put one or more files on a disk to use on your home computer for weekend overtime. (Sure, you want to do that a lot!)

To select a Windows file (called a document, remember), click that document ▼   or point to it if you've turned on the single-click option. To select more than one

5

document at a time, hold down the Ctrl key while clicking (or pointing to) each document that you want to select. You can select folders, as well as documents. When you select a folder and other document files to copy to a disk, for example, Windows Me copies all the document files within the folder, as well as the other document files you've selected, to the disk. Figure 5.2 shows an Explorer screen with several document files and a folder selected. The File, Send To command is about to send those files to the disk in the A: drive. The Send To command is useful for sending copies of selected files and folders to a disk, a fax recipient, or one of several other destinations you've set up.

FIGURE 5.2

Select multiple docu-
ments and folders if
you need to copy sev-
eral at a time.

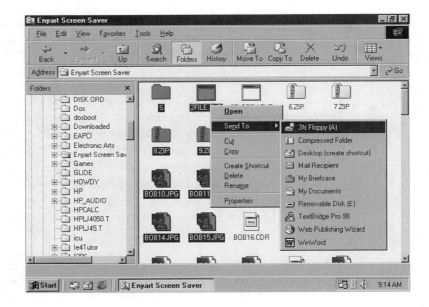

 If you want to select all but one or two documents and folders inside a window, first Ctrl+click the one or two that you don't want to select (which selects those) and choose Edit, Invert Selection to reverse the selection. All the items that were not selected are now selected, and the one or two that were selected are not selected anymore.

12. When you want to move or copy a file to another folder (the Send To command works only for disks and other non-hard disk devices), select the file (or select a group of files) in the right window and drag while holding down the *right* mouse

▼   button to the folder or disk where you want to move or copy the file. Windows opens a pop-up menu when you release the files from which you can select a move or copy operation. If you don't like to drag, you can copy or move files in two steps by clicking Move To or Copy To, selecting a destination and clicking OK.

13. Rename files and folders if you need to by selecting the file or folder and pressing the F2 shortcut key. (F2 is the shortcut for the File, Rename menu command.) Windows Me highlights the name, so you can edit or enter a new name. When you

▲   press Enter, Windows Me saves the new name.

The strength of Explorer is that your entire computer system appears in the left window at all times. When you want to drag a document or folder to a different directory on a completely different drive (or even to another computer on the network if you are connected to a network), the target disk drive always appears in the left window. As long as you've clicked the disk drive's plus sign to display that disk's directories, you can drop a file into that directory from elsewhere in the system.

The Explorer Options

Explorer supports various display options for the items inside its windows. Recall from previous hours that Windows Me supports the use of filename extensions. The Tools, Folder Options command displays tabbed dialog boxes that enable you to control the items in the Explorer display.

Different users require different output from the Explorer program. There are types of documents that you simply don't need to display during normal work inside Explorer. The system files are good examples of files that the typical user does not need to see.

In addition, the actual location of the file—its pathname—does not always match the system of embedded folders. In other words, a document might be located inside two embedded folders shown with the Explorer display, but the actual file might be embedded three levels deep on your hard disk. The system of folders—usually but not always—matches the system of directories on your disk. If you need to know exactly where folders and documents are located on your disk drive, you can request that Explorer display the full pathname of those folders and documents using these steps:

1. Select the Tools, Folder Options command to display the Folder Options tabbed dialog box shown in Figure 5.3.

2. Click the View tab to see the folder display options.

3. If you click the option labeled Display the Full Path in Title Bar, Explorer displays a full pathname of selected documents in the title bar every time you select one of the items in the left window.

5

FIGURE 5.3

The Folder Options dialog box determines the appearance of Explorer.

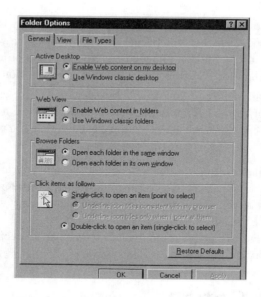

4. Another option, Hide file extensions for known file types, determines how Windows responds to known file types. Windows comes installed with several types of files already *registered*, and you might not ever need to register additional types. Registered files are files that Windows recognizes by their filename extensions. When you install a program whose data file is not registered, the installation program registers the file type with Windows.

   The file type's registration tells Windows the required program needed to process files with that extension. Once registered, when you double-click that file's icon, Windows starts the program you've associated with that file. For example, when you double-click a file with a .CDA extension, Windows starts the Media Player application because Media Player is the application associated to all files that end with the .CDA extension.

5. Look through the remaining items to see the other folder options that Windows provides. Click OK to finish your selection.

If you are familiar with MS-DOS and filenames, you might feel more comfortable if you display the file extensions on the Explorer screen documents. Hiding the extensions reduces clutter in the right window, but with the extension, you can determine the exact name of the file when you need the exact name. Fortunately, with or without the extensions, the icons next to the filenames help remind you of the file's type.

If you hide filename extensions in Explorer, Windows hides those extensions in almost every other file listing. For example, if you hide Explorer's extension display, you will no longer see extensions in WordPad's Open dialog boxes. You won't even see them in applications that you purchase in addition to Windows applications, such as Microsoft Excel.

Managing Documents with a Right Mouse Click

After you display the Explorer (or any other file list in Windows Me), you can point to any folder or document and click the right mouse button to perform several actions on the document. Here's what you can do with documents:

- Select the document
- Play sound documents or open graphics documents
- Print the document
- Copy the file to a disk
- Cut or copy selected text to the Windows Clipboard
- Create a shortcut access to the file so that you can later open the file without using the Open dialog box
- Delete the document
- Rename the document
- Change the document's system attributes

Right-clicking a file's name produces a menu that enables you to perform these actions.

The following To Do item walks you through many of these right-click actions.

To Do: Practicing with the Right-Click

▼ To Do

1. Point to a text file on your C: drive. Text files use a spiral notepad icon. Open your Windows folder if you see no text files in your C's root folder. Point to the file and right-click. A pop-up menu opens to the right of the document, as shown in Figure 5.4.

   The Open command always attempts to examine the document's native format and open the document with an appropriate program such as the Windows's Notepad program. Although the first command is Open for text files, the command is Play if you right-clicked a sound file. For now, don't select Open.

▼

5

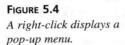

FIGURE 5.4
A right-click displays a pop-up menu.

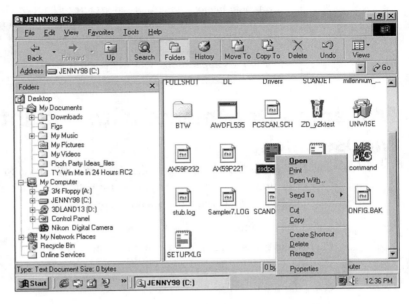

2. Find a blank formatted disk. Insert the disk in the A: drive. Right-click over the text document and select the Send To command. The disk drive appears in the list that appears when you select Send To. When you select the disk drive, Windows Me begins sending an exact copy of the text file to the disk. Windows graphically displays the sending of the document to the A: drive with a flying document going from one folder to another.

3. Point to the text file once again and right-click. Select Delete. Windows displays the message box shown in Figure 5.5. Don't choose Yes because you need to keep the text file where it is.

   The *Recycle Bin* is a special location inside Windows that holds the documents you delete. The Recycle Bin's icon appears on your Windows desktop. Windows gives you one last chance to recover deleted documents. When you delete a document file of any type, Windows sends that file to the Recycle Bin. The documents are then out of your way but not deleted permanently until you empty the Recycle Bin. Remember that you can delete documents directly from any Open dialog box.

4. Click No because you should not delete the text file now.

FIGURE 5.5

The Recycle Bin holds deleted documents for a while.

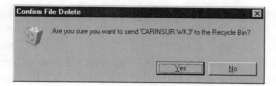

5. It's extremely easy to rename a document. Right-click to display the document's menu and select Rename. Windows highlights the name, and you can edit or completely change the name to something else. Change the filename now to XYZ. Press Enter to keep the new name. (If you want to cancel a rename operation you've started, press Esc.)

> Do not supply an extension when you rename the file unless you've turned on the filename extension display. For example, if you renamed a Readme document (that is really named Readme.txt) to NewName.txt, the document would actually be named NewName.txt.txt! Fortunately, Windows Me warns you if you change a file's extension, so you can accept or reject the change before it becomes permanent.

6. Try this: Move the mouse pointer to an area of the Explorer's right pane where no icon appears and right-click. A new menu appears.

The Undo Rename command reverses the previous renaming of the document. Select Undo Rename, and the XYZ text file you just renamed reverts to its original name.

 5

> Undo Rename remembers a long list of past names. For example, if you change a document's name three times in a row, and then select Undo Rename three times, Windows reverts the name to its original name!

You now understand the most important commands in Explorer's right-click document menu. This menu differs slightly depending on the kind of document you click (folder, sound, graphic, program, text, word processor document, and so on), but the fundamental menu of commands stays the same and works the way this section describes. If you want to make copies of files on the hard disk or move the file to a different location, you should master the techniques described in the next section.

Right-Click to Copy and Move Documents

A file icon's right-click menu offers advanced copying and moving of files. The *Clipboard* is the go-between for all Windows copy, cut, paste, and move operations. When you want to copy a file from one place to another, you can place a copy of the file on the Windows Clipboard. When you do, the file is on the Clipboard and out of your way, until you go to where you want the file copied. You'll then paste the file to the new location, in effect copying from the Clipboard to the new location. When you copy a file to another location, the file remains in its original location and a copy is made elsewhere.

The Clipboard holds one item at a time. If you copy a document to the Clipboard, a subsequent copy overwrites the first copy.

If you want to copy a file to disk, use the Send To command explained in the previous section because Send To is easier to use when copying to a floppy disk.

When you move a file from one location to another, Windows Me first performs a cut operation. This means that Windows Me deletes the file from its current location and sends the file to the Clipboard (overwriting whatever was on the Clipboard). When you find the location to which you want to move the file, Windows Me copies the Clipboard's contents to the new location (such as a different folder or disk drive).

The Clipboard

In a way, the Clipboard is like a short-term Recycle Bin, which holds all deleted files until you are ready to remove them permanently. The Clipboard holds deleted (or copied) documents and pieces of documents, but only until you send something else to the Clipboard or exit Windows Me and turn off your computer.

To Do: Practicing with Move and Copy

1. Right-click a text file's icon.
2. Select the Copy command. Windows sends a complete copy of the document to the Clipboard. The Clipboard keeps the document until you replace the Clipboard's contents with something else or until you exit Windows. Therefore, you can send the Clipboard document to several subsequent locations.

▼ 3. Right-click a folder in Explorer's right window. The menu appears with the Paste command. Windows knows that something is on the Clipboard (a copy of the text file), and you can send the file's copy to the folder by clicking Paste. Don't paste the file now, however, unless you then open the folder and remove the file. There is no need to have two copies of the text file on your disk.

4. Right-click once again over the text file. This time, select Cut instead of Copy. Windows erases the document file from the Windows folder and places the file on the Clipboard.

> Windows keeps the name of the document in place until you paste the document elsewhere. The name is misleading because it makes you think the document is still in the folder. A ghost outline of an icon appears where the document's icon originally appeared. As long as the name still appears in the folder, you can open the file and do things with it, but as soon as you paste the Clipboard contents elsewhere, the file permanently disappears from the folder.

5. Right-click a folder. If you select Paste, the text document leaves its original location and goes to the folder. Don't paste now but press Esc twice (the first Esc keypress removes the right-click menu, and the second restores the cut file).

6. Windows is as safe as possible. If you change your mind after a copy or cut operation, you can always reverse the operation! Right-click the icon area and the pop-up menu contains an Undo command that reverses the most recent copy or cut.

> Here's a much faster way to move a document to another folder listed in the Explorer windows: Drag the document to the folder! Try it by dragging a test file over to another hard disk or to another folder on the same disk. An outline of the document travels with the mouse cursor during the drag. When you release the mouse button, the file anchors into its new position. Want to restore the item? Right-click the mouse and select Undo Move or Undo Copy. Windows always enables you to undo copies and moves, no matter how you perform the move, through menus or with the mouse.

If you want to use the drag-and-drop shortcut method for copying documents, hold down the Ctrl key while dragging the document to the other folder. (The key combination is easy if you remember that both copy and Ctrl begin with the same letter.) As you drag an item, Windows displays a plus sign at the bottom of the icon to

▼

5

▼   indicate that you are copying and not moving. To cancel a copy you've started, drag the item back to its original location before releasing your mouse button or press Esc before releasing your mouse button. In addition, if you drag the item while holding the right mouse button, Windows Me displays a pop-up menu, enabling you to specify that you want to move or copy the document.

7. Sometimes, you might need a document for a program outside of the program in which you're currently working. You can place a document on the Windows desktop. Select a text file and copy the document to the Clipboard by right-clicking and selecting Copy. (You also can use drag-and-drop if you want. Hold down Ctrl and drag the document out of the Explorer window, if you've resized Explorer so that you can see part of the desktop, and continue with step 8.)

8. Move the cursor on the Windows desktop to an area of the wallpaper that has no icon on it. Right-click to display a menu and select Paste. The document's file will now have an icon on your desktop along with the other icons already there.

▲   To copy or move the desktop document, use the right-click menu or drag the document with the mouse, as explained earlier in this hour.

Placing Documents on the Desktop

The items you place on the desktop, whether by copying or by moving, stay on the desktop until you remove them from the desktop. Even after shutting down Windows Me and turning off your computer, a desktop item will be there when you return.

Although you shouldn't clutter the desktop with too many documents, you might want to work with a document in several different programs over a period of a few days. By putting the document on the desktop, it is always easily available to any application that's running. Of course, if you run an application in a maximized window, you must shrink the window to some degree to retrieve the document because you have to see the desktop to copy and move the items on it. Also, you can drag Web pages to your desktop if you've activated the Active Desktop feature.

Where Do the Deleted Files Go?

When you delete files by using dialog boxes or Explorer, you now know that those files go to the Recycle Bin. While in the Recycle Bin, those files are out of your way and deleted in every respect except one: They are not really deleted! Those files are not in their original locations, but they stay in the Recycle Bin until you empty it.

Periodically, you will want to check the Recycle Bin for files that you can erase completely from your hard disk. The following To Do item explain the Recycle Bin in more detail.

The Recycle Bin icon changes from an overflowing bin to an empty one when you empty the Recycle Bin, enabling you to tell at a glance whether your Recycle Bin is empty.

To Do: Working with the Recycle Bin

1. Display your desktop by minimizing any open windows you might have on the screen.

2. Double-click the Recycle Bin icon. The Recycle Bin window opens, as shown in Figure 5.6.

FIGURE 5.6

The Recycle Bin lists deleted files that you can recover.

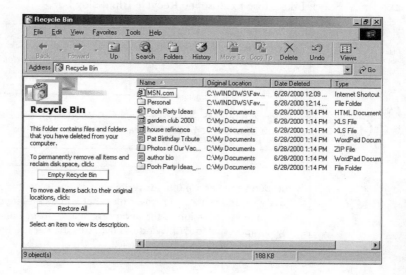

3. If you've deleted at least one file, you should have one or two files already in the Recycle Bin. There might be many more, depending on what has taken place on your system. You will recognize the format of the Recycle Bin's column headings; you can adjust the width of the columns by dragging the column separators with your mouse.

 The Recycle Bin dialog box contains all deleted files on your system—not just the deleted files on one of your disk drives. You can change the disks that the Recycle Bin uses for its storage of deleted files, but unless you change your Windows Me default values, all files that you delete through Windows Me go to the Recycle Bin (with the exception of files deleted from a diskette, which are not moved to the Recycle Bin.)

▼   4. Most of the Recycle Bin dialog box's menu bar commands are identical to the commands in Explorer. When you select an item (or more than one item by using Ctrl+click), the menu commands apply to that selected item.

5. Double-click one of the Recycle Bin's items to display a Properties dialog box for that item. It tells you additional information about the deleted item, such as the date you created and deleted the item. Click OK to close the dialog box.

6. Perhaps the most important menu command is File, Empty Recycle Bin. This command empties the entire Recycle Bin. You can select this command now or click the button (if visable), if there is nothing in your Recycle Bin that you think you will need later. Then click Yes to confirm.

▲   7. Select File, Close to close the Recycle Bin dialog box.

Double-click (or single-click if you've selected the single-click option) a Recycle Bin icon to look at a document to verify the contents before deleting the document.

When you use MS-DOS to delete a file, Windows Me erases the file as soon as you issue the command instead of sending the file to the Recycle Bin.

Although the Recycle Bin adds a level of safety to your work so that you have a second chance to recover files that you delete, if you hold the Shift key when you highlight a file and press Delete (from Explorer or any of the My Computer windows), Windows bypasses the Recycle Bin and deletes the files from your system immediately.

Making Windows Me Easier

There are numerous ways to make Windows easier for your day-to-day work. Three time-saving techniques are as follows:

- Changing the Start menu
- Adding single-key access to programs
- Shortcuts

After you create single-key access to a program or a shortcut or you change the Start menu, those time-savers stay in effect, making work inside Windows Me much more efficient.

These time-savers might not help everyone, but they often help users of Windows Me. You have to experiment with the techniques until you find the ones that help you the most. Practice using the time-savers by following this To Do item.

To Do: Saving Time with Windows

1. You can add programs to the top of the Start menu by dragging a program from Explorer or My Computer to the Start button. Open the Explorer window if Explorer is not running.

2. Click the Windows folder. The folder's contents appear in the right window.

> Before adding programs to the Start menu, you must know the command and location of the program you are adding. If you do not know the path to the program, you can use the Find commands described in Hour 9, "Finding Files, Folders, and Friends."

3. Scroll down the window to locate a game called FreeCell (the extension is .exe). FreeCell is a solitare card game.

4. Drag the FreeCell icon to your Start button. The icon stays in place, but an outline of the icon moves with your dragged mouse cursor.

5. Release the icon over the Start button. You've just added the FreeCell game to the top of your Start menu.

6. Close Explorer and click your Start button. Your Start menu now includes the FreeCell game, as shown in Figure 5.7. You can now start FreeCell without traversing several Start menu layers for those times when the boss is away for a short while. (Depending on the programs already at the top of your Start menu, you might see additional entries.) You may have noticed that the menu item reads, "Shortcut to Freecell." Right-click and select Rename to change it so that it reads "Freecell" as shown.

5

FIGURE 5.7

Your Start menu now includes the FreeCell game.

> Windows Me offers a great way to rearrange and modify your Start menu
> without going through the windows and buttons of the Settings, Taskbar
> and Start Menu option. Any time you want to move one of the Start menu's
> entries from one location to another, display that item on the Start menu
> and drag that item to another location on the menu. (Don't click the item
> and release the mouse; be sure that you click and hold your mouse button.)
> If you right-click over any Start menu item, a pop-up menu appears,
> enabling you to rename or delete that item.

7. Delete the FreeCell game from the Start menu (you can add it later if you really want it there) by selecting Settings, Taskbar and Start Menu from the Start menu, selecting the Advanced tab, clicking Remove, and selecting the Start menu entry you want to remove. Scroll to the FreeCell game and select the FreeCell entry.

8. After selecting FreeCell, click the Remove command button to remove the game from the Start menu.

9. Click the Close button, but do not close the Start menu dialog box. Scroll through the options at the bottom of the dialog box to see all the ways Windows Me enables you to modify the Start menu's behavior.

10. Click the Advanced command button. Windows opens Explorer.

11. If you click the Programs folder, Explorer displays the items in the Start menu's first set of cascaded menus.

12. Open the Accessories folder to view the contents of the Accessories group. Remember that you're viewing contents of the Accessories menu that cascades from the Start menu. The Calculator program's icon appears in this folder group.

13. Right-click the Calculator icon to display a menu.

14. Select Properties to display the Calculator program's Properties tabbed dialog box (see Figure 5.8).

15. Press Alt+K to move the cursor to the Shortcut key text prompt. Type C at the prompt. Windows Me changes the C to Ctrl + Alt + C on the screen. Ctrl+Alt+C is now the shortcut for the Calculator program. If you run a program that uses a shortcut key you've added to Windows Me, the program's shortcut key takes precedence over the Windows Me shortcut key.

16. Click OK to close the dialog box.

FIGURE 5.8

You can now add a single-key shortcut that will start the calcula-tor program.

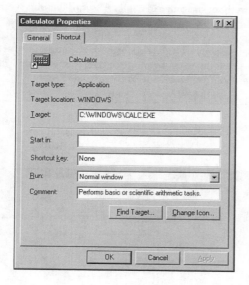

17. Select File, Close to exit Explorer and then close the Taskbar and Start Menu Properties dialog box.

Whenever you now press Ctrl+Alt+C, Windows starts its Calculator program. This single-key shortcut (actually a simultaneous three-key shortcut) enables you to start programs instantly, from virtually anywhere in the Windows system, without having to locate the program's menu or icon.

5

Shortcuts

A subfolder resides in your Windows folder called Start Menu. The Start Menu's folder contains all the items that appear on your Start menu, including the items you drag to the Start menu as you did in the previous task. If you display the contents of the Start menu in Explorer, you see small arrows at the bottom of the icons there, as shown in Figure 5.9. The arrows indicate shortcuts to the file.

The name shortcut has a double meaning in Windows Me—one of the reasons that this section's timesavers can become confusing.

A shortcut is actually better termed an *alias file*. When you create a shortcut, such as on the Start menu, Windows does not make a copy of the program in every location where you place the icon. Windows actually creates a link to that program, called a shortcut, that points to the program on your disk wherever its location might be.

If you right-click a document or folder in Explorer's right window, you see the Create Shortcut command that creates a shortcut to the document or folder to which you are pointing. Windows creates a new icon and title (the title begins with Shortcut too) but does not actually create a copy of the item. Instead, Windows creates a link to that item. The link reduces disk space taken up by multiple copies of the same files. The shortcut pointer takes much less space than a copy of the actual file would.

FIGURE 5.9

Start menu items are actually shortcuts to files.

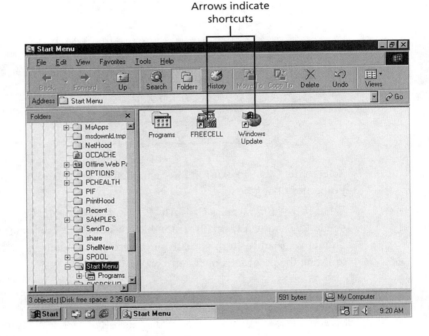

Summary

This hour showed you how to use the Explorer to search your computer system for documents and folders, as well as how to manage the computer system by using a uniform interface for all your storage devices. Copying and moving among folders and documents are painless functions when you use Explorer. You can display the item to be moved in the right window and drag that item to any device listed in the left window. Inside Explorer, you can associate file types to programs, so you can click a document and run the appropriate program that works with a document.

Three shortcuts exist that help you access your programs. You can add a shortcut to the desktop, to the Start menu system, and even to the keyboard to start programs quickly.

Q&A

Q Why does it seem as though many Explorer functions are available elsewhere, such as in the My Computer window and in Open dialog boxes?

A You can find many of Explorer's capabilities elsewhere. Windows is known for giving you the tools you need where you need them. You don't have to hunt for the tools you need.

Q I'm confused; are there three kinds of shortcuts?

A There are three versions of shortcuts in Windows Me. You can add a single-key shortcut to any program. When you press Ctrl+Alt and that key at the same time, Windows starts the program. You can be working in Explorer, at the desktop, or in virtually any other program, but when you press the shortcut keystroke, Windows starts the program you've assigned to that shortcut key.

When you right-click a document or folder and select the Create Shortcut command, Windows creates a shortcut to the item, which is really an alias name that knows the location of the original document or folder, but which acts like a copy of the item.

When you add items to the Start menu (or any menu cascading out from the Start menu), you must create a shortcut to that item because you don't want a copy of the same program all over your disk drive. Therefore, the menu command will be a shortcut to the program that, after you select that menu item, finds the program on the disk drive and starts the program.

5

Workshop

The quiz and exercise questions are designed to test your knowledge of the material covered in this hour. The answers are in Appendix C, "Answers to Quizzes."

Quiz

1. How does the new Windows Me thumbnail view display lists of files?

2. *True or false*: You should start Internet Explorer to manage your computer's drives, folders, and files.

3. Why would you want to display filename extensions in Windows Explorer?

4. How can you rearrange Start menu entries with your mouse only?

5. How can you tell at a glance that an icon represents a shortcut and not a file?

Exercises

1. Place your favorite word processing program at the top of your Start menu for quick access to the program. Then, add a keyboard shortcut to the word processor so that you don't even have to display the Start menu to start the program.

2. Open the Start menu's Settings, Taskbar and Start Menu dialog box. Click the Advanced tab. Determine how you can use the bottom scrolling list of options to change the behavior of your Start menu.

HOUR 6

A Call for Help

This hour shows you how to help yourself! That is—how to help yourself find help when using Windows Me. Although this book is *really* all you'll ever need to use Windows effectively (self-promotion was never one of my weak points), when you get confused, Windows offers a good set of online tools that you can access to find out how to accomplish a specific task.

If you've used previous versions of Windows, you will notice that Microsoft has revamped the entire help system.

In this hour, you will

- Access the help system
- Search the Internet for answers
- Access Windows application help

Introducing the Help System

Even Windows Me experts need help now and then with Windows. Windows is simply too vast, despite its simple appearance and clean desktop, for users to know everything about the system. Windows includes a powerful built-in

Help system. The Help system is online, meaning, in this case, that the help is on your disk and available from anywhere within the Windows Me environment. Help is available whenever you need it. For example, if you are working with Explorer and forget a short-cut key, you can search the online help system for the words *shortcut key*, and Windows gives advice about shortcut keys.

There are a number of ways you can request help while working in Windows. There are also a tremendous number of places from which you can get help. This hour focuses on the most common ways that you can use online help and also offers tips along the way.

To use every help feature available to you in Windows, you need Internet access. Microsoft keeps up-to-date advice on the Web, such as bug reports and add-on programs to Windows that you can download to improve your use of Windows Me.

The taskbar is always available to you no matter what else you are doing in Windows Me. Even if you've hidden the taskbar behind a running program, the taskbar is available as soon as you point the mouse to the bottom of the screen. You can find a Help command on the taskbar's Start menu. Help displays the online help's opening screen by using a Web browser format. To get started, the next To Do item shows you how to access the online help system.

To Do: Accessing Help from the Start Menu

To Do

1. Click the Start button to display the Start menu.
2. Select Help to request online help. After a brief pause, you see the Windows Help screen shown in Figure 6.1.

The Help window offers two kinds of help: local help that searches your PC's Windows Me help files for answers to your questions and Web help resources that connect to your Internet provider and accesses Microsoft's huge online help resource.

The Help window contains a toolbar that works like a Web-browsing toolbar.

FIGURE 6.1

The Windows Help screen offers all kinds of help.

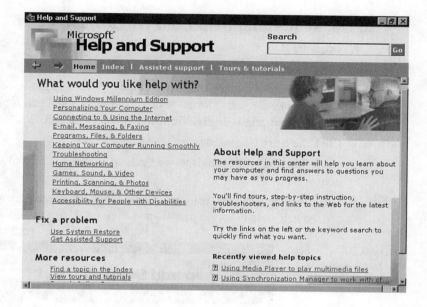

When you need help, you aren't limited to your own system help files. Although you can get many answers from your PC's local help files, Microsoft's online Help window makes it easy for you to contact the large online help databases Microsoft stores on the Web.

The Help window resides on your disk as an HTML file, which is the format behind all Web pages. Web pages can be local or on the Internet—your PC reacts to both in the same manner. Therefore, the Help window acts like a Web page. When you rest your mouse cursor over a *hot spot* (a link to another location, also called a *hyperlink*), the mouse cursor changes to a pointing hand to let you know that if you click that hot spot, another page will appear. As with all help pages, you can traverse backward through your help screen travels by clicking the toolbar's Back button.

6

Getting Local Help

If you have a question about Windows or about a certain utility program that comes with Windows, try the local help first. You will find many common Windows answers there, and searching your local disk is generally quicker than waiting on a Web search as the following To Do item demonstrates:

To Do: Requesting Help from Windows Me

1. Open the Help window if it is no longer open.

2. After a brief pause, the Help screen that you saw in Figure 6.1 appears.

   The initial Help window offers a summary of the help items available to you in an Explorer-like format. Click an item to read more about that topic. When you click a topic, more details emerge from which you can select.

3. Click the entry labeled, Games, Sound, & Video.

4. Click Working with Sounds to see the help contents related to sounds within your help system.

5. Click Playing CDs and then click Using Media Player to Play Multimedia Files to see the help details appear as shown in Figure 6.2.

Figure 6.2

The Help window offers CD help.

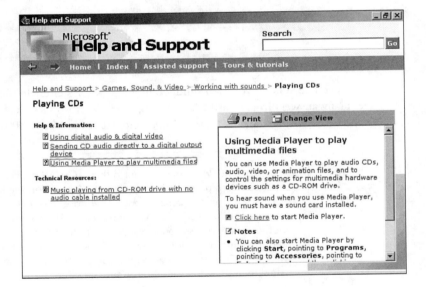

6. Press the Back button to see the Help screen before you displayed the detail. As with any Web page, you can click the Back button to return to the previous help screen. If you view several topics in succession, you sometimes want to return to a previous topic. Return to the detail page once again. You can also return to pages you've backed up from by clicking the Forward button.

   Don't close the help screen yet because the next section needs you to leave it open.

The local help's Contents page contains an Explorer-like view of the entire Windows Help system on your disk. You move from general to more detailed topics as you dive deeper into the help system.

Searching the Index

The help system offers an index search that helps you zero in to a more specific item for which you need help.

Follow this To Do item to use the index.

To Do: Using the Index in Your Search

1. Click the Index icon at the top of the Help window. An alphabetical list of all items within the help system appears in a scrollable window pane, as Figure 6.3 shows. If you know exactly which Windows Me element with which you need help, you might prefer the Index page over the regular contents page you have been working with throughout the first part of this hour's lesson.

FIGURE 6.3

The Index enables you to find details quickly.

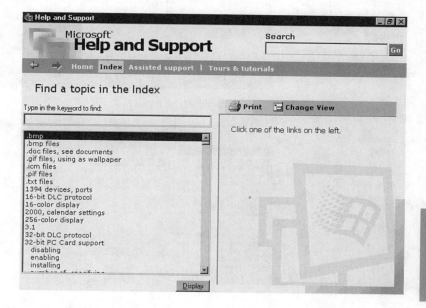

2. To find an index item, scroll the indexed list to the item you want to find. You can quickly move to an item by clicking the text box and typing your requested entry. As you type, the index item that matches your typed letters begins to appear.

3. Scroll through the entries, looking at the various index items.

4. Locate the indexed entry, `Direct Cable Connection` and double-click the `overview` entry below the main topic. A detailed overview window opens in the right window pane. A hot spot appears in the right window labeled `Click Here`. The help pages are often cross-referenced to other related help pages and Windows accessory programs, so you can read all the information related to the topic in which you are interested and start that topic's program when needed. For example, if you clicked `Click Here`, the Direct Cable Connection setup program would begin. (Don't click the entry now.) You can move to other topics by clicking on the index pane's items or by selecting hot spots in the right pane. As you move to various hot spots, the Back button always returns you to the previous help page, so you can always get back from where you came in the Help system.

5. Every once in a while, an indexed topic requires additional information. Sometimes the Help system narrows a search to a more specific item. For example, if you click the indexed item labeled `assistance, product`, the Topics Found dialog box appears like the one in Figure 6.4. When you select one of the dialog box's topics and click the Display button, that topic's Detail page appears.

FIGURE 6.4

Help needs you to be more specific.

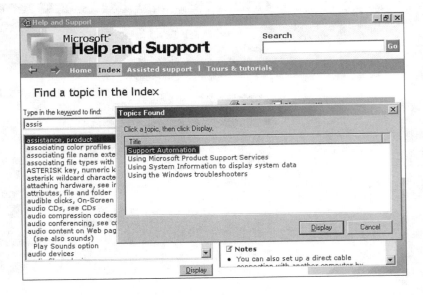

6. Close the help window to return to the main Help window.

If you know with which specific Windows Me element you need help, you can often locate the help quicker by selecting from the Index page instead of the more general Contents page that first appears when you request help.

Searching the Internet

As new information becomes available, Microsoft adds help sites, set up for you, to the Internet. You cannot update your version of Windows Me as fast as Microsoft can update its Internet site, so it makes sense for Microsoft to extend the Help system to the online world. When you search the Internet for help topics, you're certain to get the latest information available on Windows Me topics, including bug fixes, suggested system file replacements, and the latest news about new technology.

The following To Do gets you started locating help on the Internet.

To Do: Using the Internet to Get Help

1. From the Help screen, select the Assisted Support hot spot on the Help window's toolbar. The Help window lists online sites in which you can connect to the Internet for more help. Log onto the Internet and select a link, such as MSN Computing Central Forums.

2. After selecting a forum from the right pane, such as Hardware Forum, a technical support page appears, such as the one shown in Figure 6.5, where you can perform extensive detailed searching of the site for information you need.

FIGURE 6.5

The Web Help button takes you to the Web to locate in-depth answers you cannot find locally on your disk.

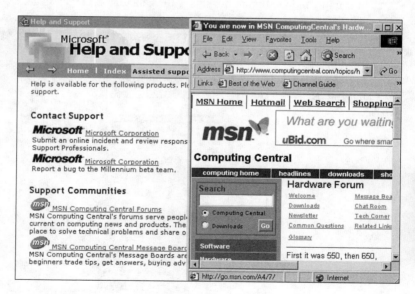

3. After you find the answer you need, close the Internet Explorer window to return to your own computer's online help page.

If you cannot find the answer you need in your local Help files, search the Internet. Microsoft's staff constantly updates online sites to provide the latest support information Windows Me users need.

Other Forms of Help

The help you obtain in Windows does not always come from the help system itself but from auxiliary help systems that add support to the tasks and programs you work with.

Using Application Help

When you use a Windows program, you often need help with the program rather than Windows. Almost every Windows application's menu bar includes a Help option you can click for help with that program.

For example, if you select Help, Help Topics from the Calculator program, a Help dialog box appears with tabs at the top of the window that list helpful help divisions such as Contents, Index, and Search. The Contents pages offer a general overview of the program. You're already familiar with the Index page because it mimics the Index page in the Help window. Figure 6.6 shows the Calculator's Index page.

FIGURE 6.6

You now will be acquainted with the Index page of Windows Me's programs' help screens.

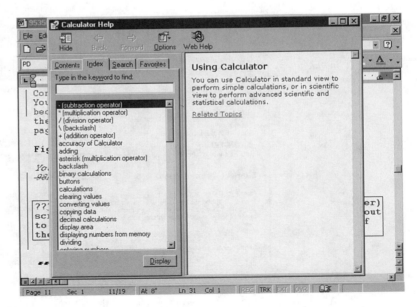

Some Windows applications do not yet support the Web-like browser style that the Windows Help window supports. Therefore, the Web-like, two-window summary and Detail dialog boxes aren't available for all programs that you use. As Windows usage grows, more software firms should begin incorporating the Web-style browser into their help engines.

The Search page makes looking for a particular topic not indexed on the Index tab easier. To search for a topic, click the Search tab, enter a topic, and then click the command button labeled List Topics. If the help engine locates your search candidate, a list of all help pages that include your search topic appears, and you can open that help page to view its details in the right pane by clicking the Display button. Calculator Help also includes a Favorites tab, on which you can store Help topics you might want to locate again.

For those programs that do not fully support the Windows Me Web-like help system, you must adjust the way you look for help keywords. Instead of a Search tab, you might see a Find tab. (The Contents and Index pages still exist but do not display in the 2-pane Web-style of the Windows Me help interface.)

Using Pop-Up Help

Sometimes, you'll be in the middle of a dialog box working inside Windows when you spot a command button or other control that you do not understand. Look in the upper-right corner of the window for a question mark command button. If you find such a question mark, you've found the Windows *Pop-Up Help* command button and cursor (sometimes called *Roving Help*).

The Pop-Up Help lets you narrow the focus and request help on a specific screen item. Not all dialog boxes or screens inside Windows contain the Pop-Up Help feature, so look for the question mark command button, which is to the left of the window minimizing and resizing buttons.

As long as the dialog box contains the Pop-Up Help button, you can request Pop-Up Help for any item on the dialog box as the following To Do item demonstrates.

To Do: Requesting the Pop-Up Help

1. Display the Taskbar and Start Menu dialog box from the Start, Settings menu option. The dialog box displays the Pop-Up help button with the question mark in the upper-right corner.

2. Click the question mark once and your mouse cursor changes to a question mark that follows the mouse pointer as you move the mouse.

▲ To Do

6

▼ 3. Point the question mark mouse cursor over the Always on Top option and click the option. Windows displays the Pop-Up Help message box shown in Figure 6.7.

FIGURE 6.7
The Pop-Up Help helps you when you point to a place on the screen.

▲ 4. Press Esc to get rid of the pop-up description box and return to the regular mouse cursor shape.

Another way exists that produces the Pop-Up help. Point your mouse cursor over an item. Right-click and select What's This? from the single-option menu that appears to display the pop-up description.

Summary

This hour showed you how to access the powerful Help features in Windows Me. When you have a question about Windows Me, you can ask Windows Me for help. There are several ways to access the helpful dialog boxes about a variety of topics. The most common method of getting detailed help is to select the Help command from the Start menu. You can access your local PC's help files or search the Internet for the answers you need. Most Windows Me programs contain a Help command that displays a tabbed dialog box containing different kinds of help search screens.

Q&A

Q **There are so many kinds of help available; which one should I use?**

A The method of help that you access depends on the task you're trying to accomplish. Generally, there are several ways to get help on the same topic. If you want help on a procedure such as moving files, you can probably find related topics grouped together in the Index listing. There, you can find topics, grouped by subject, which you can browse.

For help on a dialog box element that you don't understand, click the question mark button (if one is available in the dialog box's upper-right corner) and click over the item you want help with. A description pops up that describes that item in more detail.

If you cannot find help on a topic, especially if you want help with the Windows Me Internet interface, check out Microsoft's Web site for help.

Workshop

The quiz and exercise questions are designed to test your knowledge of the material covered in this hour. The answers are in Appendix C, "Answers to Quizzes."

Quiz

1. What two kinds of help does Windows Me provide?

2. In what ways do the Windows Me help system mimic an Internet Web browser?

3. What is a hot spot?

4. If you know exactly which Windows Me topic you need help with, which is the fastest way to go directly to that topic's help information?

5. *True or false*: Programs compatible with Windows Me must use the same help system format as Windows Me uses.

Exercises

1. Read all about Windows Explorer from the Windows Start menu's Help window.

2. Open the Display Properties dialog box by right-clicking on your Windows desktop's wallpaper area. Select the Pop-Up Help for the various items that you see. By doing so, you get a preview of the material you'll learn in the next hour's lesson.

6

HOUR 7

Desktop Management

This hour differs somewhat from the other hours. Instead of studying a single central aspect of Windows Me, such as Explorer, this hour contains a potpourri of desktop-management tips and procedures that improve the way you use the Windows Me environment. Previous hours studied topics in depth, but this hour offers advice that you might want to use while you work within Windows.

One way to activate your desktop is to use the Windows Active Desktop feature. Place Web pages and other files directly on your desktop to customize your Windows wallpaper. Windows Me comes with several screen saver designs, and you can purchase and download additional screen savers. Screen savers not only provide something for your computer to do while it is idle, but also offer security features.

This hour also offers a collection of tips that helps you customize Windows to suit your preferences. Start Windows and walk through this hour, trying the shortcuts and advice, to decide which topics best suit your needs. Now that you've mastered the major Windows tools, such as Windows Explorer and the Settings menu, you are ready to streamline the way you use Windows.

In this hour, you will

- Place Web pages on your desktop as wallpaper
- Use screen savers to personalize your PC
- Add security to your PC with screen savers
- Locate the computer's time and date settings

Activate Your Desktop

Whereas this hour introduces you to the Windows Me Active Desktop feature, Hour 14, "Understanding the Internet's Push and Channel Content," takes the Active Desktop to its next level by describing the *push technology* that you can integrate into your Active Desktop. You will learn how to subscribe to various online services, such as news agencies that send Web content directly to your PC at preset time intervals. You don't have to go as far as push technology, however, to enjoy many benefits of the Active Desktop. The Active Desktop is Windows's way of more seamlessly integrating your Windows desktop into the online Internet world.

Web pages are the result of their underlying language, *HTML*, which defines the colors, pictures, embedded *applets* (small programs that activate Web pages by using yet another language called *Java*), and information that appears on those pages. HTML stands for *Hypertext Markup Language*.

Why use a Web page on your desktop as wallpaper? Perhaps the page is a support page that you need to tweak Windows. Perhaps the page contains a game applet that you want to play in your spare time. Whatever the reason, you easily can change your wallpaper to any HTML file.

HTML documents end with the .html filename extension and use a Web page icon in Explorer views. Some document names still follow the pre-Windows 95 filename limitations that require a maximum 3-letter extension, so some HTML documents end with a filename extension of .HTM.

You can work with the Windows desktop by following along with this To Do item.

To Do: Working with the Windows Desktop

1. Right-click over the Windows wallpaper to display the pop-up menu.
2. Select Active Desktop, Customize My Desktop and click the Background tab if the Background page is not already displayed. The Display Properties dialog box appears, as shown in Figure 7.1. (As with most of Windows, you can access the Display Properties dialog box from other locations, such as right-clicking the desktop and selecting Properties.)

FIGURE 7.1

You can set wallpaper to any HTML or graphics file.

3. The Background page enables you to set up a wallpaper file. You can select one of the supplied wallpaper files by scrolling and selecting from the list box, or you can click the Browse button and search your disk for an HTML file.

4. When you locate the HTML file you want as your wallpaper, click the Open button to select the file. The file and its pathname now appear in the Wallpaper list for subsequent selections.

Your desktop must be set up for active content before you can use HTML wallpaper. If your desktop is not currently set up for active content when you select the HTML wallpaper file, Windows asks if you want to enable the Active Desktop option. You must click Yes before Windows can use the HTML file as wallpaper. If you do not enable the Active Desktop, Windows cannot display the selected HTML file as wallpaper.

5. When you click OK and return to your desktop, the HTML file appears as wallpaper.

The wallpaper on your desktop can hold graphics or HTML files. You can easily select HTML files as your desktop wallpaper from the Background page in the Display Properties dialog box.

7

> You will learn additional ways to activate your desktop in Hour 14. With the help of the Internet Explorer Web browser (you will learn all about IE in Hour 11, "Surfing the Web with Internet Explorer 5.5"), you can place Web items on your desktop on-the-fly.

SOS—Save Our Screens!

Want to know an insider's computer industry secret? Here it is: Screen savers really don't save many screens these days. In the past, computer monitors, especially the monochrome green-letters-on-black kind, would *burn in* characters when left on too long without being used. In other words, if you left the monitor on for a long time and did not type anything, the characters on the monitor would begin to leave character trails that stayed on the monitor even after you turned it off.

To combat character burn-in, programmers began to write *screen savers* that blanked the screen or displayed moving characters and pictures. The blank screens had no burn-in problems, and the moving text never stayed in one place long enough to burn into the monitor. The screen savers kicked into effect after a predetermined length of non-use. Therefore, when you left your computer, the screen saver began after a few minutes. Upon returning, you could press any key to restore the computer screen to the state in which you left it.

Almost everybody has heard of screen savers. Computer software stores contain shelf after shelf of screen saver programs that display pictures of your favorite television characters, cartoons, and geometric and 3D designs. Microsoft designed Windows Me to include several screen savers, so you don't have to buy one.

Getting back to that industry secret: Today's monitors don't have the burn-in problem that previous monitors had. Screen savers aren't needed. Why, during an age when they are not needed, are screen savers more popular than ever before? The answer is simple: Screen savers are fun! Screen savers greet you with designs and animated cartoons when you'd otherwise look at a boring screen. It's *cool* to use a screen saver. After you master Hour 14, you will be able to use even live Web pages as your screen saver!

Screen savers aren't just for fun and games. Windows screen savers offer an
additional benefit over entertainment: The Windows screen savers provide
password protection. If you need to walk away from your screen for a while
but you want to leave your computer running, you can select a password for
the screen saver. After the screen saver begins, a user has to enter the correct
password to use your computer. This ensures that payroll and other depart-
ments can safely leave their computers without fear of disclosing confidential
information. Often, computer stores display their PCs with password-protected
screen savers to keep customers from tampering with the systems.

Setting Up a Screen Saver

Windows contains several screen savers from which you can choose. Through the Screen
Saver dialog box, you can set up a blanking screen saver or one that moves text and graphics on the screen. You control the length of time the monitor is idle before the screen
saver begins. The following To Do item explains how to implement a screen saver.

To Do: Requesting a Screen Saver

1. Right-click over the Windows wallpaper. The display menu appears.

2. Select the Properties command. The Display Properties tabbed dialog box appears
   (shown earlier in Figure 7.1).

3. Click the tab labeled Screen Saver. Windows Me displays the page shown in
   Figure 7.2.

FIGURE 7.2

*The Screen Saver tab
controls the screen
saver's timing and
selection.*

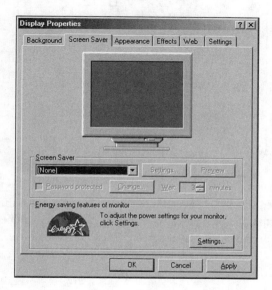

▼ To Do

7

▼   If your monitor is designed to be *Energy Star-compliant*, meaning that your moni-
     tor supports energy-efficiency options, the lower dialog box settings will be avail-
     able to you. You can adjust these options to save electricity costs. The Energy Star
     controls work independently and override any screen saver settings you might use.

4.   The drop-down list box—directly below the Screen Saver prompt—that you display
     when you click the down arrow contains a list of Windows screen savers. Click the
     box now to see the list. When (None) is selected, no screen saver will be active on
     your system.

5.   If you select Blank Screen, Windows uses a blank screen for the screen saver. When
     the screen saver activates, the screen goes blank, and a keypress (or password if
     you set up a password) returns the screen to its previous state.

     The remaining screen savers are more fun than a blank screen saver. If you want to
     see the other screen savers, click any one of the remaining screen savers in the list
     (such as 3D Flying Objects or 3D Maze), and Windows will display a preview of it
     on the little monitor inside the dialog box, as shown in Figure 7.3.

FIGURE 7.3

*You can preview any of
the screen savers.*

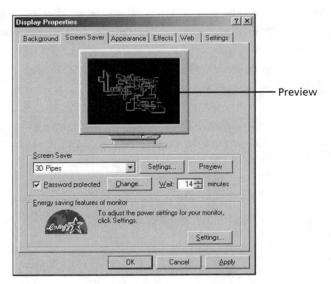

6.   The animated screen savers can move fairly fast. To adjust their speed, click the
     Settings button. In some cases, you also can adjust the number of animated items
▼   that appear on the screen saver screen. Click OK when done.

▼   7. The Preview button enables you to view, full-screen, the screen saver if you want a
         better preview than the small screen inside the dialog box provides. Click Preview to
         see the actual screen saver in action. Press any key or move the mouse to terminate
         the screen saver preview and return to the dialog box.

     8. The Wait prompt determines how many minutes your computer must remain idle
         for the screen saver to activate itself. By pressing Alt+W (the shortcut key combi-
         nation for the Wait prompt), you can enter a new minute value or click the up and
         down arrow keys to change to a new minute value.

     9. When you click the OK command button at the bottom of the dialog box, Windows
         activates the screen saver program. The screen saver remains active in all future
         Windows Me sessions until you change it again by using the Screen Saver dialog box.

     10. The screen saver operates in the background but never shows itself, even on the
         taskbar of program buttons, until your computer sits idle for the specified time
         value. Don't touch the keyboard or mouse for the waiting time period, and you'll
         see the screen saver go into action. Press any key (or move the mouse) to return to
▲   the desktop.

> Windows Me now lets you create your own screen saver! Store pictures in
> the following folder: c:\My Documents\My Pictures. You can capture these
> pictures from a digital camera or scan the pictures with an attached scanner.
> Select the My Pictures Screensaver and Windows randomly displays
> your pictures on the screen when the screen saver begins its work. You can
> adjust settings such as the length of time each picture appears by clicking
> the Settings button once you select the My Pictures Screensaver option from
> the Screen Saver tabbed page.

Securing Your Screen Saver

Using the Display Properties box, you can add a password to any of the Windows screen
savers, including the blank screen saver. After the screen saver executes, your PC requires
a password before relinquishing control to you or anyone else who wants to use your
computer. The following To Do item explains how to set up the password.

To Do: Setting Up a Password

    1. Display the Display Properties tabbed dialog box once again by right-clicking over
        your screen's wallpaper and selecting Properties.

    2. Click the Screen Saver tab to see the Screen Saver dialog box.

    3. Click the Password-protected check mark prompt.

To Do

7

▼   4. Click Change. You must tell Windows the password it requires before releasing a screen saver. The Change Password dialog box opens, as shown in Figure 7.4.

FIGURE 7.4

Tell Windows the secret screen saver password.

5. Windows requires you to type the password twice. The password appears on the screen as asterisks so that no one looking over your shoulder can read it. Because of the asterisk protection, Windows asks that you enter the password twice to ensure that you make no mistakes as you type the new password. Type the same password at both prompts.

▲   6. Press the OK command button. Now when Windows starts the screen saver, you must enter the password to use the computer.

> The screen saver password does not guarantee total computer security. Someone can reboot your computer and still use the computer's files. The password-protected screen saver does, however, keep people from looking at the work you were performing before you left the computer idle.

Check the Time

A clock showing the current time appears to the right of your taskbar. (The clock's position might differ depending on where you moved your taskbar.) In addition to the time, your computer and Windows also keeps track of the date.

There are several reasons why you might want to change the computer's time and date settings. Perhaps you've moved to a different part of the world and need to change the computer's clock. Perhaps your computer contains a time and date memory kept current with a battery that has gone bad. Perhaps the person who set up your computer didn't know the right time or date when he installed Windows. Whatever the reason for setting the time and date, these settings are easy to adjust.

Windows uses the international settings, found by double-clicking the Regional Settings icon in the Control Panel, to format all date and time values displayed from within Windows. Therefore, the selected country in the Windows international settings determines the appearance of all time and date values.

As you saw in Hour 4, "Understanding the My Computer Window," the Control Panel contains many of your system's hardware and software settings. You can change your computer's date and time settings by double-clicking the Date/Time icon inside the Control Panel. There's a much faster and easier way, though, as the following To Do item explains.

If you don't see the time on your taskbar, select the Settings, Taskbar and Start Menu command on the Start menu and check the Show Clock option.

To Do: Changing the Date and Time

1. Double-click your taskbar's clock. Windows displays the Date/Time Properties tabbed dialog box shown in Figure 7.5.

2. This is the easiest clock you will ever set! The arrow controls enable you to change the month or year. If you click a day inside the month, the date instantly changes to that date.

FIGURE 7.5

A double-click displays the Date/Time Properties dialog box.

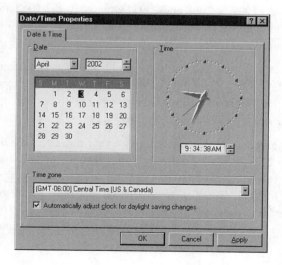

▼   3. Click the hour, minute, or second to change the time. If you highlight the hour (by
dragging the mouse cursor over it), minute, or second, click either the up or down
arrow next to the time. That highlighted value increases or decreases by one unit.
As you change the time value, the analog clock face changes also. (You can also
type a new number after highlighting an hour, minute, or second value.)

4. Windows Me is smart and can handle time zones easily. Select the appropriate time
zone by clicking the down arrow next to the list labeled Time zone and choosing
your time zone.

5. When you are done modifying the date and time, click OK to close the dialog box,
and the taskbar's time reflects your changes. You can now turn off your computer,
and the computer's new settings will still be in effect (up to the second) when you
▲   turn on the computer again.

> Not all time zones respect daylight savings time. For example, people who
> live in the state of Indiana don't have to change their clocks every six months
> because they don't follow daylight savings time. For those who don't want
> Windows to adjust for daylight savings, uncheck the option at the bottom
> of the dialog box before closing the Date & Time Properties window.

Working into the New Millennium

Microsoft released Windows Me after Y2K, the year 2000, began. The two-digit year
problem still persists even though the turning point of January 1, 2000 didn't cause problems that many expected. Should Windows interpret two-digit year values, such as 68
and 97 as 1968 and 1997 or 2068 and 2097? Obviously, the 1968 and 1997 values are
probably accurate in this case, but for other two-digit year values Windows runs into,
such as 01, the answer is different.

When you select the Start menu's Settings, Control Panel option and open the Regional
Settings dialog box, Windows gives you the ability to determine exactly how to handle
two-digit years that Windows will come across in various applications. Click the Date
tab to display the Date page shown in Figure 7.6.

Notice the option that enables you to specify a year range for two-digit values. If the
range is 1930 to 2029, you are informing Windows that any two-digit year value from 30
to 99 should be interpreted as 1930 to 1999 and any two-digit year value from 00 to 29
should be 2000 to 2029. This Y2K interpretation technique is known as *windowing*, but
the name has nothing to do with the Windows operating system. The window in this case
is the 100-year range you specify that tells Windows Me how to interpret two-digit years.

If you were working with historical data, as might be the case with genealogy records, your dates could very well fall before 1930 and a two-digit year of 11 might very well mean 1911 and 2011. In that case, you might want to change the range used so that two-digit year values are assumed to be 1900.

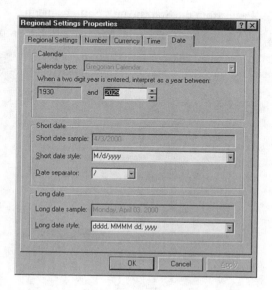

Obviously, the windowing technique for repairing two-digit years is limiting at best. Only when four-digit years appear in every application and every database in the world will we be past the Y2K problem. Fortunately, enough computer programs and data files were fixed in time to keep havoc from raging through computer systems. The Date page inside the Regional Settings dialog box is just an extra safe-guard that you can use to help Windows Me determine where two-digit years might fall even though Windows will run across fewer and fewer two-digit years as time goes by because of new programming standards that use four-digit years to eliminate the confusion.

Paint Windows Me

Windows offers several color schemes for you to select. Microsoft designed several color schemes that work well together. Depending on your taste, you can choose from conservative to very wild colors.

The color schemes that you can select have nothing to do with the colors of icons, wallpaper, or screen savers on your system. The color schemes determine the color for various systemwide items such as screen title bars, window backgrounds, and dialog box controls.

7

By selecting from various color schemes, you can determine the colors Windows Me uses for common system-level items such as window controls. The Control Panel contains a Display icon that you use to change the color of your Windows Me installation as the following steps show:

1. Select Control Panel from the Start menu's Settings menu.

2. Double-click the Display icon. The now-familiar Display Properties tabbed dialog box appears.

3. Click the Appearance tab to display the Appearance dialog box shown in Figure 7.7.

FIGURE 7.7

Change system colors using the Appearance dialog box.

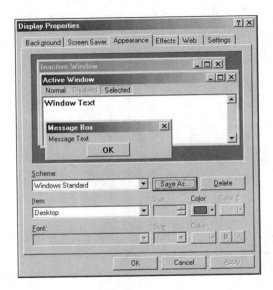

4. If you want to take the time, you can change the colors of every item on the Windows screen including dialog boxes, window borders, and title bars. However, it's much easier to pick a color scheme from the list of the many choices that Microsoft supplies.

On the Appearance page, the top half contains the currently-selected color scheme. If you select a different color scheme, you'll see that scheme's color appear at the top of the dialog box. For example, suppose that you're taking your powerful color laptop to Egypt to write with while cruising down the Nile River. Open the drop-down list box labeled Scheme and select Desert from the list. Instantly, the top half of your dialog box changes colors to a desert scheme. Now you can compute like a true Egyptian!

5. The color scheme of your Windows installation does not instantly change. You're still in the process of selecting colors at this point. If you don't like the desert color scheme, try another. As a matter of fact, try *all* of them to find one you really like.

There are some color schemes that include the additional benefit of large text sizes. As Figure 7.8 illustrates, you can select a color scheme that makes window text easier to see by enlarging the character size of the Windows Me characters when they appear in dialog boxes and title bars. In addition, high contrast color schemes might work well for times when you take your Windows laptop outdoors.

FIGURE 7.8

You can change not only system colors, but also common Windows Me character sizes.

6. When you find a color scheme that you really like, click the OK command button to close the dialog box and change the color scheme to your selected colors. You can now begin working with the new color scheme; as soon as you open a window, you'll see the difference.

As you change your color scheme, feel free to change the Windows display font as well. By default, Windows displays icons and window titles and messages in the MS-DOS Sans Serif font. From the Appearance dialog box, you can select a different font for almost every kind of text Windows Me displays.

7

Summary

This hour took a brief detour from the style of surrounding hours and gave you some tips and desktop-management tools that can help you work with Windows more effectively. After completing the first part of this book, you should have a good understanding of the tools that are available to you as a Windows user. Now that you've become more comfortable with these aspects of Windows, you will appreciate some of this hour's time-saving tips.

In this hour, you learned how to improve your computer's desktop wallpaper by adding your own graphics or HTML-based wallpaper. You will build on the HTML-on-desktop concept as you progress through the remaining 17 hours. Your PC's idle time can be taken up by setting up a screen saver. By password-protecting that screen saver, you can add security to your system so that you can safely leave for a few minutes without exiting the program in which you're working.

There are many customization features inside Windows. You now know how to change the computer's time and date. These customization tools help both the novice and the advanced user enjoy Windows Me more fully.

Q&A

Q How does the wallpaper pattern differ from the screen saver pattern? Are they the same thing?

A The wallpaper is your desktop's background. You always see the wallpaper when you first start Windows and when you minimize or close programs you are using within Windows. You will never see the screen saver unless you quit working on your computer for a few minutes and the screen saver begins running.

The screen saver must be a moving pattern (or be completely blank) to accomplish the goal of a screen saver. A screen saver is primarily a running program that keeps the screen's characters from getting burned into the screen's phosphorus. The burn-in problem is not too common today, so a secondary goal of a screen saver is to display an animated and often fun screen during your computer's idle times. As mentioned earlier in this hour, you can turn your Web-based wallpaper into a screen saver so that a designated Web page (or HTML document on your disk) appears when the screen saver wakes up.

Q How do I adjust my computer's clock when daylight savings time occurs?

A You don't have to do anything when daylight savings time occurs, as long as you've checked the daylight savings time option in the Date/Time Properties dialog box. When you check this option, Windows monitors the calendar and adjusts your computer's time appropriately. If you live in an area that does not follow daylight savings time, leave the option unchecked so that your computer won't change the clock every six months.

Workshop

Quiz

1. Where are HTML files often used?

2. *True or false*: Without a screen saver, characters can burn themselves into your monitor.

3. What does Energy Star monitor?

4. How can a password-protected screen saver help secure your system?

5. Name two ways the Display Properties Appearance tab helps you see your Windows work better.

Exercises

1. Create your own screen saver by storing graphic pictures in your C:\My Documents\My Pictures folder.

2. Change the color scheme of your desktop to a different color. Try setting your own colors for individual Windows elements, such as title bar text. You can really get colorful. If you get *too* colorful, Windows might not be as easy to use as before because some colors do not work well together. You can always return to one of the supplied Windows color schemes after you experiment. If you create a good color pattern, save the scheme under a filename that you'll remember. You then will be able to switch back and forth between your scheme and others without having to re-enter the color settings.

7

PART 3

Windows Accessories in the Afternoon

Hour

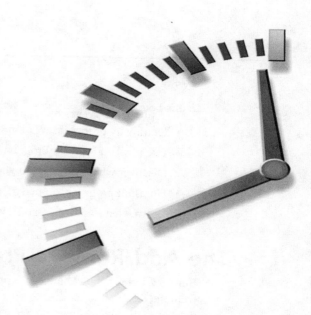

HOUR **8**

Installing Programs with Windows Me

By itself, Windows Me doesn't do work for you. Your application programs do your work. You use application programs to write documents, create graphics, explore the Internet, manage database files, and play games. Somehow you've got to get application programs onto your PC. Programs come on CD-ROMs (or, less commonly, on disks), and you must run those programs through an *installation routine* so that Windows Me properly recognizes them.

Although every application program requires a unique, one-of-a-kind installation routine, you'll install most of today's programs the same way. This hour looks at Windows support for adding programs, discusses unique installation problems you might encounter, and reviews how to remove programs that you've installed and no longer need.

In this hour, you will

- Learn why proper installation is critical
- Use the Add/Remove Programs dialog box effectively
- Discover where to go when you need to add or remove a Windows component
- Uninstall programs properly
- Learn what to do when no adequate uninstall procedure exists

The Add/Remove Programs Icon

Before Windows, you could add a program to your computer simply by copying a file from the disk you purchased to your hard disk. To remove the program, you only had to delete the file. Things get messier with Windows, however, because Windows expects a lot from application programs. Those programs are no longer simple to add or remove, so you must familiarize yourself with the proper techniques.

 If you don't follow the proper program-installation techniques, your application probably won't run correctly. Even worse, with the Windows integrated set of files, a program you add to your PC incorrectly might make other programs fail.

The Windows Control Panel contains an entry that you'll frequently visit to manage the programs on your PC. This icon is labeled Add/Remove Programs. When you open this icon, the tabbed dialog box shown in Figure 8.1 appears. Depending on the number of your PC's installed applications, you'll probably see different applications listed in the lower half of your PC's Add/Remove Programs window.

The dialog box's top half contains an Install button that you can click to install new software. Surprisingly, you'll rarely, if ever, use this button when installing Windows Me programs because most programs install somewhat automatically, as explained later in this hour. The dialog box's lower half contains a list of application programs on your PC. Not every program on your PC appears in the list. The list contains programs that you can *uninstall* from your system. If you uninstall using the Add/Remove Programs Properties dialog box, you can be assured that the application will completely go away.

FIGURE 8.1

You manage your installed programs from the Add/Remove Program Properties dialog box.

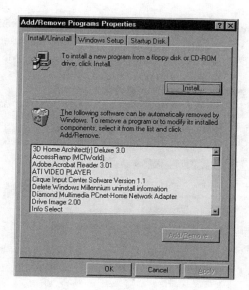

Although you can uninstall most Windows applications, occasionally an application will share a support or system file with another application. Even more common, sometimes the uninstallation routine detects *incorrectly* that the file is shared by another program. Therefore, during some uninstallation routines, you might see a dialog box message asking if you want the routine to remove one of the shared files. Generally, it's difficult to know what to do. The safest advice is to keep the file by responding as such to the dialog box if it appears. Although in many cases retaining the file simply wastes disk space, you'll avoid possible trouble with other applications that might use the file.

If you make a system backup before uninstalling an application, you can safely remove the file and then keep the backup handy until you're convinced that the system is stable. Again, it's often simpler just to keep the file in question when the uninstallation program prompts you about it. These orphaned files often make for heated discussions among the PC community—and rightly so. Windows and uninstallation routines should be written so that they work together more accurately without requiring the user to make such ambiguous file-deletion decisions.

The Windows Setup Page

After you've opened the Control Panel's Add/Remove Programs dialog box, click the Windows Setup tab to display the page shown in Figure 8.2. Unlike your applications, you'll never remove Windows because you would be removing the operating system that controls your PC. (You wouldn't sit on the same tree branch you're sawing off, would you?) When you update to a future version of Windows, the new version will remove Windows Me, but you've got plenty of time to worry about that later. For now, the Windows Setup page lets you add and remove various Windows Me options.

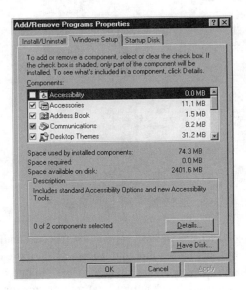

Sometimes you'll rerun an application program's installation routine to change installation settings, just as you change Windows options from the Windows Setup page. Program installations are sometimes the only place where you can modify the program's installed options. This is true for Microsoft Office as well as some other major software titles. When you need to change such a program, you will have to run its install procedure once again (perhaps by clicking the Install button on the Install/Uninstall page), but the program won't really install a second time. Instead, the program will prompt you for changes you want to make to the installation.

If a program stops working properly, you might have to reinstall it completely. Although you can rerun the installation again in some cases, you're probably better off uninstalling the program first to remove all traces of it and then running the installation from scratch again. (Be sure to back up your data files before you do that.)

When you make a change to a Windows Me setting, that setting might not show until you restart Windows Me.

The following To Do item shows you how to change Windows Me installation settings. Although the various Properties menu options you find throughout Windows Me let you change settings that affect Windows' performance, appearance, and operation, the Windows Setup page lets you add or remove parts of Windows properly.

> You'll need your Windows Me CD-ROM in order to change Windows Me options, so place it in your CD-ROM drive. If the Windows banner automatically appears when you insert the CD-ROM, close the window. Some systems come with the Windows Me operating system stored on the hard disk, so don't worry about locating the Windows CD-ROM unless prompted for it.

To Do: Modifying Installation Settings

1. Display the Windows Setup page. The Components scrolling list box shows which groups of Windows Me options you've installed. An empty check box means that none of those options are installed to run. A grayed-out checkmark means that some of the programs in the group are installed. A regular checkmark means that the entire group is installed. If you didn't install Windows, or if you installed Windows using all the default options, you might not be completely familiar with all the groups that appear. As you work through this 24-hour tutorial, you'll learn more about the various options available for Windows.

   The checked options indicate that every program in that group is installed. For example, rarely will all of Windows' Accessories group be installed, so you'll see a grayed-out checkmark there.

2. Click the title for Accessories (if you click the checkmark, you'll change the setting) and then click the Details button. You'll see a scrollable list of Accessories programs (these are the programs that appear when you select the Start menu's Programs, Accessories option) like the one shown in Figure 8.3. Click Cancel to close the dialog box.

3. Select System Tools and click Details. Select the System Monitor option. Rarely will Windows users have this option checked. If you do, uncheck it to remove it from your Windows. (You can repeat this task afterwards to put it back.) If your System Monitor is not installed, check it.

> When you check or uncheck options, Windows will not completely reinstall. Instead, Windows adds or removes the programs necessary to make the changes you request on the Windows Setup page. Whether you install or remove the System Monitor, you'll see the same procedure occur when you begin the update process in the next step.

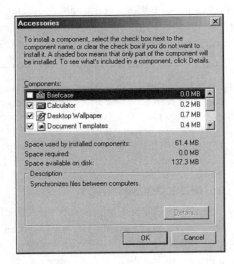

FIGURE 8.3

See which Accessories options are installed.

4. Click OK to close the System Tools window.

5. In the Windows Setup page, click OK once again to start the Windows setup modification. A dialog box appears, telling you the status of the update. The update can take a while if you add or remove several Windows components.

6. Close the Control Panel. When you restart Windows, you'll see the System Monitor on the Start menu's Programs, Accessories, System Tools menu.

The System Monitor appears in an Accessories menu group called System Tools. The System Monitor is called a *utility program* because it works in the background, enabling you to analyze Windows Me's performance. If your PC ever begins to act sluggishly, run the System Monitor to see which Windows resources you need.

With the personalized menus that Windows Me introduces, you might not see the System Monitor program on the System Tools menu until you click the down arrow at the bottom of the menu to view the hidden menu options. Remember that Windows Me hides infrequently-used menu options and displays only those menu options you use frequently to save time.

Installed Applications

Almost every time you purchase a new application program to install on your PC, you'll insert its CD-ROM into the drive, close the drive door, and see a message such as the one shown in Figure 8.4.

FIGURE 8.4

An application program is about to install.

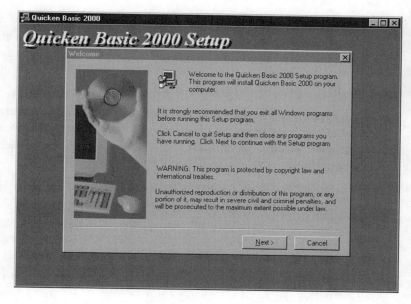

8

In most cases, such an application checks your PC to see if the program is already installed. If it isn't, the program gives you a prompt like the one shown in Figure 8.4. The software authors know that you probably wouldn't be inserting the CD-ROM in the drive if you didn't want to install the program.

If the program is already installed, the program often begins executing (without the installation prompt) after you close the CD-ROM drive door.

If the CD-ROM doesn't start, or if you have AutoPlay disabled and you want to leave it that way, you can choose Run from the Start menu and type **d:\Setup**. (Replace the d with the letter of your CD-ROM drive.)

If you're installing from disks, you'll have to insert the first installation disk into the disk drive, choose Run from the Start menu, and type **a:\Setup**.

If you get an error message, choose Start, Run once again to make sure that you've entered the drive, backslash, and Setup command properly. If you get an error message again, your program might require a different command. Replace Setup with Install to see what happens. If the Run command still fails, you must check the program's owner's manual to locate the correct command.

Each application's setup is different! Therefore, unless every reader had identical software to install, this book could not describe every scenario that occurs past the original installation window. Nevertheless, the following list provides guidelines that almost every installation follows:

- You can often read installation notes (often called a *Readme* file) by clicking the appropriate selection in the installation window.
- Sometimes multiple installation options are available. Check the manual, if one comes with the program, for the installation that suits you if you can't determine from the opening window which one to use.
- When you start the installation, a wizard usually guides you step-by-step through the process.
- You can often accept all installation defaults if you're unsure whether to install an option during the wizard's performance. The wizard asks questions such as which disk drive and folder you want to install to.
- If you don't have adequate disk space, the installation program will tell you. You'll have to remove other files, get more disk space, reduce the installation options, or do without the program if you don't have space for it.
- At the end of the installation, you will probably have to restart Windows in order for all the installation options to go into effect. If you're asked whether you want to restart Windows, you can answer No, but don't run the installed program until you restart Windows.

Uninstallation Procedures

Most application programs written for Windows Me include a standard uninstallation routine that removes the application from Windows and from your PC. Remember that an application program is often made up of several files. The program's installation routine stores those files in several different locations. Therefore, without an uninstallation routine, removing the application is a tedious task.

Before displaying the Control Panel's Add/Remove Programs window to uninstall a program you've installed, check the menu group the program resides in. Sometimes, in a program's menu group, the installation routine sets up the uninstallation routine that you

8

can run from that group. For example, if you installed a game called Side-to-Side, you might start the game by selecting from a series of menus that might look like this: Programs, Side Game, Play Side-to-Side. Look on the same menu and see if there's an uninstall option that you would select, such as Programs, Side Game, Uninstall Side-to-Side. When you begin the uninstallation process, a wizard begins that steps you through the program's removal.

If there isn't a menu option for the uninstallation, you should again look to the Control Panel's Add/Remove Programs dialog box. Scroll through the list of items in the lower part of the dialog box to see if the program you want to remove appears in the list. If so, select that entry and click the Add/Remove button to begin the uninstall wizard.

If no entry appears, you are running out of options! Insert the program's CD-ROM once again and see if the opening window contains an uninstall option. If not, look through the Readme file to see if you can get help. Also, look in the program's owner's manual. Lacking any uninstall routine at all, you should try one more place if you have access: the Web. See if you can find the company's Web page somewhere in the Readme file or owner's manual. If you can't find it, try going to the Web address http://www.companyname.com/ and see if something comes up. (If you have no idea how to get on the Web, you'll learn how in Hour 11, "Surfing the Web with Internet Explorer 5.5.")

A Last Resort

If your search for an uninstall procedure comes up empty, you are forced to do one of two things:

- Leave the program on your system if you have ample disk space
- Manually remove as much of the program as you can

That last option can get messy. You'll need to search for the program files (perhaps you remember the folder where you installed them). In the next hour you'll learn how to search for files, so you might want to browse Hour 9 before attempting to manually remove the application. After you've removed the program's files and the folder where the application resides (just ignore any related program files that might be scattered across your disk because they're almost impossible to find), you need to remove the menu entry as well. Follow the next To Do item to remove the application from the Start menu.

To Do: Removing an Application from the Start Menu

1. From the Start menu, select Settings, Taskbar and Start Menu.

2. Click the Advanced tab.

3. Click the Remove button to open the Remove Shortcuts/Folders dialog box, shown in Figure 8.5.

FIGURE 8.5

You can remove menu items and menu groups from the Remove Shortcuts/Folders dialog box.

4. Locate the program group that the application resides in. You might have to click one or more of the plus signs to expand a group to get to the one you need. If you only want to remove one or more entries within the group, open the group to display those entries using the Explorer-like techniques you now know.

5. Highlight the group and click the Remove button to remove the group from the Start menu. When you close the dialog box, the entry will be gone from the Start menu.

Several software companies offer uninstallation utility programs that you can purchase. These programs attempt to remove all traces of unwanted programs from your disk. If you purchase one, the program should be able to remove most programs known about before the uninstall product was released. As new programs appear on the market, these software companies update their uninstallation utility programs, so upgrade the utility to ensure that you've got the latest when you need it. (Often you can download updates from the company's Web site.)

Summary

This hour described how you install application programs on your PC and also how you remove them. Before Windows came along, program installation and removal was simple because rarely did a program reside in more than one file on your disk. Today's Windows programs, however, install with multiple files in multiple locations, and their removal can get tedious.

The next hour describes how you use Windows Me's file-searching capabilities to locate files on your computer. You might need to search for a file if you manually need to remove a program from Windows, as described in the last section.

Q&A

Q Why don't I ever use the Add/Remove Programs dialog box's Install button to install programs?

A Nobody seems to have a good answer for that! It seems as if software companies don't want to access this already-supplied installation resource. If they did, all program installations would basically require the same steps, and, you would think, users would be happier. Nevertheless, companies seem to prefer that the installation routine begin automatically when the user inserts the CD-ROM.

The drawback of this approach is that many times such an installation won't work as expected. Either the AutoPlay feature is turned off, or the user bought the program on disks. (Disk drives don't support the AutoPlay feature.)

Workshop

The quiz and exercise questions are designed to test your knowledge of the material covered in this hour. The answers are in Appendix C, "Answers to Quizzes."

Quiz

1. What Windows Control Panel option helps you install and uninstall application programs?

2. What happens if you insert an application program's CD-ROM in your PC's CD-ROM drive and the application is not already installed?

3. From where can you modify the Windows installation options?

4. What are some ways to uninstall application programs?

5. Why would you never want to uninstall Windows Me?

Exercises

1. Open the Install/Uninstall page on the Add/Remove Programs dialog box. Scroll through the list to make sure old programs that you do not use are no longer installed. If one or more of these programs appear, select them and click the Add/Remove button to remove the application. By regularly checking the installed application list, you will keep your hard disk free of programs you no longer use that consume disk space.

2. Open the Windows Setup page on the Add/Remove Programs dialog box. Make sure that all the Windows Me's Accessibility, Accessories, and Multimedia options are installed. By doing this, you help ensure that your system is ready for all the remaining lessons in this tutorial.

HOUR 9

Finding Files, Folders, and Friends

Hard disks are getting bigger, more information appears on the Internet by the minute, and you've got to find things fast! Fortunately, Windows Me comes to your rescue with powerful searching tools. Windows can quickly find files and folders that you need. You can search by filename, date, and location. In addition, Windows includes several Internet searching tools that enable you to find people and Web sites that match the exact specifications you want to match.

In this hour, you will

- Master the Start menu's Search command
- Specify wildcard searches
- Learn which search options help you find information the fastest
- Learn how the Internet search tools help you wade through huge mounds of data
- Locate people in other parts of the world

Introducing Search

Click the Start menu to see the Search menu. Table 10.1 explains each of Search's options.

TABLE 10.1   Using Search to Locate Information

Target	Description
For Files or Folders	Locates a file or folder on your PC system, including networked drives if you have them.
On the Internet	Searches the Internet for information.
People	Searches for people on your own computer as well as over the Internet.
Using Microsoft Outlook	Searches through the Microsoft Office program named Microsoft Outlook (if you have Outlook installed) for information.

This book doesn't cover searching with Microsoft Outlook because you must have the Microsoft Office software in order to use the Microsoft Outlook search feature.

You should master the Start menu's Search command so that your computer can look for files and folders. You won't have to wade through disks, folders, and subfolders looking for a document you created in the past. Let Windows do the work for you.

Explorer's Search button option contains many of the same searching capabilities as the Start menu's Search command. Therefore, after you master the Search command, you'll also know how to look for information from inside Explorer. By the way, you can quickly display the Search Files and Folders window by right-clicking the Start menu and selecting the Search option or by pressing the Windows key on your keyboard and then pressing F (for Find) before releasing both keys.

Improving Your Searches

You'll often use *wildcard characters* when performing searches. A wildcard character stands for one or more groups of characters, just as a joker often functions as a wild-card in card games. Search supports two wildcard characters: * and ?.

* acts as a wildcard for zero, one, or more characters. For example, if you wanted to see all files that end with the .txt extension, you could specify *.txt as your search *criteria* (search instructions). The asterisk wildcard tells Find to locate every file that ends in .txt, no matter what appears before the file extension. The criteria ABC*.* represents all files that begin with the letters ABC, no matter what follows the letters and no matter what extension the file has. (ABC*.* even locates files that begin with ABC and have no extension.)

The question mark wildcard replaces single characters within a criteria. Therefore, ACCT??.DAT finds all files that begin with ACCT, have two more characters, and end in the .DAT extension. The following files would successfully match that criteria: ACCT97.DAT, ACCT98.DAT, and ACCT99.DAT. However, neither ACCT.DAT nor ACCTjun98.DAT would match because the two question marks specify that only two characters must replace the wildcards in those positions.

Searching Files and Folders

You'll probably use the Start menu's Search command to search for files and folders on your PC. Search gives you access to many different search criteria. You can search for files in a specific folder, on a disk, or on your entire computer system, including net-worked drives if you have any.

If you know a partial filename, you can find all files that contain that partial filename. If you want to search for a file you changed two days ago, you can find all files with modification dates that fall on that day. You can even save searches that you perform often so that you don't have to create the search criteria each time you need to search, as discussed in the next section.

The following To Do item explains how to perform the search.

To Do: Using Search

1. Display the Start menu and select Search.
2. When the menu appears, select For Files or Folders. The Search Results dialog box appears, as shown in Figure 9.1. Your screen might differ slightly if your Search window's toolbar is displayed.

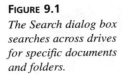

FIGURE 9.1

The Search dialog box searches across drives for specific documents and folders.

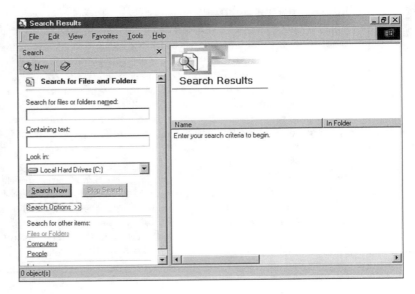

3. Type **winmine.*** at the Search for Files and Folders Named prompt. This wildcard specification looks for all files and folders that begin with the letters winmine.

    You will accept the defaults in the other fields. Windows automatically searches subdirectory folders, although you can click Search Options, Advanced Options to limit the search to top-level, root-folder directories only.

4. Click the Search Now button to start the search. (If you press Enter, Search clicks the Search Now button for you because Search Now is the default button.) After a brief pause, your dialog box should resemble the one shown in Figure 9.2. The list contains not only the document's filename, but also the folder that the document resides in, the size of the document, the type of file, and the date and time that the file was last modified.

    Your search results appear in the right portion of the search window. You can drag the edge of any column title left or right to expand or shrink the width of that column. If you click a column title, Search sorts the found information in alphabetical, numerical, or date and time order.

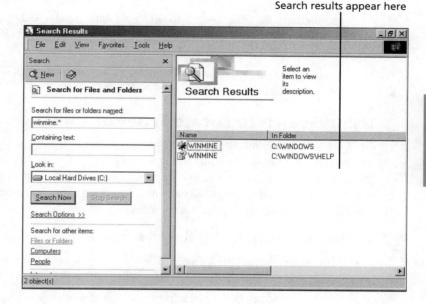

Search results appear here

FIGURE 9.2
Search locates your files.

9

If you don't see filename extensions but you want to, select the window's Tools, Folder Options, click the View tab, and uncheck the option labeled Hide File Extensions for Known File Types.

At least four files should appear, and they'll appear in your Windows folder. One of these files has an .exe extension, meaning that you can run (execute) that file.

If your filename extensions are turned off, the executable file is the file with the land mine icon to the left of its Name entry. Now that Windows Me has located the executable file, you can run the program directly from the Search window.

5. Double-click the winmine.exe entry, and a Windows game named Minesweeper appears. Start clicking away on the squares, but be very careful!

Windows is smart. If the file you click isn't an executable file, Windows attempts to open the file using other resources. For example, if you click a Microsoft Word document, Windows automatically looks for the Microsoft Word program on your PC and opens the document using Word (assuming that you have Word). If you

▼

select a help file, Search opens a help window with that file displayed. If you select an email message file, Search locates your email reader and displays the message there. As long as the file is registered (explained in Hour 5, "Using Explorer to Navigate"), Windows can associate the file's parent program and display the file.

▲

6. After you've played Minesweeper for a while, close its window and then close the Search window.

Using Search to Locate Types of Files

Not only will Search locate files if you know a partial or complete filename, but you can also search for a file that you modified two days ago or find all files of a specific type. You can even save searches that you perform often so that you don't have to create the search criteria each time you need to search. The following To Do item illustrates the other options available from the Search window.

To Do: Searching Using the File Type

1. Display the Start menu and select Search.

2. Select For Files or Folders.

3. Type **C:\WINDOWS** in the Look In prompt. By doing so, you request a search of drive C's Windows folder, looking for specific files.

If your Windows folder is located on a different drive, type that drive's letter instead of C, or open the Look In drop-down list box and select the correct drive and folder.

4. Search searches the Windows folder as well as all subfolders within the Windows folder. If you want to limit the search to the Windows folder only, select Search Options, Advanced Options, Search Subfolders as explained in the previous section.

5. Select Search Options, Date to open the Date subwindow shown in Figure 9.3. If you want to limit your search to specific dates, the window enables you to search only for files modified, created, or last accessed between a beginning and ending date or within the last few days or months. For now, click Date once more to hide the Date options.

▼

FIGURE 9.3

You can narrow the search to specific dates.

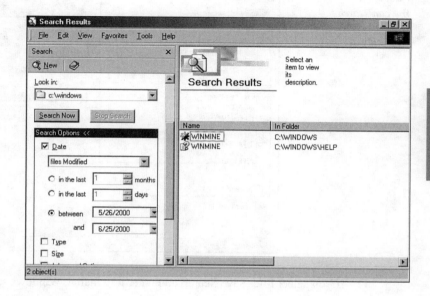

9

6. Click the Type option.

7. Open the All Files and Folders list box to display a list of file types, as shown in Figure 9.4. These file types are all the file types that are currently registered inside your Windows Me installation. If you want to search for files of a certain type, such as Microsoft Word documents only, you can select that file type from the list, and Search ignores all the files that don't match the selected type. You can also search for files that meet a specific size criteria by selecting from the Size Is fields.

8. Select Cursor from the Type list box. You are directing Search to find all mouse cursor files within the Windows folders.

9. Click the Search Now button and wait a bit while Windows scans your disk drive. The search might take a while, depending on the speed of your computer and the number of files in your Windows folder.

10. When the search is complete, the Search window lists the files that meet your search criteria in the bottom portion of the dialog box. If there are several cursor files in the Windows folder (as there should be), Windows displays vertical scrollbars so that you can scroll through the list of choices.

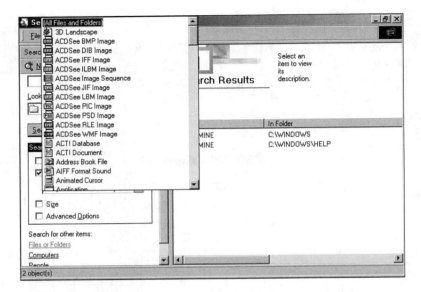

FIGURE 9.4

You can search through specific file types only.

11. If you select File, Save Search and enter a filename, Windows saves your search in a file that you can later reuse for another search without having to enter the options again.

If you save a search file to your Windows\Desktop folder, an icon immediately appears on your desktop along with the other icons there. When you click that icon, the search begins! By placing common searches on your desktop that you perform regularly, you'll save yourself some effort later when you want to find files and folders. Although you can select the Windows\ Desktop folder from the Save Search dialog box, you can also click the Desktop button to the left of the dialog box, as shown in Figure 9.5, to save the search to the desktop without having to locate the Windows folder first.

▼   12. Select File, Close to close the Search window.

Click here to save to desktop

FIGURE 9.5
*Quickly save searches
to your desktop for
later use.*

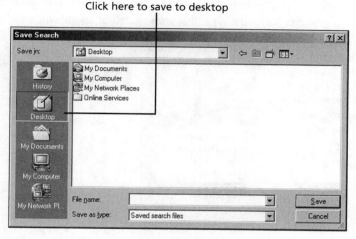

9

Searching for Internet Information

The Internet provides a wealth of information, but with that richness often comes *information overload.* A lot of material appears on the Internet, and you must wade through stuff you don't want in order to get to the stuff you do want. The Start menu's Search command helps you make sense out of Internet searching by providing you with an interactive desktop tool that you can use to look for information as the following To Do item demonstrates.

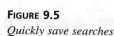

To Do: Searching Using Windows' Internet-based Search Capabilities

1. Open the Start menu. Suppose that you want to search the Internet for information on *Mardi,* a Herman Melville work.

2. Select Search, On the Internet. If you aren't already connected to the Internet, your Internet sign-in dialog box appears so that you can enter your ID and password. (Depending on your Internet connection, you might have to initiate the dial-in sequence to connect to your Internet provider. If you have a connection that's always on, such as a DSL or cable modem, or a network connection to the Internet, you won't have to log on.)

▼   When you've signed in to your Internet account, Internet Explorer opens so that
           you can select the type of search you want, as shown in Figure 9.6.

FIGURE 9.6

Search the Internet for a Web page, person's address, business, redo an old search, or locate a map of a given area.

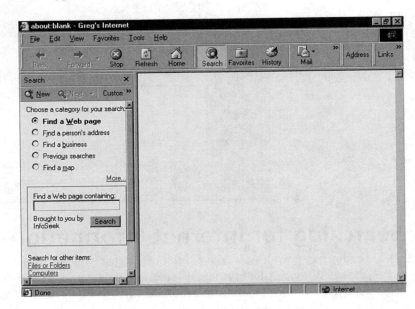

3. Type **Mardi** and click the Search button to begin the search through Web pages.

   When the search finishes, the left window shows the results. Often, unless you search for very specific information, you'll get several resulting Web locations where your search engine found the information. Most search engines give you the choice of scrolling through a summary list of 10 or 20 sites at a time, looking for the sites you want to view. Figure 9.7 shows how such a listing from the Infoseek search engine might look. Depending on the search engine that Internet Explorer uses, your results might look different from the ones in Figure 9.7. Nevertheless, you should see a similar list, one with several topics that match your search term.

> Expect to find lots of advertising on the search engine pages. This advertising means revenue for the search engine to fund the service that's free to you.

▼

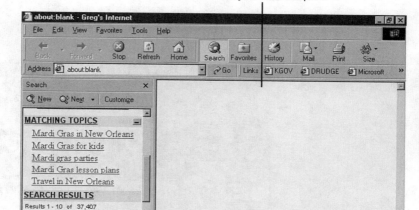

Detail appears here
when you click a topic

FIGURE 9.7

*Many times, too much
information is found,
and you'll be over-
loaded!*

9

4. By now, you've figured out that searching for Mardi turns up more information
   about Mardi Gras celebrations than about a literary classic! You can search through
   lots of topics or narrow your search a bit. Generally, you can improve your search.
   Scroll up to the Search box and type **+Melville +Mardi** and click the Search button to ensure that you get only Web sites that list Melville's name as well as the
   word Mardi. The plus signs in front of each word ensure that the resulting Web
   page will contain both words. (The words don't have to appear together or in order,
   as they would in a phrase.) When you click any of the found links that contain your
   search topic, the corresponding Web page appears in the right window. (You can
   close the left search engine window when you've found the Web information you
   want in order to give the Web page more screen room.)

   As you become more familiar with search engines and their options, you'll learn
   ways to narrow your Internet searches. Most search engines support the same
   options, and most have an options button you can click to get help on the options
   available. If you enclose a phrase in quotation marks, you're telling the search
   engine to look for Web pages that contain your exact search phrase. Use lowercase
   letters unless you are searching for a proper name. As you've seen, a plus sign in
   front of a word forces that word to appear in the resulting Web page. A minus sign
   would require that the word be absent before a successful search is determined.

▼   When you narrow your search, you'll find fewer Web pages and a more meaningful
result. You can scroll through the results and click any topic that describes Melville's
book. Clicking a topic produces the detail for that topic as Figure 9.8 shows.

Detail appears here

FIGURE 9.8

The topic's detail now
appears.

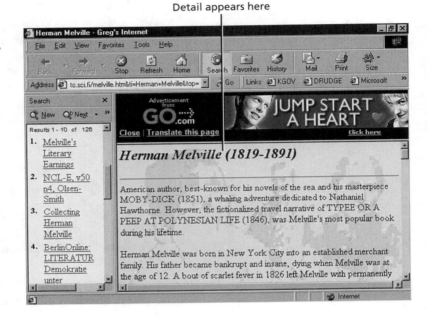

5. When you finish reading about *Mardi,* you can close the Search window and return
to the Windows desktop.

If you prefer to try another search engine, click the down arrow to the right
of Next above the search topics and select something else, such as Yahoo! or
Excite.

▲

Finding People

You can search for an old pal or a long-lost love using the Search menu. Windows uses a
collection of people-finding search engines to look for people you want to find as the
following To Do task demonstrates.

To Do: Searching for People

To Do ▼

1. Open the Start menu and select Search, People to see the Find People dialog box shown in Figure 9.9.

2. The people-search engines that Windows Me uses are subject to change. Microsoft could add or remove one or more as you receive Windows updates. The search engine shown next to Look In might be Contacts if you use Outlook or the name of an Internet search engine such as Lycos. For example, you might search for your favorite movie star's email address by typing the star's name in the Name field and selecting an Internet search engine. (You know the star's email address is not in your Outlook Contacts database if your Outlook Contacts folder is selected when you start the search.)

   You can enter a name, email address, or other known information to help narrow your search. Some searches come up with addresses and phone numbers, and other searches come up empty.

FIGURE 9.9

Search locally or on the Internet.

3. If you aren't successful, you might want to go to another people-search engine's Web page by selecting the engine name and clicking Web Site. The page should offer hints that will help you find the person.

4. Close the Find People dialog box and sign off your Internet account to return to your Windows desktop.

▲

Summary

This hour helped you find information you need on both your own PC and the Internet. Get in the habit of using Find for your PC files when you need them. You can search for the file you want to find and then select the file to open it and begin working with it.

Internet search engines help convert the Internet's information overload to a manageable repository of information. You can search Web sites that fit your exact criteria, as well as look for people's names and addresses.

The next hour's material really gets fun. You'll learn how to use the Windows Accessories programs. Even if you haven't yet purchased a word processor or a paint program, you can use the ones supplied with Windows to generate virtually any material you want to publish.

Q&A

Q I just bought my PC, and I don't have many files yet. Why will I need to search for anything?

A Sometimes you save a file in an unexpected folder, forget an exact filename, or save multiple copies of the same file on a disk across different folders. Even though you don't yet have many files, you could easily forget what you recently named a file or where you saved it.

Q I don't yet have Internet access. Can I still access the Internet searching tools?

A Sadly, no. You must sign up with an Internet service provider to gain Internet access before you can use Search's full potential. You will need to subscribe to an Internet service before you can search the Internet for information or people's addresses and phone numbers.

Workshop

The quiz and exercise questions are designed to test your knowledge of the material covered in this hour. The answers are in Appendix C, "Answers to Quizzes."

Quiz

1. Where are some of the areas Windows Me looks for data?
2. What is a wildcard character?
3. What is the difference between the * and the ? wildcard characters?
4. *True or false*: You can execute any found programs from within the search window.
5. What is a search engine?

Exercises

1. Locate all the files you edited, created, or accessed on your most recent birthday.
2. Search for your favorite sports team member's email address. If you don't succeed at first, select a different Internet people search engine and try again.

HOUR 10

Using the Desktop Accessories

Windows Me comes with several application programs you can use right away to do work. These programs—Calculator, WordPad, and Paint—all appear on your Start menu's Accessories menu list. As their names suggest, you can perform calculations, create text documents, and paint pictures by using these three accessory programs.

The Calculator program comes in handy when you want to perform quick calculations without the need of a more powerful program such as an electronic spreadsheet. WordPad does not offer the power of Microsoft Word, but you can create formatted word-processed documents quickly with WordPad, which is simple to learn. Paint is a simple but effective drawing program that you can use to create colorful pictures. If you're a good artist, you might want to paste one of your creations on your Windows desktop as wallpaper!

In this hour, you will

- Use the Windows Calculator program
- Discover what differences exist between the scientific and standard calculator views

- Create word-processed documents with WordPad
- Use Paint to create colorful graphics
- Learn which of Paint's advanced editing tools professionally manipulate your images

Calculate Results

The Calculator program performs both simple mathematical and advanced scientific calculations. You will find the Calculator program in the Programs, Accessories menu.

The Calculator program provides you with all kinds of computing benefits. Throughout a working day, you use your computer constantly, writing letters, printing bills, and building presentations. As you work, you often need to make a quick calculation and, if you're anything like computer book authors, your calculator is probably covered up beneath papers stacked a foot high. As soon as you start the Windows Calculator program, it is never farther away than the taskbar.

> The Calculator program actually contains two calculators, a *standard calculator* and a *scientific calculator*. Most people need the standard calculator that provides all the common mathematical operations required for day-to-day business affairs. The scientific calculator contains additional operations, such as statistical and trigonometric operations.

Working with the Standard Calculator

The Windows standard calculator provides full-featured calculator functions. When you use the Calculator program, you can sell your own desktop calculator at your next yard sale. Windows even enables you to copy and paste the calculator results directly into your own applications. The following To Do item guides you through the use of the standard calculator.

To Do: Using the Standard Calculator

1. Start the Windows Calculator program, as shown in Figure 10.1. The Calculator appears on the Start menu's Programs, Accessories menu option. If you see a calculator window with many more buttons than the figure's, select View, Standard to work with the non-scientific calculator.

2. To steal from an old cliché—it doesn't take a rocket scientist to use the calculator. The calculator performs standard addition, subtraction, multiplication, and division. In addition, the standard calculator includes memory clear, recall, store, and memory add.

FIGURE **10.1**

*The Windows
Calculator program
goes beyond a pocket
calculator.*

You cannot resize the calculator window. You can only minimize the
Calculator program to a taskbar button and move the window.

10

All of the calculator operations produce *running totals*, meaning that you
can continuously apply operations, such as addition to the running total in
the calculator's display.

The calculator has keyboard-equivalent keys. Instead of clicking with your
mouse to enter 2 + 2 for example, you can type **2 + 2 =** (the equal sign
requests the answer). Not all keys have obvious keyboard equivalents, however. For example, the C key does not clear the total (Esc does). Therefore,
you might need to combine your mouse and keyboard to use the calculator.

3. Click the numbers 1, 2, and then 3. (You can use your keyboard if you like, but
   make sure that your Num Lock key is turned on first.) As you click, the numbers
   appear inside the display.

4. Click the multiplication sign (the asterisk).

5. Click the 2.

6. Click the equal sign or press Enter, and the calculator displays the result of 246.

7. Click C or press Esc to clear the display.

> The Backspace key erases any character that you type incorrectly.

8. The percent key produces a percentage only as a result of multiplication. Therefore, you can compute a percentage of a number by multiplying it by the percent figure. Suppose that you want to know how much 35% of 4000 is.

   Type **4000** and then press the asterisk. Type **35** followed by the % key (Shift+5 on the keyboard). The value **1400** appears. The result: 1400 is 35% of 4000. (The word *of* in a math problem is a sure sign that you must multiply by a percentage. Calculating 35% of 4000 implies that you need to multiply 4000 by 35%.)

9. When you want to negate the number in the display, click the +/– key. Suppose that you want to subtract the display's current value, 1400, from 5000. Although you can clear the display and perform the subtraction, negate the 1400 by clicking the +/– key, press the plus sign, type **5000**, and press the equal sign to produce 3600.

> The calculator displays a letter M above the four memory keys when you store a value in the memory.

10. To store a value in memory, click MS. Whenever you want the memory value to appear in the display, click MR. MC clears the memory and M+ adds the display to the total in memory. If you want to store a running total, click the M+ button every time you want to add the display's value to the memory. The M disappears from the memory indicator box when you clear the memory.

> When you want to switch from your application to the calculator to perform a calculation and then enter the result of that calculation elsewhere (such as in your word processor), select Edit, Copy (Ctrl+C) to copy the value to the Clipboard. When you switch back to the other Windows application, you will be able to paste the value into that application.

Using the Scientific Calculator

The second Windows Calculator program, the scientific calculator, supports many more advanced mathematical operations. Despite its added power, the scientific calculator operates almost identically to the standard calculator. The standard keys and memory are identical in both calculators.

To see the scientific calculator, select View, Scientific. Windows displays the scientific calculator shown in Figure 10.2. The scientific calculator offers more keys, operators, and indicators than the standard calculator.

FIGURE 10.2

The Windows scientific calculator provides advanced operations.

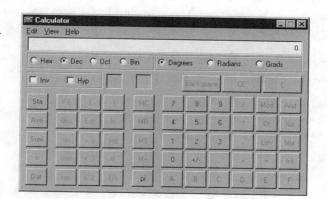

10

Write with Flair

Windows contains a word processor called *WordPad*, which appears on your Programs, Accessories menu. Although WordPad does not contain all the features of a major word processor, such as Microsoft Word, WordPad does contain many formatting features and can accept documents created in several word processing programs. This section introduces you to WordPad.

Notepad also appears in your Accessories menu group, but Notepad is a scaled-down version of WordPad and offers very few of the formatting capabilities that WordPad offers.

WordPad edits, loads, and saves documents in all the following formats: Word for Windows, Windows Write (the word processor available in Windows 3.1), text documents, and RTF (*Rich Text Format*) documents. As a result, when you open an RTF or Write or Word for Windows 6 document that contains formatting, such as underlining and boldfaced characters, WordPad retains those special formatting features in the document.

WordPad contains a toolbar that you can display to help you access common commands more easily. WordPad also supports the uses of a Ruler and format bar that help you work with WordPad's advanced editing features. When you type text into WordPad, you won't have to worry about pressing Enter at the end of every line. WordPad wraps your text to the next line when you run out of room on the current line. Press Enter only when you get to the end of a paragraph or a short line such as a title that you don't want combined with the subsequent line. (Two Enter presses in a row adds a blank line to your text.)

WordPad contains features for the novice as well as for advanced writers. If you have no other word processor on your system, you can use WordPad to produce virtually any kind of document that you need. The following To Do item leads you through the basic WordPad procedures.

To Do: Using the WordPad Program

1. Start the WordPad program from the Accessories menu. You'll see the WordPad screen shown in Figure 10.3.

2. For this task, you'll practice entering and formatting text. Type the following text:
   A large line.

FIGURE 10.3
WordPad offers many word-processing features.

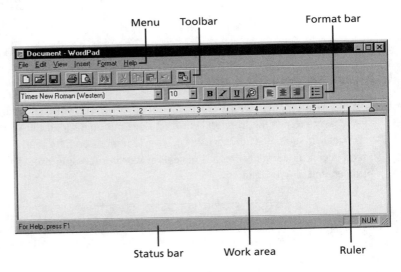

If your WordPad screen does not look exactly like the one in Figure 10.3, you can use the View menu to add a check mark to each of the first four commands—Toolbar, Format Bar, Ruler, and Status Bar—so that you display each of these four optional tools.

3. Select all three words by highlighting them with the mouse or keyboard. With the mouse, select by pointing to the first character and dragging the mouse to the last character. With the keyboard, you can select by moving the text cursor to the first letter and pressing Shift+Right Arrow until you select the entire line.

4. Click the format bar button with the letter B. The text stays selected but something changes—the text becomes boldfaced. Press any arrow key to get rid of the highlighted text and see the boldfaced text.

5. Select the three words once again. Click the second format bar button with the letter I. WordPad italicizes the text. Now click the third format bar button with the letter U. WordPad instantly underlines the selected text. Keep the text highlighted for the next step.

6. By default WordPad selects a *font* (a typestyle) named Times New Roman. You can see the font name directly below the format bar. The font's size, in *points* (a point is 1/72 inch), appears to the right of the font name (the default font size is 10 points).

You can change both the font and the font size by clicking the drop-down lists in which each appears. When you select text, select a font name, WordPad changes the font of the selected text to the new font name style. After selecting the text, display the font name list by clicking the drop-down list box's arrow and select a font name. If you have the Comic Sans MS (Western), use that font to correspond to Figure 10.4. If you do not have that font name, select another font name that sounds interesting.

10

FIGURE 10.4

The text is formatted to your exact specifications.

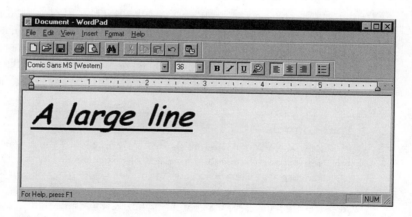

Open the point size drop-down list box and select 36. (You can type this number directly into the list box if you want to.) As soon as you do, you can see the results of your boldfaced, underlined, italicized, large-sized text displayed using the font name you selected. Press the left or right arrow key to remove the selection. Figure 10.4 shows what your WordPad window should look like.

WordPad applied all the previous formatting on the three words because you selected those words before you changed the formatting. If you select only a single word or character, WordPad formats only that selected text and leaves all the other text alone.

Don't overdo the formatting of text! If you make text too fancy, it becomes cluttered, and your words will lose their meaning amidst all the italics, underlines, and font styles. Use italics, boldfacing, and underlining only for emphasis when needed for certain words and titles.

7. Press Enter. Click the B, I, and U format bar buttons and return the font name to Times New Roman. Lower the font size to 10. Type the following: `Windows is fun` and press the spacebar. If you do not like the font size, click the down arrow to the right of the font name list and select a different size.

8. Suppose that you want to italicize your name. If you now click the format bar for italics, all subsequent text you type will be italicized. Click the italics format bar button now and type your first name. The name will be italicized, but the other text will not be italicized.

9. Click the italics format bar button once again and continue typing on the same line. Type this: `and I like to use WordPad`.

10. As you can see, you don't have to select text to apply special formatting to it. Before you type text that you want to format, select the proper format command and then type the text. WordPad then formats the text, using the format styles you've selected, as you type that text. When you want to revert to the previous unformatted style (such as when you no longer want italics) change the style and keep typing.

Font Controls

Ctrl+B, Ctrl+I, and Ctrl+U are the shortcut keys for clicking the B, I, and U format bar buttons. You can also change the formatting of text characters by selecting Format, Font. WordPad displays a Font dialog box, as shown in Figure 10.5, on which you can apply several formatting styles.

As you change the style, the Font dialog box's Sample area shows you a sample of text formatted to the specifications you provide. When you close the Font dialog box, WordPad formats subsequent text according to the Font dialog box settings.

FIGURE 10.5

The Font dialog box provides all formatting specifications in a single place.

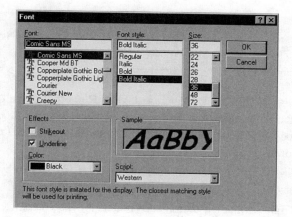

10

11. Select File, Print Preview to see a *thumbnail sketch* of how your document will look if you were to print it. By looking at a preview before you print your document, you can tell if the overall appearance is acceptable and if the margins and text styles look good. You can quit the preview and return to your editing session by pressing Esc.

▲ 12. Close WordPad for now. Don't save your work when prompted to do so.

You've only seen a taste of the text-formatting capabilities available, but there's just enough time left in this hour to discuss one final accessory program called *Paint*. Before moving to Paint, however, browse some of the following word-processing features that WordPad supports:

- The Ruler indicates where your text appears on the printed page when you print the document. Each number on the Ruler represents an inch (or a centimeter if your computer is set up for a metric setting in the View, Options dialog box). As you type, you can watch the Ruler to see where the text appears as you print the document. If you select the Format, Paragraph command, WordPad displays the Paragraph dialog box in which you can set left and right indentations for individual paragraphs as well as tab stops.

You can place tab stops quickly by double-clicking the Ruler at the exact location of the tab stop you want.

- The toolbar's Align Left, Center, and Align Right toolbar buttons left-justifies, centers, and right-justifies text so that you can align your text in columns as a newspaper does. The center alignment format bar button is useful for centering titles at the top of documents.
- If you have a color printer, consider adding color to your text by clicking the toolbar's color-selection tool.
- The far-right format bar button adds bullets to lists you enter. Before you start the list, click the Bullets button to format the list as a bulleted list.

Paint a Pretty Picture

Paint provides many colorful drawing tools. Before you can use Paint effectively, you must learn how to interact with Paint, and you also must know what each of Paint's tools does. Start Paint by selecting the Start menu's Programs, Accessories, Paint option. The Paint screen contains five major areas, listed in Figure 10.6. Table 10.1 describes each area.

FIGURE 10.6

The five major areas of the Paint screen enable you to create and edit your graphic images.

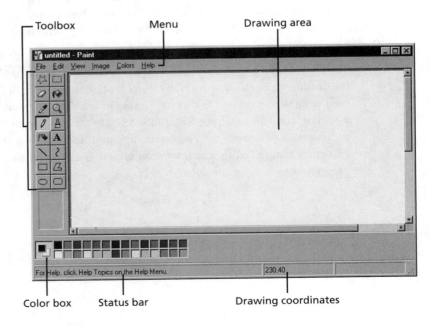

Toolbox   Menu   Drawing area

Color box   Status bar   Drawing coordinates

Paint does not contain a toolbar with buttons as do WordPad and other Windows programs. Paint contains a toolbox that is the most important area of Paint. It is from the toolbox that you select and use drawing tools.

TABLE 10.1   Paint's Five Areas Help You Draw Better

Area	Description
Drawing area	Your drawing appears in the drawing area. When you want to create or modify a drawing, you work within this area.
Color box	A list of possible colors you can choose to add color to your artwork.
Menu bar	The commands that control Paint's operation.
Status bar	Displays important messages and measurements as you use Paint.
Toolbox	The vital drawing, painting, and coloring tools with which you create and modify artwork.

10

The two scrollbars on the drawing area enable you to scroll to other parts of your drawing. The drawing area is actually as large as a maximized window. If, however, Paint initially displays the drawing area maximized, you cannot access the menu bar or the tool box or read the status bar. Therefore, Paint adds the scrollbars to its drawing area so that you can create drawings that will, when displayed, fill the entire screen.

The following To Do item helps you learn how to start Paint and navigate around the screen a bit. Practice using Paint and learn Paint's features as you work with the program.

▼ To Do: Getting Artistic with Paint

1. Start Paint. Paint is located on the Programs, Accessories menu.

2. Maximize the Paint program to full size. Paint is one of the few programs in which you'll almost always want to work in a maximized window. By maximizing the window, you gain the largest drawing area possible.

3. If you do not see the toolbox, the status bar, or the color box, display the View menu and check each of these three important screen areas to ensure that all five areas show as you follow along in this hour.

4. Take a look at Figure 10.7. This figure labels each of the toolbox tools. Each tool contains an icon that illustrates the tool's function. The tools on the toolbox comprise your collection of drawing, painting, and coloring tools. When you want to add or modify a picture, you have to pick the appropriate tool. As you work with Paint in subsequent tasks, refer to Figure 10.7 to find the tool named in the task.

▼

▼

FIGURE 10.7

The tools on the toolbox.

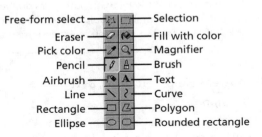

Free-form select —— Selection
Eraser —— Fill with color
Pick color —— Magnifier
Pencil —— Brush
Airbrush —— Text
Line —— Curve
Rectangle —— Polygon
Ellipse —— Rounded rectangle

5. Click the Pencil tool.

6. Move the mouse cursor over the drawing area, and the cursor changes to a pencil (the same icon that's on the pencil tool).

7. Hold down the mouse button and move your mouse all around the drawing area. Make all sorts of curves with the mouse. Notice that Paint keeps the pencil within the borders of the drawing area. Figure 10.8 shows what you can do when you really go crazy with the Pencil tool.

FIGURE 10.8

The Pencil tool enables you to doodle.

8. The default color for the pencil drawing is black. Click a different color on the color bar, such as red or green, and draw some more. The new lines appear in the new color. Select additional colors and draw more lines to beautify the picture even more.

▼

Every time you change a tool or color or draw a separate line, Paint saves the next group of changes to the drawing area. As with most Windows accessory programs, Paint supports an Edit, Undo feature (Ctrl+Z or Alt+Backspace). You can undo up to three previous edit groups. Therefore, if you've just drawn three separate lines, you can remove each of those lines by selecting the Undo command three times.

9. Erase your drawing by selecting File, New. Don't save your current drawing. Paint clears the drawing area so that you can start a new document image.

10. Click the Line tool. Use the Line tool to draw straight lines.

   A straight line is defined by two coordinates: the starting coordinate position and the end coordinate position. To draw a line, you must anchor the line's starting position and extend the line to its ending position. Paint automatically draws a straight line from the starting position to the end position. You can draw lines, using the Line tool, in any direction.

11. Get used to reading *coordinate pair* numbers in the status bar. The numbers tell you the number of drawing points from the left and top of your window. Move the mouse around the drawing area (do not press a mouse button yet) and watch the pair of numbers at the right of the status bar change.

12. Select a different color and draw another line. Paint draws that line in the new color.

Now that you've selected the Line tool, look at the area below the toolbox. You'll see five lines, with each line growing thicker than the one before. By clicking a thick line, the next line you draw with the Line tool appears on the drawing area in the new thickness. You can change the thickness, using this line size list, for any of the geometric shapes.

13. Click the thickest line in the list of line sizes. Draw a couple of lines to see the thicker lines. If you change colors before drawing, the thicker lines appear in the new color.

14. The rest of the geometric shapes are as easy to draw as the lines are. Select File, New to clear the drawing area. Don't save any changes.

15. Click the Line tool to change the line thickness size to the middle line thickness (the third thickness size). Always change the Line tool's thickness before selecting one of the geometric drawing tools. The Line tool's line size determines the line thickness for all the geometric tools.

16. Select the Rectangle tool. Rectangles, like lines, are determined by their starting *anchor position* and the rectangle's opposite corner's position. Begin drawing a rectangle at coordinates 190,75. After anchoring the rectangle with the mouse button, drag the mouse until it rests at 385,270. The status line indicator will show 200,200, meaning that the rectangle is 200 by 200 drawing points. When you release the mouse, you will have drawn a perfect square.

> Drawing a perfect square is not always easy because you have to pay close attention to the coordinates. Paint offers a better way to draw perfect squares. Hold down the Shift key while dragging the mouse, and the rectangle always appears as a square. Shift also draws perfect circles when you use the Ellipse tool.

The three rectangles below the toolbox do not represent the line thickness of the rectangles. They determine how Paint draws rectangles. When you click the top rectangle (the default), all of the drawing area that appears beneath the next rectangle that you draw shows through. Therefore, if you draw a rectangle over other pictures, you see the other pictures coming through the inside of the new rectangle. If you click the second rectangle below the toolbox, the rectangle's center overwrites any existing art. As a result, all rectangles you draw have a blank center, no matter what art the rectangle overwrites. If you select the third rectangle, Paint does not draw a rectangular outline but does draw the interior of the rectangle in the same color you've set for the interior. (The default interior color is white.)

17. Now that you understand the rectangle, you also understand the other geometric tools. Click the Ellipse tool to draw ovals (remember that Shift enables you to draw perfect circles). Click the Rounded Rectangle tool to draw rounded rectangles (or rounded squares if you press Shift while dragging).

    Click the top rectangle selection (to draw see-through shapes) and click the Ellipse to draw circles. Click the Rounded Rectangle tool and draw rounded rectangles. Fill your drawing area with all kinds of shapes to get the feel of the tools.

18. A blank drawing area will help you learn how to use the Polygon and Curve tools, so select File, New (don't save) to clear your drawing area.

19. Select the Polygon tool. The Polygon is a tool that draws an enclosed figure with as many sides as you want to give the figure. After you anchor the polygon with the mouse, drag the mouse left or right and click the mouse. Drag the mouse once again to continue the polygon. Every time you want to change directions, click the mouse once more. When you finish, double-click the mouse, and Paint completes the polygon for you by connecting your final line with the first point you drew.

▼ 20. Clear your drawing area once again. The Curve tool is one of the neatest but strangest tools in the tool box. Click the Curve tool (after adjusting the line thickness and color if you want to do so).

Draw a straight line by dragging the mouse. After you release the line, click the mouse button somewhere just outside the line and drag the mouse around in circles. As you drag the mouse, Paint adjusts the curve to follow the mouse. When you see the curve that you want, release the mouse so that Paint can stabilize the curve.

21. The Eraser/Color Eraser tool erases whatever appears on the drawing area. The Eraser/Color Eraser tool comes in four sizes—a small eraser that erases small areas up to larger erasers that erase larger areas at one time. When you select the Eraser/Color Eraser tool, you can also select an eraser thickness. Select the Eraser/Color Eraser tool now and drag it over parts of your drawing to erase lines you've drawn.

▲ 22. Clear your drawing area and exit Paint.

The geometric tools generally require you to select a line width, a drawing style (such as rectangles that hide or don't hide their backgrounds), and an exterior and interior color and then draw the shape. You draw most of the shapes by anchoring their initial position and then by dragging the mouse to extend the shape across the screen. If you make a mistake, you can use the Eraser/Color Eraser tool to correct the problem.

10

Although Paint can only create bitmap files with the .BMP filename extension, the Paint program can read both bitmap and PC Paintbrush files. PC Paintbrush filenames end with the .PCX filename extension. If you read a PCX file and save the file, Paint saves the file in the bitmap file format when you select File, Save.

Drawings often have titles. Graphs often have explanations. Maps often have legends. Pictures that you draw often need text in addition to the graphics that you draw. The Text tool enables you to add text by using any font and font size available within Windows. You can control how the text covers or exposes any art beneath the text. After clicking the Text tool, drag the text's outline box (text always resides inside this text box that appears). When you release your mouse, select the font and style and type your text. When you click another tool, your text becomes part of the drawing area.

Summary

This hour showed you three desktop accessory programs. The Calculator program offers advantages over its real-world desktop equivalent because the calculator always is available on your Windows desktop as you work with other programs.

WordPad gives you introductory word-processing features that enable you to create documents which contain special formatting. WordPad is limited compared to the word processors sold today. For example, WordPad contains no spell checker. Nevertheless, WordPad offers simple introductory word-processing features and supports several file formats so that any WordPad documents you create will be available in other word processors you eventually purchase.

The Paint accessory program enables you to draw. Paint's drawing tools rival many of the drawing tools supplied in art programs that sell for several hundred dollars. Paint includes geometric tools that help you draw perfect shapes. You can color the shape outlines, as well as their interiors, with Paint's coloring tools. The menu bar provides commands that resize, reshape, invert, and stretch your drawn images. If you want precision editing, you can have it by zeroing in on the fine details of your drawing by using the Magnifier tool.

> If you work with photographic art files, you might benefit from the program named Imaging (located on the Accessories menu). The Imaging program enables you to manage and view photographic image files, such as those you receive as faxes and scans.

Q&A

Q Why can't I read all the text on the Print Preview?

A The Print Preview feature was not designed to let you read text necessarily. The Print Preview feature simply draws a representation of your document when you print the document on the printer. Instead of printing the document and discovering there is a margin or formatting error, you can often find the errors on the Print Preview screen, so you can correct the problem before printing the document.

Q I'm no artist, so why should I learn Paint?

A As just stated, there are many applications that combine text and graphics. In the world of communications, which ranges from business to politics, pictures can convey the same meaning as thousands of words can. Graphics catch people's attention more quickly than text. When you combine the details that text provides with the attention-grabbing effect of graphics, you're sure to have an audience.

There are many other graphic reasons to master Paint, as well. You might want to use Paint to produce these graphic publications:

- Flyers for volunteer or professional organizations
- Holiday greetings
- Letters that include drawings by the kids
- Sale notices for posting on bulletin boards

Perhaps the best reason to learn to use Paint: It's fun!

Workshop

The quiz and exercise questions are designed to test your knowledge of the material covered in this hour. The answers are in Appendix C, "Answers to Quizzes."

Quiz

1. What are the two kinds of calculators available in Windows Me?
2. How does WordPad differ from Notepad and from major word processors such as Microsoft Word?
3. A common type size is the size of *pica,* which is 12 points. What is the actual height, in inches, of pica?
4. How can you center text in WordPad?
5. How can you draw perfect squares in Paint?

Exercises

1. Pick up a daily newspaper and try to mimic the look of the headline article in WordPad. WordPad will not format the text into multiple columns, but you can still learn WordPad by mimicking the headline typeface, size, and attempt to make the subheadlines and text look like your newspaper's.
2. You can learn Paint really fast if you have any children or know of some who can show you. Just start Paint and show them the mouse, they'll figure out the rest. Watch and learn!

10

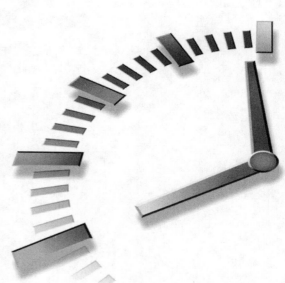

PART 4

Late Afternoon Internet Integration

Hour

HOUR 11

Surfing the Web with Internet Explorer

In today's world, the Internet is a much larger part of computer users' lives than ever before. Windows includes Internet Explorer 5.5, an Internet *browser* that enables you to access the Internet from within Windows. In designing Windows, Microsoft kept the Internet firmly in mind by providing access to the Internet throughout Windows rather than just from the separate Internet Explorer browser, as in the past. As you will learn throughout this part of the book, the Internet Explorer concept runs throughout Windows, and you can access the Internet or your desktop from almost anywhere in Windows.

This hour introduces the Internet to you and shows you some of the ways Windows integrates itself with the Internet. You will learn how to access the Internet with Internet Explorer.

In this hour, you will

- Learn what makes the Internet such an important online tool
- Learn why modern Internet access techniques, such as Web pages, make the Internet more manageable

- Start and use Internet Explorer to surf the Internet
- Navigate the Internet and view the multimedia information you find there
- Enter Web information faster with Internet Explorer

Introduction to the Internet

The Internet is a world-wide system of interconnected computers. Whereas your desktop computer is a standalone machine, and a network of computers is tied together by wires, the Internet is a world-wide online network of computers connected to standalone computers through modems. Hardly anyone understands the entire Internet because it is not one system but a conglomeration of systems.

The Internet began as a government- and university-linked system of computers, but it has grown to be a business and personal system that contains almost an infinite amount of information. The Internet is so vast that nobody could access all of its information today.

 No central Internet computer exists. The Internet is a system of connected computers. *Internet* is the term given to the entire system.

The Internet's vastness almost caused its downfall. How does anyone access or find information on the Internet? Fortunately, Internet technicians began standardizing Internet information when it became apparent that the Internet was growing and becoming a major information provider. With the Windows Me interface assisting Internet Explorer's search tools, locating information is simple.

The WWW: World Wide Web

The *WWW*, *World Wide Web*, or just *Web*, is a collection of Internet pages of information. Web pages can contain text, graphics, sound, and video. Figure 11.1 shows a sample Web page. As you can see, the Web page's graphics and text organize information into a magazine-like, readable, and appealing format.

URL address entry/display

FIGURE 11.1

Web pages provide
Internet information in
a nice format.

FIGURE 11.1

Web pages provide
Internet information in
a nice format.

Web page display area

11

Generally, a Web site might contain more information than will fit easily on a single Web page. Therefore, many Web pages contain links to several additional extended pages, as well as other linked Web pages that might be related to the original topic. The first page you view is called the *home page*, and from the home page you can view other pages of information.

Each Web page has a unique location that includes the source computer and the location on that computer, but such locations would be difficult to keep track of. Therefore, the Internet has standardized Web page locations with a series of addresses called *URLs*, or *uniform resource locator* addresses. You can view any Web page if you know its URL. If you do not know the URL, the Internet provides several search engines that find Web pages when you search for topics.

Surely you've run across computer addresses that look like this: `www.microsoft.com` and `www.mcp.com`; these are URLs that access the Web pages. These two happen to be the URLs for Microsoft Corporation and Macmillan USA, respectively.

Introducing the Internet Explorer Web Browser

Before you can access and view Web information, you need a program that can display Web page information, including text, graphics, audio, and video. The program you need is called a *Web browser*—or just a *browser*. Although several companies offer browsers, Windows integrates one of the best Web-browsing programs, called Internet Explorer. Although Internet Explorer has been around for a few years, the Windows Me release is Internet Explorer version 5.5.

This 24-hour tutorial uses Internet Explorer in the figures and descriptions. Some people prefer to use a competing Web browser, such as Netscape Navigator, and you can use that browser from Windows to access Web pages. Internet Explorer 5.5 generally integrates the best with Windows (because Microsoft wrote both products).

Before you can access the Internet's Web pages, you need to get Internet access through an *ISP*, or *Internet service provider*. Hour 13, "Exploring Online Services," describes how to connect to the Internet through one of several services available to Windows users from the Windows desktop. If you want Internet access through another ISP, such as a local Internet provider in your town, your provider will tell you how to use Internet Explorer or another Web browser to access the ISP's Internet system.

Internet Explorer is easy to start. You literally can access the Internet with one or two clicks by running Internet Explorer. This task explains how to start Internet Explorer. You must already have Internet access through the Microsoft Network or another provider, and you must know the phone number to that provider. (Your provider will have to give you the specific access and setup details.)

The following To Do item explains how to start Internet Explorer.

To Do: Starting Internet Explorer

1. Double-click the Windows desktop icon labeled Internet Explorer. If you get an Internet Connection Wizard dialog box, you must contact your service provider to learn how to hook up Internet Explorer to the Internet.

2. If required, enter your Internet ID and password and click Connect to dial up the Internet. For users with a DSL or cable modem system, the connection will not always require an ID and password.

3. Assuming that you have set up an account with a service provider, Internet Explorer dials your provider and displays the page setup to be your initial browser's *home page*. Depending on the amount of information and graphics on the page, the display might take a few moments or might display right away.

Internet Explorer's Home toolbar button displays your browser's opening home page. At any time during your Internet browsing, you can return to Internet Explorer's home page by clicking this Home button. You can change your browser's home page address by entering a new home page address within the Tools, Internet Options dialog box's General page. When you enter a new home page address, Internet Explorer returns to that page whenever you click the Home toolbar button or when you start Internet Explorer in a subsequent session.

Using Internet Explorer to access the Internet and Web pages requires just one or two clicks. Other Windows Me tasks you perform might automatically start Internet Explorer as well. Internet Explorer automatically displays an initial start Web page from which you then can access additional Web pages and surf the Internet!

Internet Explorer makes it easy to navigate Web pages. Before looking at a lot of Internet information, take a few minutes to familiarize yourself with the Internet Explorer screen by following this To Do item:

To Do: Managing the Internet Explorer Screen

11

1. Study Figure 11.2 to learn the parts of the Internet Explorer screen. Internet Explorer displays your home page and lists its address in the address area. Your screen might differ slightly depending on your Internet Explorer configuration. Internet Explorer is fully customizable. For example, you can hide a toolbar or drag one toobar next to another one (as shown) to make more room for the Web page content.

You probably recognize most of the Internet Explorer's toolbar buttons. Windows intentionally puts similar buttons throughout all its windows so that you can navigate the Web from Windows Explorer, My Computer, and other locations.

2. Some Web site addresses are lengthy. Drag the Address text box left or right (giving more or less room to the link buttons) to adjust the address display width. The more room you give the Address text box, the less room there is for the other toolbar buttons. You can maximize and minimize the Address text box by double-clicking its slider control.

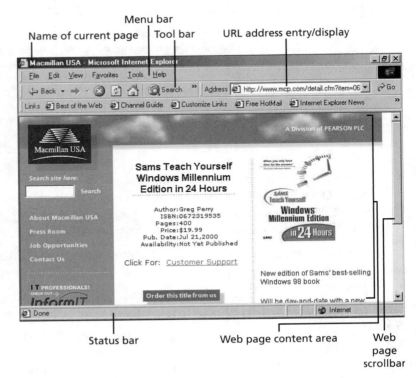

FIGURE 11.2

Learn the Internet Explorer screen so that you can maximize the Internet Explorer browser.

Menu bar

Name of current page | Tool bar | URL address entry/display

Status bar   Web page content area   Web page scrollbar

3. Click the down arrow at the right of the address entry to open a list of recently traversed site addresses. If this is the first time you or anyone has used your computer's Internet Explorer, you might not see sites other than the current start page sites. The toolbar's History button opens the left window pane shown in Figure 11.3, enabling you to return to sites you've gone to in past Internet visits. If you click any of the sites (you might click another day's name to open its site), the display area (now at the right of the screen) updates to show that site. You can return to a single-page view by clicking the left window pane's Close button.

4. Click the scrollbar to see more of the page. Most Web pages take more room than will fit on one screen.

5. Select View, Full Screen (or press the F11 shortcut key) to dedicate your entire screen, except for part of your toolbar at the top, to the Web page.

6. When viewing a full screen view, your menus still work so that you can once again change the view by clicking Alt+V to display the View menu.

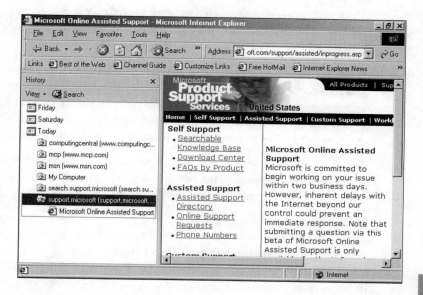

FIGURE 11.3
Internet Explorer uses the left side of the screen for various Internet-traversal functions such as this history list.

Familiarize yourself with Internet Explorer's screen elements. As you traverse the Internet, Internet Explorer will aid you—as you see throughout the rest of this hour's lesson.

11

Surfing the Internet

Remember that the Web is a collection of interconnected Web pages. Almost every Web page contains links to other sites. These links (also called *hot links* or *hypertext links*) are often underlined. You can locate these links by moving your mouse cursor over the underlined description. If the mouse cursor changes to a hand, you can click the hand to move to that page. After a brief pause, your Web browser displays the page.

> A link is nothing more than a URL address to another Web site. The link often displays a description and not a technical URL address. (As you move your mouse cursor over a link, your Web browser's status bar displays the actual URL address to the link.) Therefore, you can traverse related Web pages without worrying about addresses; just click link descriptions to move to those sites. In the next hour, you will learn that if you change the display properties of the Windows desktop, you can make your desktop act like hot links and view areas on your own PC inside Internet Explorer's Web page.

Suppose that you view the home page of your financial broker. The page might include links to other related pages, such as stock quotation pages, company financial informational pages, and order-entry pages in which you can enter your own stock purchase requests.

One of the most useful features of Internet Explorer and every other Web browser is the browser's capability to return to sites you've visited, both in the current session and in former sessions. The toolbar's Back button returns you to a site you just visited, and you can keep clicking the Back button to return to pages you've visited during this session. The Forward toolbar button returns you to pages from where you've backed up.

Keep in mind that you can click the Address drop-down list box to see a list of URL addresses you've visited. In the History pane, you'll find addresses from the current as well as previous Internet Explorer Web sessions.

If you know the address of a Web site you want to view, you can type the site's address directly in the Address text box. When you press Enter, Internet Explorer takes you to that site and displays the Web page. In addition, you can select File, Open to display a URL dialog box and type an address in the dialog box. When you click OK, Internet Explorer displays the page associated with that address. From the Start menu, you can even enter a URL in the Run dialog box to see any page on the Web.

As discussed previously, Internet Explorer 5.5 more fully integrates into Windows and Windows applications than any previous Windows version. Most of the Microsoft Office products, for example, include an Internet Explorer-like interface in many areas, and they link directly to Internet Explorer when you perform certain Internet-related tasks from within an Office product. In some cases, you can bypass Explorer when you want a file listing or when you want to view a file while surfing the Internet. From Internet Explorer's own Address text box or the File, Open dialog box, instead of entering a URL address, type a disk, pathname, and filename. If Internet Explorer recognizes the file's registered type (see Hour 4, "Understanding the My Computer Window"), you see the file's contents.

If you find a location you really like, save that location in Internet Explorer's Favorites list. (This is the same Favorites list found on your Start menu if the Start menu's Settings, Taskbar and Start Menu Properties dialog box's Advanced page has the Display Favorites option checked. By putting the Favorites list on the Start menu, Windows puts all your favorite Web sites at your fingertips from wherever you are working inside Windows.) For example, if you run across a site that discusses your favorite television show and you want to return to that site again quickly, click the Favorites toolbar button and the site is added to your Favorites list. The Address history does not keep track of a lot of recently visited addresses; you can, however, store your favorite sites in the Favorites folders so that you can quickly access them during another Internet session.

You can practice moving among Web pages by using the Internet Explorer browser. After you visit a site, you can return to that site very simply. The following To Do item demonstrates how you traverse the Web using Internet Explorer.

To Do: Moving Between Pages

1. If you have not started Internet Explorer, start it and log on to the Internet.

2. Click the Address list box to highlight your Start page's URL address.

3. Type the following Web page address: **http://www.mcp.com**. Macmillan USA's home page appears, as shown in Figure 11.4. (Depending on the changes that have been made to the site recently, the site might not match Figure 11.4 exactly.)

FIGURE 11.4

Macmillan USA's home page contains a wealth of information.

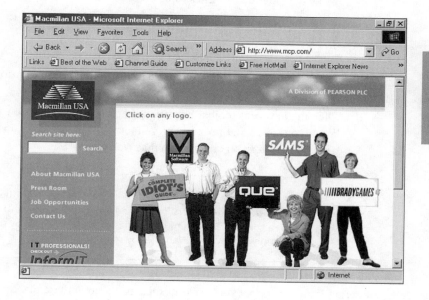

Often, you see Web addresses prefaced with the text http://. This prefix enables you and your browser to both know that the address to the right of the second slash is a Web page's URL address. Internet Explorer does not require the http:// prefix before URLs. Be sure to type forward slashes and not the MS-DOS backslashes you might be used to typing on PCs.

Most Web addresses begin with www and end with com. Knowing this, Microsoft added a time-saving feature to the Address list box: Type the *middle* portion of any Web site that follows the general format http://www.*sitename*.com, such as mcp, and then press Ctrl+Enter. Internet Explorer surrounds your entry with the needed http://www and com to complete the address.

4. Click any link on the page (indicated by a hand mouse pointer or a text color change when you move the mouse over a link's hot spot). After a brief pause, you see the linked Web page.

5. Click the toolbar's Back button. Almost instantly, the first page appears.

6. Once back at Macmillan Publishing's home page, practice building a favorite site list by clicking the Favorites toolbar button.

7. Select the Favorites, Add to Favorites menu option. Internet Explorer displays the Add to Favorites dialog box.

8. Type a description for the page (such as **Macmillan Computer Book Publishing**).

9. Click Create In, then click on a folder in which you want to store your favorite site and click OK.

10. Click the Favorites toolbar button once again. You see the new entry in its folder. When you select that favorite entry, Internet Explorer looks up the entry's stored URL address for you and goes to that Web page.

If you add too many favorites, your Favorites list might become unmanageable. Utilize the folders inside the Favorites dialog box to organize your Web content. By setting up a series of folders named by subjects, you can group your favorite Web sites by subject.

Internet Explorer makes your Favorites list available in these places:

- The Windows Start menu
- The Favorites toolbar button in Internet Explorer and other Windows Me menus that display the toolbar such as the My Computer window
- The Internet Explorer Favorites menu option

As with all the Windows Me menus, the Internet Explorer menus are personalized to display only your most recent selections. By providing only the most recently accessed sites, the sites you are most likely to look for again, Internet Explorer keeps you moving quickly to the information you want to access. If you've turned off the Windows Me personalized menus on the Start menu's Settings, Taskbar and Start Menu option, Internet Explorer always displays all your favorites when you select from the Favorites menu option.

Locating Information

When you want to find something on the Internet, just turn to the tools you already know: the Windows Search feature. You learned how Windows Me searches for data in all kinds of places in Hour 9, "Finding Files, Folders, and Friends." Internet Explorer displays the same search window as Windows displays when you click the Internet Explorer toolbar's Search button. When you want to locate a Web site, just click the Internet Explorer's Search button and your browser window is broken into two vertical panes. As Figure 11.5 shows, you can specify the search in the left pane and the results appear in the right. When you finish with the search pane, click its Close button and your browser window returns to its normal appearance.

FIGURE 11.5

Internet Explorer offers the same search window options as Windows Me.

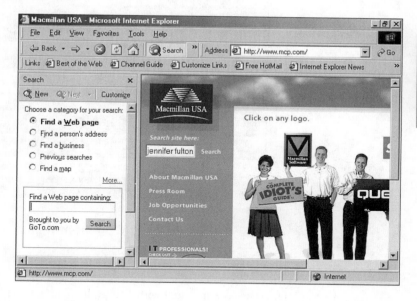

11

Most of the search engines are case sensitive; that is, you need to type words and phrases exactly as you expect them to appear if you want the search to match your search case exactly. Otherwise, if you enter a search criteria in all lowercase letters, the search engines generally do not base the match on case. Therefore, if you want to locate the city named Flint (in Michigan), enter Flint. Otherwise, if you enter the name in all lowercase letters, the search engine will probably search both for the city name as well as the rock.

Helpful Browsing Tools

Internet Explorer provides several features that help you accomplish your Web-browsing job. You will use these tools to speed your online access as you browse the Internet.

Keeping Links Handy

If you want your most important Web sites located even closer than the Favorites list, add the site to your Links bar. You can right-click the top of Internet Explorer taskbar and click the Links option to display a series of links to Web sites. Although the links consume a row of Internet Explorer browser content space, they provide yet another quick way to get to your frequent Web sites. Figure 11.6 shows the links at the top of the browser window.

FIGURE 11.6

Your links are ready for one-click access.

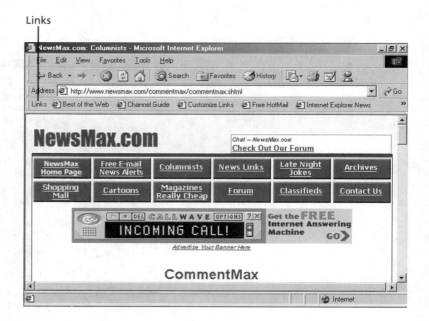

Internet Explorer comes pre-installed with a set of links to get you started, but you can add your own and remove those that are already there. To remove or change a link, right-click over the link and select the appropriate menu item from the pop-up menu. To add a link, drag its Web site icon from the Internet Explorer Address text box to the Links bar. You can rearrange links by dragging them one at a time to a different location. To see the links that don't fit on the Links bar, click the arrow at the far right of the Links bar.

Using Shortcut Keys

Internet Explorer supports these two shortcut keys that will save you time:

- *F4*—Opens the Web address's drop-down list box so that you can quickly jump to a site you have visited recently.

- *F6*—Places the text cursor in the Web address list box so that you can type a Web address to display.

As Internet Explorer searches and locates Web sites, you might hear sounds coming from your PC speakers. This occurs as the Windows Me sounds are turned on for Internet Explorer (Hour 22, "Using Multimedia and Sound," discusses how to work with sounds). A bell rings when a Web page that you search for appears in the browser window, for example. The sounds are helpful when you work in multiple open program windows simultaneously. You can enter a Web address and press Alt+Tab to switch to your word processor and type more of a letter. When Internet Explorer locates and begins to display that site, you will hear the bell ring and know that it is time to return to Internet Explorer to view the Web page.

11

Open Multiple Browser Windows

You can open multiple Web pages from Internet Explorer. Suppose that you have been viewing a Web page with links to another page. You want to read both pages, perhaps to compare notes in resized windows. You can open a second Internet Explorer browser window by right-clicking over the hyperlink and selecting Open in New Window from the pop-up menu that appears. In addition, you can hold the Shift key while clicking on that hyperlink to open the page in the second window.

When you open a second window, the browser window opens with your Web site shown there, and your original browser window will still be open, displaying the Web site you started from. By judiciously opening new Web sites in additional windows, you can view several Web pages at the same time without having to browse between them each time you go back to one.

AutoComplete Works for You

Internet Explorer, as well as parts of Windows Me, support many *AutoComplete* features with which you can begin typing items such as dates, times, days of the week or month, names, and recent Web site addresses you've looked for. When you start typing such an item familiar to Internet Explorer, Internet Explorer completes the entry for you. If you begin typing a month name such as Nov, for example, Internet Explorer displays a small box with November above your month abbreviation. If you press Enter, Internet Explorer completes the month name for you! If you type a full month name, such as July, Internet Explorer offers to complete your entry with the current date, such as July 7, 2004. You can accept the complete date by pressing Enter or ignore it by typing the rest of the sentence, as you want it to appear.

Summary

This hour introduced you to the Internet, a vast collection of interrelated computers all around the world. You can access the Internet as long as you have access through an Internet Service Provider. Although Internet information appears in many forms, the most useful information often appears on Web pages that contain text, graphics, sound, and video.

Windows supports the Internet Explorer Web browser with which you can view Web pages. Internet Explorer includes searching tools as well as a history system that keeps track of recent Web pages. Not only can you view Web pages with Internet Explorer, but you also can view other kinds of files on your computer. As the Internet becomes more organized and as Internet access gets faster and cheaper, you will make the Web browser a greater part of your daily computing routine. One day, you might find that you do most of your work with Web browsing software such as Internet Explorer.

Q&A

Q I've clicked the Windows Me Internet icon, but I don't see Web pages. What do I have to do to get on the Internet?

A Do you have Internet access from Microsoft Network or from another Internet service provider? Generally, unless you work for a company that offers Internet access to its employees, you must sign up for Internet access, get the access phone number, pay a monthly fee (most Internet service providers offer unlimited access for a flat monthly rate), and set up your browser, such as Internet Explorer, to access that provider.

If you want to use one of the services inside the desktop's Online Services folder, Hour 13 tells you how to access the services by following wizards that sign you up for a subscription.

Q How do I know whether I'm viewing a Web page from the memory buffer or from the actual site?

A If the page appears almost instantly after you enter the address, the chances are great that you are looking at the page from your browser's memory. In most cases, the memory's page will match the actual Web site. Nevertheless, if you want to make sure that you're viewing the latest and greatest version of the Web page, click the Refresh toolbar button. Refresh forces Internet Explorer to reload the page from the actual site's address.

Workshop

The quiz and exercise questions are designed to test your knowledge of the material covered in this hour. The answers are in Appendix C, "Answers to Quizzes."

Quiz

1. Where is the central Internet computer located?
2. What is a URL?
3. What is the purpose of the ISP?
4. How do hypertext links help you maneuver around the Web?
5. How does Internet Explorer 5.5 make searching for data familiar to you?

Exercises

1. If you've never tried the Internet, you're burning daylight so don't hesitate any longer. Sign up with an ISP. If you don't like your ISP, you can usually change with no penalty unless you sign up with a long-term contract. (Don't do that!) Browse the Web and see the fun you've been missing. It's not so difficult, is it?

2. Go to the Microsoft home page at `http://www.Microsoft.com/` and, from that page, open four separate windows from four separate hyperlinks that you find there. Notice that you cannot return to a page in a different window; when you open a new window, your Back key does not return you to the previous window. To move between separate browser windows, you must use the same techniques that you use to move between Windows Me windows such as closing or resizing a window to see another window underneath.

11

HOUR 12

How Windows Ties into the Web

Windows Me offers a tight Web connection. If you aren't connected to the Web, you probably soon will be, and Windows takes advantage of that connection.

Actually, Windows blurs the line between online and desktop computing. In parts of Windows, it's difficult to tell if you're working on the Internet, on a local disk file, or a combination of both. You will find Web-related features throughout all areas of Windows. Even the Windows desktop, for years the local PC's wholly owned area, now might contain live content, sent there from the Internet.

In this hour, you will

- Learn why the Web-like Windows interface eliminates desktop and Internet access differences
- Learn how an Internet connection can sometimes hamper your Web usage

- Use your taskbar for simple access to the Internet
- Set up a Web-page element as wallpaper
- Learn why any HTML file works as a desktop component
- Apply any Web page as a desktop component

Your Desktop and the Web

In Hour 3, "Take Windows Me to Task," you learned how to add Web-like selection and execution to your desktop icons. On the Web, when you click an icon that links you to another spot, the single-click takes you to that remote spot. In Windows a single-click selects (highlights) an icon, but a double-click normally opens the program window beneath the icon. By underlining icon titles and offering single-click program execution, your desktop becomes more Web-like, blurring the distinction between your desktop and the online world. Figure 12.1 shows the Web style as opposed to the classic Windows style.

FIGURE 12.1
*The Windows desktop
can respond as the
Web responds.*

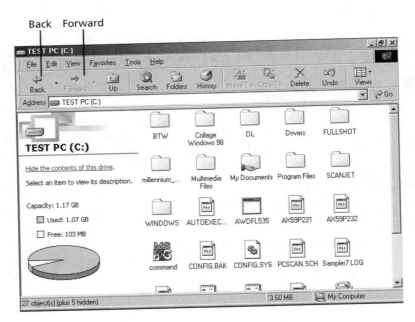

With Windows Me, Microsoft pushes the desktop/Web integration for a good reason: The Internet is part of today's computing environment. Although millions of PC users don't use the Internet, the Internet's growth has outpaced all expectations, and the sheer number of current users plus the expected growth in the next five years makes the Internet the most important component in the computing world.

If you've used the Internet to search various online sites with a browser (the previous hour explained all about browsers and the requirements you need to go online), you know how to move from site to site. Unlike a book that you read from beginning to end, the Internet has no sequential nature. When you traverse the Internet, you move from site to site by clicking the hot spots that you find on the Internet pages. Rarely will you read an entire page before you click a link to take you to a different page. The Back and Forward buttons enable you to move back and forth between Web pages that you've already read. By the time you've spent an hour or more on the Web, you have looked at Web sites that are related and often unrelated.

When you work at your desktop PC without being on the Web, you also work in a seemingly random fashion. For example, you might open a document that you've been working on for an annual report. During your lunch break, you might write a letter to your aunt. Your boss might knock on your door and request that you update sales figures in the spreadsheets for which you are responsible. You might continue editing the annual report before you finish the spreadsheets. In other words, you move back and forth between data documents, spreadsheets, word-processed reports, and other kinds of data such as email, databases, and setting windows as you use your PC. The Back and Forward buttons found in Windows enable you to traverse the typical data tree you've traveled during your work sessions.

Why should the desktop be distinct from the online world? You access files on your disk drives, perhaps on networked drives, and also on the Internet. Shouldn't you use the same browser to access all of them? Shouldn't your interface for any file, no matter where that file resides, be the same so that you don't have to learn two separate programs to manage your data?

Perhaps you can be reassured that such Internet connections are probably not going to last forever. Wireless (satellite-based) Internet connections are here and getting less costly every day. The Internet's slow modem speeds are being worked on. Although more and more people use the Internet each day, your speed should never get *worse* than today's speed, and many companies are working on making the Internet faster for all. Therefore, the seamless Web-style desktop is worth the trouble even if you still use a modem for Internet access. Although you still face the modem connection woes that often arise, your Windows desktop is prepared for the arrival of that fast Internet connection.

12

Online via Modems and T1 Connections

The tight Web and desktop combination does fall apart in one respect—at least for the time being. If you access the Internet through a company's *T1 connection* (a high-speed wired Internet connection that gives you constant Web access), you will more likely understand how the desktop and Web can work together. If, however, you use a modem to access the Internet, as millions do each day, the desktop and Web distinction blur as much as possible, but you still face two real walls: speed and connection.

If you have a quick Internet connection such as a T1, and if you don't have to fight busy signals to log in, moving from a one-PC desktop to a connected desktop is not a leap. Your own files as well as those on the Internet are available when you want them. A Web page that you traverse appears almost as quickly as a word-processor file you stored yesterday on your hard disk. If, however, you must fight busy signals, log in, and use a fairly slow connection (as you have to do even with the fastest of today's modems), you are painfully aware that even though the Windows desktop provides access to a seamless Internet connection, the reality is that you always must make some effort to get onto the Internet.

To experience the Web directly from Windows, take a moment to follow this To Do item to prepare your taskbar for Web access.

To Do: Accessing the Web from the Taskbar

1. Right-click your taskbar and select the Toolbars menu.

2. If Address has no check mark next to it, select Address to add the address text box to your taskbar.

3. If Quick Launch has no check mark next to it, select Quick Launch to add the Quick Launch toolbar to your taskbar, as shown in Figure 12.2. Follow these same steps to add the Address Toolbar as well. As always, you can drag the taskbar's slider controls left or right to give more room to any of the elements there. The Internet Explorer icon launches Internet Explorer and takes you to your browser's home page. The Show Desktop icon minimizes all open windows. The View Channels button gives you access to your push content, as explained in Hour 14, "Understanding The Internet's Push and Channel Content."

4. Click the Internet Explorer icon (the blue letter *e*) to sign on to the Internet (if you're not already signed on) and to view your browser's home page.

5. Although you can use your browser to enter a URL, click your taskbar's Address field, and enter a Web address such as www.microsoft.com to see its page. Even if you are not on the Internet and even if you do not have your browser running from step 4, the page tries to appear when you enter its address in the taskbar's Address text box because it is typically copied from the Internet to your hard disk to speed up your initial login.

FIGURE 12.2
Your taskbar is now ready for the Web.

As you can see, after you've set up the taskbar's Quick Launch toolbar, you can get to your Internet browser's start-up home page by clicking one of the Internet Explorer icons on your taskbar. In addition, if you add the Address toolbar to your taskbar, you can type Web addresses directly on your taskbar and explore Web sites.

Your desktop is not the only place that you can put icons to launch programs quickly. You can add icons to your taskbar. Sometimes, the one taskbar area is called the *Quick Launch* bar because of its capability to hold program icons that you can click at any time to start the programs.

As a summary, here are the Web-related options you find when you right-click over your Windows Me taskbar and select the Toolbars option:

- Address—Display or hide the address text box in which you can enter Internet addresses to view without having to start your Internet browser first.

- Links—Display or hide buttons that hold Internet sites (you can add to the buttons from within your Internet browser program or by dragging Internet Web page icons to the Links taskbar area).

- Desktop—Place or remove all your desktop icons on the taskbar so that you don't have to minimize your open windows to launch any desktop program.

- Quick Launch—Display or hide buttons from which you can start your Internet browser, retrieve email messages, minimize all open windows (with the Show Desktop button), or view your *Internet channels* (special Internet sites that send Web content to your browser).

- New Toolbar—Create your own toolbar of buttons that correspond to any folder on your system, including your Printers folder. The toolbar you create will subsequently appear on the taskbar's right-click menu. By placing shortcuts in your new toolbar's folder, such as a shortcut to Windows Explorer, you can enable one-click launching of any program on your PC.

12

If your taskbar gets too cluttered with icons, you might have to drag the top edge up to give more room to the taskbar.

You do not have to set up your active Windows desktop in the Web style before using the Web-related icons on the taskbar.

The Active Desktop

Windows Me's Active Desktop is so simple, you might not realize the power behind it at the beginning. You can use *anything* that appears in your Web browser on your desktop as wallpaper. If you access a Web page with a graphic, a link to another page, an *ActiveX* or *Java applet* (ActiveX and Java applets are miniature programs that arrive in your browser with a Web page), or straight text, you can place that Web page element on your desktop for later reference. Check out www.msnbc.com or www.ESPN.com sites for common examples of sites with ActiveX and Java components.

Suppose that you want to use Web content as your Windows Me desktop. The following To Do item explains how to do that.

To Do: Sending Web Page Information to Your Desktop

1. Display a Web page from your browser.
2. Right-click a graphic or title on the Web page.
3. Select Set as Wallpaper. After a brief pause, click your taskbar's Show Desktop button to see your new wallpaper. Depending on your Display Properties settings, your wallpaper might be centered, *tiled* (repeated to cover your entire desktop), or stretched to fill your whole screen.

If you open your Display Properties dialog box (by right-clicking the desktop area), you see your new wallpaper listed in the Background page's Wallpaper list.

▼   4. Display your Web browser again.

     5. Locate a link to another site.

     6. Drag that link to your desktop. After a brief pause, your desktop holds a shortcut
        to that page. You can subsequently go to that link simply by clicking the new
▲   desktop icon.

You can set any Web element, such as a graphic or active applet, as wallpaper by right-
clicking that element on a Web page. Your new wallpaper either fills your entire screen
(if you've set up a properly tiled or stretched display property) or sits in the middle of
your desktop.

> If your wallpaper element changes on its original Web site, your wallpaper
> might not reflect the change until you right-click the wallpaper element and
> select Refresh. If, however, the Web site contains an ActiveX or Java compo-
> nent (such as you can find at www.ESPN.com), you can drag that active com-
> ponent (such as a news or stock ticker) to your desktop, and the component
> will continue to change just as it does on the Web page. Of course, if you
> close your Internet connection (by logging off the Internet), the active com-
> ponent cannot update from its live data.

Add Desktop Components

You can add components to your desktop. A *component* is any Web-based document. A
Web document generally has the filename extension `.html` after the *Hypertext Markup
Language* used for Web page layout. You can create your own HTML files and place
them on your desktop or use Web pages as a component.

> The difference between a component and wallpaper is that you can place as
> many components on your desktop as you have room for and resize them.
> You can activate one and only one element to be used as your desktop's
> wallpaper background at any given time.

Almost any program written for Windows recently enables you to save the data as an
HTML file. These files can serve as desktop components, as you will see in the following To Do item. If you have wallpaper, the components do not replace the wallpaper but
sit atop the desktop wallpaper. The following steps teach you how to create your own
HTML file and use that file on your desktop as a component.

12

To Do: Adding Desktop Components

To Do

▼

1. Select your Start menu's Programs, Accessories, Notepad program. Notepad, a text editor, appears on your screen.

2. Type I want to activate my desktop.

3. Select File, Save As to open the Save As dialog box.

4. Type c:\ and press Enter to change the directory listing to the highest directory in the C: drive.

5. Type **Trial.html** in the Filename field and click Save.

6. Exit the Notepad application.

7. Right-click your desktop.

8. Select Active Desktop, Customize My Desktop.

9. Click the Web tab to display Figure 12.3's dialog box page. (Your dialog box might differ slightly because of items you might see in the list box.)

FIGURE 12.3

Set up Active Desktop items from the Web page.

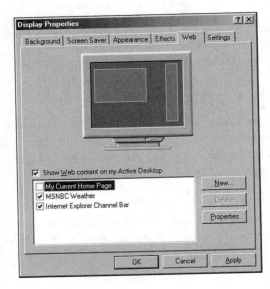

10. Click New. Click the Browse button. You now must locate the HTML file you created in the earlier steps.

11. Double-click the Trial.html file (the filename extension might not show), and then click OK. Windows adds that file to the list of components you can place on your Active Desktop. A check mark should appear next to the Trial.html file, but if one does not, click the check box to add the check mark.

▼

12. Click OK. After a brief pause, a new box with your Notepad file appears on your desktop, as shown in Figure 12.4. If you move your mouse over the new component, the note turns into a window with resizing handles and a Close button, enabling you to treat the window just like any other window.

FIGURE 12.4

Your Notepad file now appears as a desktop component.

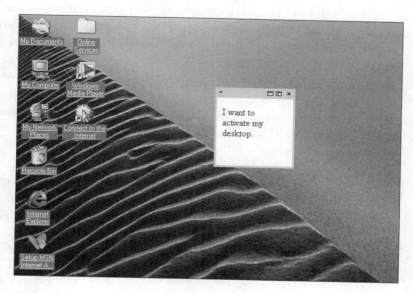

Desktop Components

If all Web pages are created as HTML files (and they are) and if you can use any HTML file as a desktop component (and you can), why not create a more active desktop by placing a complete Web page or two on your desktop? The following To Do item demonstrates how you can make a component out of any Web page because of the Web's adherence to HTML files.

To Do: Adding Active Components

1. Right-click your desktop.

2. Select Active Desktop, Customize My Desktop.

3. Click the Web tab. You see the Trial.html file, which you created in the previous task, in the list.

4. Click New to create a new component.

5. Type **http://** followed by the Web address you want to use, such as **http://www.microsoft.com**.

6. Click OK. Windows logs you on to the Internet if you are not already logged on. Windows displays the Add Item to Active Desktop dialog box. Click OK.

7. If the site you entered requires a password (most public sites require no password), you will be prompted for one. The Web page address appears in the Active Desktop list with a check mark next to the Web page's address. Uncheck Trial.html that you added in the previous section if the check mark is still there. You might see the Synchronizing dialog box appear as Windows downloads the Web page information to your computer.

8. Click OK. After a brief pause, your desktop shows a new box with the Web-page component in it, as shown in Figure 12.5. When you rest your mouse over the top edge of the Web-page component, the component turns into a typical window with resizing handles, enabling you to resize or close the component if you want to change it.

FIGURE 12.5

Your desktop now contains an active Web component, and you can add others as well.

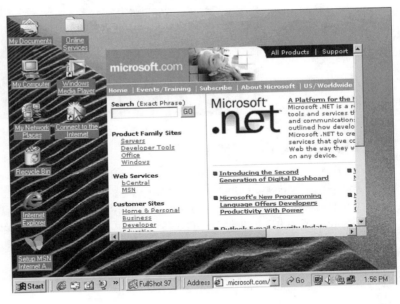

You can now place Web pages on your desktop as components. Resize and move the components as needed. The components act like regular windows with one exception: When you click the Show Desktop taskbar icon, all open windows minimize, but the components stay open. Therefore, live Web pages remain on your desktop. Keep up with the latest scores or stock ticker if you access Web sites with such information.

Summary

This hour showed how Windows integrates with the Internet. Although your Internet connection might hamper the true invisible marriage between Windows and the Internet, the Windows desktop does open itself up to full Internet integration so that you can access the Internet as easily as you access files on your own disk. As you saw in this hour, you can even place live Web pages on your desktop as wallpaper elements or as components so that you can view information when you need it.

Q&A

Q I use the Internet for email but for nothing else. Can the Active Desktop help me?

A Perhaps not right now. Nevertheless, you probably will be using the Web before long. As the Web becomes faster, and as more content is put on the Web, it should become more of a staple for all PC users. At that time, your desktop and Internet relationship will be critical.

Q I've added a Web page to my desktop, and its small window now appears on the desktop. Why, however, when I click Show Desktop, does that Web page window stay open when my other application windows minimize?

A You must remember that when you add a Web page to your desktop, that Web page might act like a window just as your other open windows act, but the window is actually a part of your desktop. As long as you are logged on to the Internet, that window remains open and current.

Q I've added a Web page as a desktop component. Everything works fine, but why does Internet Explorer open when I click a desktop component's link?

A Although a Web page component looks and acts like a Web page inside your Web browser, the component is not a browser. You can only keep the Web page on your desktop that you added to the desktop. Nevertheless, you can click a component's hyperlink and Internet Explorer automatically opens and displays that link's Web site. (You may encounter some exceptions to this rule, however. For example, Microsoft's own Web site will display linked pages within its component window.)

Workshop

The quiz and exercise questions are designed to test your knowledge of the material covered in this hour. The answers are in Appendix C, "Answers to Quizzes."

12

Quiz

1. How do the windows in Windows Me mimic your Web browser?

2. What is the purpose of the Address bar on your Windows taskbar?

3. *True or false*: You can only send text files, such as those that you create in Notepad, to your active desktop.

4. What does HTML stand for?

5. What is the difference between wallpaper and an active component that you place on your desktop?

Exercises

1. Open your My Computer window. Select the View As Web Page option from the Tools, Folder Options menu if the window does not appear like a Web page. Click on your C: drive icon and then click on a folder. If that folder contains additional folders, double-click on one of those. Now, click the toolbar's Back key and you will see that Windows Me backs you up to the most recent folder you visited just as you can back up to revisit Web pages.

2. Place your favorite Web page on your desktop.

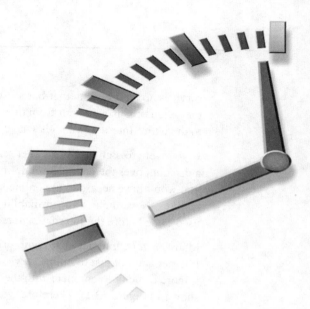

HOUR 13

Exploring Online Services

This hour helps you locate an Internet service provider (ISP) by using one of the services available in the Windows Online Services desktop folder. Although you can sign up for Internet service through a local ISP, Windows provides you with the software needed to try out several popular online services that provide Internet capabilities, as well as other kinds of online benefits.

In this hour, you will

- Determine if you need an online service for your Internet service provider (ISP)
- Learn what advantages online services offer over a straight ISP
- Sign up for online service
- Try different services by signing up for trial memberships

Why Online Services Are Less Critical Today

In the past, online services provided a unique interface so that you'd have to learn specific commands and controls for each service you used. Today, the services are entirely Internet-based, so their distinctions are less important. Although they each organize content from their opening screen differently, they all provide access to the entire Internet, which is where the vast collection of data resides.

If you were to sign up for Internet service through a local ISP, which is often available at a discount over the national online services, you will be able to access the Internet, but you won't have access to the online services' organized content or special information features. Nevertheless, the availability of the organized content is not as important as it used to be before the Internet matured to the consistent entity that it is today.

Many *portals*, Internet pages with organized content, are available free to anyone on the Internet and not just to online service providers. The online service providers are finding it more difficult to compete with the major portals such as *Excite* and *Yahoo!*. (Yahoo! is shown in Figure 13.1). Therefore, you don't have to use an online service to reap the same benefits.

FIGURE 13.1

Portals such as Yahoo! offer organized access to Internet content.

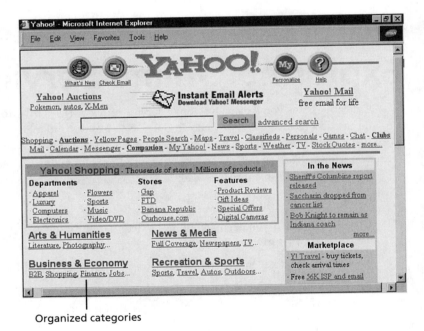

Organized categories

As you learn more about your local options, you will be able to determine better whether an online service such as America Online, or a straight ISP that provides no-frills Internet access is for you. The choice is made even more difficult (or easier depending on your view) by the availability of fairly low-cost, high-speed DSL and cable modem ISPs popping up in major cities around the world. If your choice is a $19 modem-based online service, or a $29 high-speed, always-connected, DSL Internet service, the extra $10 is almost always a bargain because of the time you save logging on and transferring data as opposed to a modem's slower line.

Most online services now work in conjunction with DSL and cable modems. You use the high-speed access provider as your primary ISP and pay the online service a smaller monthly fee than normal to access the software and features specific for their members. Staying with an online service is especially important if you have been with one for a while and want to retain the same email address you've always had.

Introduction to Online Services

When you open the Online Services desktop folder, you see the set of icons shown in Figure 13.2. America Online (AOL) and Prodigy are more than just Internet providers; the services offer unique advantages for the Internet user who wants more than straight Internet Web access. (AT&T WorldNet and Earthlink provide only an Internet connection.) If your Online Services window does not contain all four icons shown in Figure 13.2, run Windows Setup from the Control Panel's Add/Remove Programs dialog box.

FIGURE 13.2
You can sign up with any of these service providers.

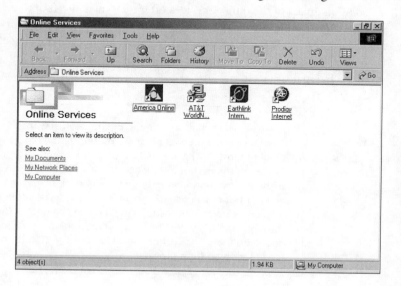

13

If you do not see the Online Services on your desktop, you must run the Control Panel's Add/Remove programs and add the online services from the Windows Setup dialog box page.

All the services charge a fee for their access. Although they all offer somewhat different pricing plans, most services compete with one another, so you must decide which is right for you based on your needs, the reliability of the service, the capabilities each provides, and recommendations from others. Some services provide different access in different areas. For example, one might not support ISDN or DSL access in your area, but provide only modem access.

Don't discount recommendations; if most of your co-workers and friends subscribe to a service, such as Prodigy, you should consider Prodigy because you will communicate with the others without problem, and they can help you get started quickly.

All the online services offer *flat-rate pricing plans*. With a flat-rate plan, you pay one monthly fee no matter how much (or how little) you use the service each month. In addition, the services provide local numbers, so you don't have to pay long distance charges in most areas.

The primary difference between using one of the Windows-supplied online services for your Internet connection and a local ISP that provides more of a generic Internet connection is that the online services offer unique content available only to their subscribers. In addition, many of the online services offer their own interface to the Internet and its content. The drawback to online services is that they offer abundant advertisement at virtually every turn. These ads, as well as the extra graphics and menus they provide on their home pages, mean somewhat slower access in some cases than you can get from a stand-alone Internet service provider.

The companies that provide the online services want the services made available to as many users as possible. Therefore, they try to make these services simple to install. The very nature of online communications requires fiddling even with the best of installation routines, but these services generally install without a lot of intervention on your part. If, however, you use a local ISP and opt not to use one of the online services, you often face somewhat-difficult setup routines, and depending on the quality (or lack) of support through your ISP, you might not get much help. These setup risks might not outweigh the lower cost of a local ISP, but you should consider the risks when shopping for a provider.

The growth of the Internet, with its millions of Web sites, takes much of the uniqueness out of the *unique content* provided by online services. For example, CompuServe might offer movie reviews, but so do a plethora of Web sites, many of which offer as many or more movie reviews as America Online. Most daily newspapers, magazines, and entertainment services now offer Web sites. If you're willing to search the Internet for a specific reviewer's take on a new movie, you can often find as good a review or better outside your particular service provider's unique content.

However, one reason online services are successful is that they offer more than just unique content. The online services generally utilize a proprietary interface. Although you can often use the service in conjunction with Internet Explorer, for example, to access the Web, you can also use the online service's customized interface to access information. For example, Figure 13.3 shows America Online's opening screen. From this screen, you can access one of several categories easily, whereas with a more generic Internet service provider, you would need to know the Web locations to find such information using Internet Explorer.

FIGURE 13.3

Online service providers offer their own managed interface to the Internet and its information.

Perhaps you've heard of the online service named CompuServe. A few years ago, America Online purchased CompuServe. Windows Me does not provide sign-up access for CompuServe, but most of CompuServe's features are in America Online.

13

Newcomers to online technology often prefer the organized content available through an online service. Setting up Internet Explorer or another browser is not always a trivial task with generic ISPs. In addition, the dedicated toolbar buttons and menu structure of the online services get the newcomer (as well as the pros in many cases) to their information destinations faster.

One of the benefits of using the supplied online service if you don't have an Internet provider or if you want to make a change is that all the software for the service setup comes with Windows. You've got everything you need to set up America Online, Prodigy, Earthlink, and AT&T WorldNet, so you don't have to wait to get started.

One of the benefits of using Windows to set up an online service is that you can try a service free for a month before deciding if you want to keep it. The services compete heavily with one another and you, the user, benefit from that competition. Try all the services free for a month and explore their benefits before you decide which one is right for you. (The section "Comparing the Online Services," later in this chapter, compares and contrasts all the services.)

When you choose which online service you want to try, you'll need to set up that service in Windows and subscribe to it. All the online services require that you set up the service before you can use it. Each service is compressed to save disk space until you are ready to use it.

Each Online Services folder icon starts a wizard that sets up one of the services. The following To Do item gets you started by starting you with the Prodigy service. America Online and AT&T WorldNet both provide similar sign-up routines.

▼ To Do: Signing Up For Prodigy

1. Open your desktop's Online Services window.
2. Select the Prodigy Internet icon. A dialog box, shown in Figure 13.4, appears to verify your intent to begin the sign-up process.

FIGURE 13.4
You are getting ready to begin the Prodigy sign-up routine.

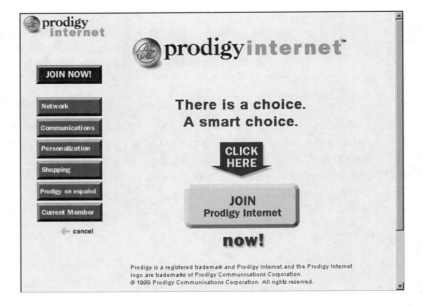

▼ 3. As you continue with the sign-up process, the routine will make a toll-free call to gather recent information, such as local phone numbers in your area.

Consider Online Security

All the online services provide fairly adequate levels of security. Although no online service can ensure that your every keystroke's privacy is guarded, online services do provide more security than regular voice calls, credit card purchases in stores, and purchases you make by mail. The stories you might have heard about online privacy issues are generally overblown.

Use common sense when you provide information over an online service or over the Internet. If you order products from a reputable dealer, the odds are vastly in your favor that you'll have no security troubles. Almost every financial transaction made today over an online service uses a *secure connection*, meaning that information you supply is encrypted on your end before being sent and then decrypted on the receiving end.

---

4. Before you complete the sign-up routine, you must supply a credit card for the monthly billing. Generally, you will have the choice to call in the credit card number instead of issuing it online if you prefer. In addition, you will have to provide a username and password. The name must be unique, so if someone else already has your name, you will have to provide another one. The username and password are required for subsequent access to the service and identifies you as a valid member
▲ of the service.

America Online, Earthlink, and AT&T WorldNet all provide similar sign-up routines. Upon completion, you should see a new icon representing the online service on your Windows Me desktop. You can select the icon to start the online service. When you double-click the icon, such as the Prodigy icon if that's the one you installed, your computer will dial the Prodigy number and display the opening Prodigy screen such as the one shown in Figure 13.5. You're online!

13

FIGURE 13.5
You are now online with Prodigy.

Comparing the Online Services

Which online service is right for you? Only you can answer that question. Perhaps none of the four included with Windows Me are right for you. The following sections briefly explain advantages of each service so that you can better choose between them.

In comparing the services, keep in mind that competition makes all of them worthwhile contenders, and they each provide some advantages over the others. All the services provide the typical Internet-based online service features described in Table 13.1. Each online service, however, goes about implementing the features in different ways.

TABLE 13.1 Look for These Features in Your Online Service Provider

Feature	Description
Chat	Lets you interactively communicate with others who are signed on at the same time you are. All online services, including a straight Internet connection, provide text-based chats in which you type messages back and forth to others who have joined your *chat room*. Chat rooms are areas of interest sorted by topic, such as *PC Support*, *Teen TV*, *Religious Talk*, *Windows Troubleshooting*, *Politics*, and *Movies*.
Email	Stands for *electronic mail* and describes the service with which you can transfer messages and files to other users on your online service and across the Internet. The receiving user does not have to be signed in to receive mail you send.

Feature	Description
FTP	Stands for *File Transfer Protocol* and lets you transfer files to and from other Internet-based computers. Online services almost always provide their own FTP alternative when you want to retrieve files from the service. Generally, a service will offer a file-search section in which you can search for files of particular interest and download them by clicking a button.
Internet Phone	If you have a multimedia PC (and who doesn't these days?) with a microphone and speaker, you can speak to others anywhere in the world. You are not charged the long distance connect rates, but you are charged for your regular online service (some exceptions apply). Internet Phone is not all peachy, however, because the quality is low, both you and the other party must be signed on at exactly the same time, and you both must know which Internet location the other will be at to connect. Internet Phone holds promise, but for now not too many people use it despite its initial appeal.
Mailing Lists	Free (usually) subscription-based Internet services that send you any and all new messages and files posted to the mailing lists you choose via email.
Newsgroups	An area of the Internet accessed through your online service that contains files and messages, organized by topic that you can read, download, and send to. (Newsgroups have nothing to do with Web pages that contain world headline news.)
Web	Web pages you browse from your Windows desktop using Internet Explorer and your online service.

Keep in mind that you get the standard Internet service explained in Table 13.1 no matter which online service provider you subscribe to. In addition, if you prefer to subscribe to a local ISP that offers nothing but an Internet connection, you can access any of the services listed in Table 13.1. Remember, however, that most online services put a friendly interface in front of these Internet services which make them much simpler to use. In addition, the online services provide you with support, news and current events, and entertainment areas that are more complete than you'll find with a straight Internet connection.

13

Most online services provide nice, friendly interface layers between you and the Internet. In addition to the interface, each service provides unique content such as online magazines that you cannot get elsewhere. Generally, an online service costs more than an Internet-only connection you can get locally, but you'll see a cost in another area as well: disk drive space. Most of the online services require between 30 and 50 megabytes of disk space. The unique content and interface requires a presence on your hard disk.

America Online

AOL is the number one online service in use today. Its sheer number of users makes AOL a mixed blessing sometimes. Although AOL's content is some of the most complete and its service offers perhaps the largest selection of specialized benefits, some users have a difficult time getting onto the service during peak hours. In addition, AOL throws a lot of advertising at you while you use the service. This advertising keeps your costs down and the content massive.

AOL provides a wide variety of daily news, periodicals (newspapers and magazines), local weather, movie reviews and previews, and health forums.

 AOL lets you sign on up to five members in your household. Each member can have her own distinct account and can send and receive email separately from the primary account holder. You don't pay an additional fee for the extra users, but only one user can be signed into AOL at a time.

AOL lets you send and receive email between AOL and every other service and Internet user. The email area is simple to use and you are nicely reminded, verbally through your speakers, when you have new email (you can turn this off). Another AOL service that should weigh into your online selection is that AOL offers you up to 2MB of storage for your own personal Web page. You'll have your own URL address and be registered so that others on the Internet (both AOL and non-AOL users) can access your Web page.

AT&T WorldNet Service

AT&T WorldNet service is not a true online service with unique content but an Internet service provider available from within Windows. Billing is simple for most customers because AT&T WorldNet Service bills through the AT&T long-distance service if you use AT&T. (If you have a credit card that offers extras such as airline miles, you might opt not to bill through your AT&T long-distance carrier but select a credit card billing option to rack up those miles.)

AT&T WorldNet offers nothing fancy. You'll use Internet Explorer or another Web browser to surf the Internet, and the Microsoft Outlook email and newsgroup reader works fine for the AT&T WorldNet access. AT&T WorldNet charges extra for 2–5MB of Web page storage if you want a Web page.

Earthlink

Like AT&T Worldwide Service, Earthlink does not offer any unique Internet content, but instead provides you with fast Internet access. You'll use Internet Explorer or another Web browser to navigate the internet through your Earthlink connection. You'll need an email program as well; Outlook Express works just fine.

Earthlink offers two basic packages through its modem service: Earthlink and Earthlink Gold. The Gold package provides priority technical support, an additional email account, and a CD-ROM mailed four times a year, containing the latest and greatest Internet-related software. In addition, you can sign up for the Family Pack, which costs two dollars more a month, but provides you with up to five extra email boxes, 6 MB Web space, and Personal Start Page.

If you use Sprint long distance service, you can combine it with Earthlink service and save money at the same time.

Prodigy

Prodigy's interface takes place entirely within Internet Explorer. Unlike America Online, you work in a regular Internet browser without additional controls that are unique to Prodigy.

Prodigy does give you 2MB of storage for your own Web site, but you must use tools you find elsewhere to create your Web page. Prodigy supplies no Web site creation programs. You can also use Word 97 to create Web pages or any number of Web page development programs on the market.

Prodigy's Internet Explorer interface, as do the other online services, enables you to use Microsoft Outlook and Windows 95's Newsreader and Internet Mail program, so you don't have to learn new commands to access newsgroups and email. Hour 16, "Mail and Newsgroups with Outlook Express," explains how to use Microsoft Outlook to access email and newsgroups from the Internet.

Summary

This hour explained how you can use one of the Windows online services to access the Web, newsgroups, and email if you don't already have access to a service. Both Prodigy and America Online provide unique content that you cannot get from a Web ISP alone. You will have access to forums, news, entertainment, and other links that offer more structured content than an Internet-only ISP. In addition, the online services offer a simpler interface to Web services than an ISP and a Web browser.

13

Q&A

Q Should I subscribe to more than one service?

A Probably not, although you might want to sign up for multiple services for a trial month. The services compete with one another greatly, and, although they differ, every one of them offers vast content as well as standard Web capabilities such as email and newsgroup access.

If your service is frequently busy when you dial in, a secondary service offers a backup number so that you can get to the Web when you need access. Too many busy signals for a certain service might make you decide against that service provider because you want to be able to access it when you need it. Nevertheless, a few dial-in attempts usually gets you through if you're patient.

Q Do I have to provide my credit card number if I want to try the service for a trial period?

A Unless you use AT&T WorldNet and bill your AT&T long-distance carrier, you must provide a credit card number even if you sign up for a trial, one-month period. The online service wants your business, and at the end of the trial period, they want your money. By requesting a credit card number when you first sign up, the service ensures that you will pay for each month you stay with the service. All the services offer email customer support, so you can let them know if you want to cancel the service.

Workshop

The quiz and exercise questions are designed to test your knowledge of the material covered in this hour. The answers are in Appendix C, "Answers to Quizzes."

Quiz

1. What is the difference between a premium content online service and a regular Internet service provider?

2. Of the four services listed in your Online Services window, which ones are *not* a premium content online service?

3. What if you don't want to provide your credit card online when you sign up for a service?

4. What is the difference between a portal and an online service?

5. *True or false*: The online services allow you to create and store your own Web page on the site.

Exercises

1. Sign up for one of the online services and give it a spin. If you already have Internet access, you can still go to the America Online (http://www.aol.com/) or Prodigy (http://www.prodigy.com/) Web site to access some of the nonmember services there.

2. Look around for free sign-up bonuses. Almost all the online services offer free trial periods for a month or more. Although you must supply a credit card number at sign up, you can cancel within the free time frame and not be charged. By trying the free sign-up bonuses, you can try each service yourself to find the one that suits you best.

HOUR 14

Understanding the Internet's Push and Channel Content

The Internet is a vast collection of data, much of it random. When you want something, you have to locate it. Even when you know the location of a Web site or the information that you need, you must traverse the Web to get to that information. All that is changing, however. Instead of searching for Internet data, you can now have that data sent to you.

This hour explains how to use Windows's new *push technology* to receive Internet data on your desktop. Push technology refers to information that comes to your desktop from the Internet without your having to first locate the data. Push technology involves much more than receiving email (although some push technology-based sites incorporate email), as you will learn in this hour.

In this hour, you will:

- Discover what push technology is all about
- Learn why push technology delivers what you want
- Place push content on your desktop
- Learn why channel technology gives you more specific information than push technology
- Subscribe to the channels you want

Introduction to Push Technology

When you receive push technology, information comes from the Web to your desktop or Web browser. Several forms of push technology exist. In its simplest form, you can sign up to receive regular email, such as the morning news, so that when you start your PC, the information is waiting for you.

Windows offers more advanced push technology than regular email, however. As you learned in Hour 12, "How Windows Ties into the Web," Windows Me enables you to place Web components right on your desktop. You can have Web pages and specific content sent to your desktop or your Web browser automatically. In addition, you can view only the information that has changed since the last time you visited a Web site. The push information might appear on your taskbar (such as a scrolling stock ticker with your personalized stock quotes) or in a screen saver during your PC's lull times. Internet Explorer contains special window panes in which you can view push technology information.

Push Is a Development Nightmare

You, the user, benefit from push technology. The Web site developer, however, faces some challenges to offer push content. For one thing, Microsoft's implementation of push technology differs somewhat from other vendors such as Netscape (the makers of Netscape Navigator, Internet Explorer's primary competitor). Microsoft's proposed standard for push technology content is called *Channel Definition Format* (*CDF*) that enables existing Web pages to incorporate push content. In addition to CDF, Microsoft promotes a modified version of HTML (the Web page language), called *Dynamic HTML* that supports modern push technology better than current HTML.

CDF is based on a service that enables you to subscribe to channels of push content. The channels enable you to design exactly the content you want. Instead of receiving an entire newspaper, you can subscribe to your own channel that sends you the sports and weather.

All the various push technologies require some Web site developers to supply the same Web page in a variety of formats, depending on the user's tools. Microsoft Internet Explorer users might need a page that differs somewhat from Navigator users. As with most new technologies, the push technology is evolving, and a *de facto* standard will surely take over. Microsoft has a big headstart, considering that most Windows users have access to Microsoft's push technology.

Active Desktop Push

In Hour 12, you previewed how to send push content directly to your desktop. By using push technology to place Web page content on your desktop, you can incorporate images and other Web controls such as stock tickers on your desktop as wallpaper or as a component. Windows updates the Active Desktop components while you are signed on to the Internet.

The following To Do item explains, by example, how you set up Active Desktop content as it relates to push technology. Microsoft provides active content sites that you can access to place Web topics on your desktop. The desktop links remain active as long as you're signed on to the Internet.

To Do: Placing Active Desktop Content

1. Right-click over your desktop.
2. Select Active Desktop, Customize My Desktop to display the Desktop Properties.
3. Click the Web tab.
4. Click the New button. The New Active Desktop Item dialog box, shown in Figure 14.1, appears.

FIGURE 14.1

Microsoft enables you to sign on to the Internet to retrieve Active Desktop content.

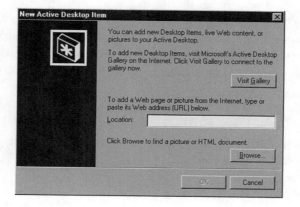

14

▼ 5. Click the Visit Gallery button to visit Microsoft's active content. If needed, your Internet sign-in window appears, so you can sign on to the Internet. After a brief pause, the Web page shown in Figure 14.2 appears. The page offers active content that you can place on your desktop.

FIGURE 14.2

Microsoft gives you a gallery of Active Desktop choices from which to select.

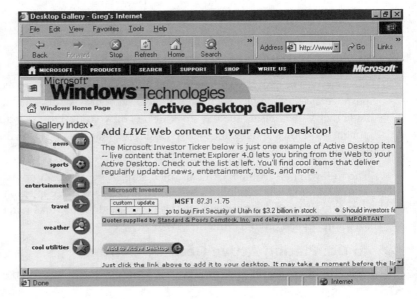

The Active Desktop Web site you see might differ from Figure 14.2 because Microsoft adds to and changes the Web site frequently. Visit the site often to see if new active content that you want appears.

6. Select one of the active components, such as news or entertainment, and the Web site displays a description for you.

7. If you want any of the content you find, click the Description page's button labeled Add to Active Desktop. If your browser's security options are set to confirm whether you want to add the item to your desktop, a Security dialog box will appear.

8. A final dialog box appears asking if you want to add the active desktop item to your own computer's desktop. Click Yes to begin the download to your desktop. One final click of OK confirms the entire process, and the item's information
▲ begins the download process.

Once downloaded to your desktop, you don't have to close specific windows to see the new item on your desktop. Always remember to use the Show Desktop icon, available on your taskbar, when you want to see your desktop because Show Desktop minimizes (but does not close) all open windows. (The Quick Launch toolbar must still be on your taskbar, or you won't see the Show Desktop icon.)

Click the Show Desktop taskbar button to see the active content. Figure 14.3 shows entertainment headlines inside a window. You could also add scrolling information such as a stock ticker if the content provides for one. Microsoft's site contains just about any content for just about any interest. (The scrolling news and tickers, as with most of the active content, contains buttons that enable you to customize the item to see your favorite information, such as stocks that you own.)

FIGURE 14.3

You can view entertainment news and other kinds of headlines.

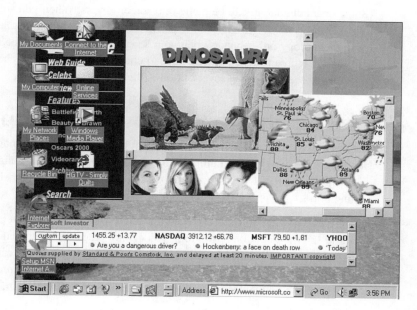

Place active push content on your desktop. You don't have to search the Web every time you want a stock quote or any other piece of information. Instead, direct your Internet Explorer to capture and place the information on your desktop.

Some channel content comes to you via audio and even video. You can listen to the channel content and watch a moving video when you select such content.

14

Notice that the Windows Me icons sit atop the desktop's active content. You should expect this. The icons are to remain in focus, just as they do when you display a background wallpaper image. Windows Me ensures that you maintain access to your icons no matter what kind of active content you place on the desktop. However, if you want to hide the desktop icons to provide more room for content, right-click the desktop and select Active Desktop, show Desktop Icons. You can then access the icons through the Desktop toolbar on the taskbar.

Turn Push Technology into a Screen Saver

Some channel content can be made into screen savers. When you subscribe to the content's channel guide, you learn if a screen saver is available. You can then request that push technology only appear when your screen saver activates. Not all channel sites are available as screen savers, so you have to check with the specific channel content provider to see if a screen saver option is there.

Favorites on the Windows Desktop

In previous versions of Windows, Microsoft used an Internet Channel bar that held active, online content. Beginning with Windows Me, Microsoft maintains the Active Gallery Web site that you saw in the previous section, and a channel bar with that active content no longer is available for your desktop.

Nevertheless, Microsoft has replaced the active channel bar with a bar that holds your favorite Internet locations. Although you cannot place the Web content onto your desktop, your favorites retain a handy status on your desktop and you can make the content available offline, meaning that you can collect the site's data and read the Web pages once you close your Internet connection. The following To Do item demonstrates how.

To Do: Using Channels

1. Right-click over your desktop.
2. Select Active Desktop, Internet Explorer Channel Bar. The Favorites Channel bar, like the one in Figure 14.4, will appear on your desktop. If you've displayed other active desktop content, as you might have done in the previous section, that content will also show on your screen. Remember, unlike wallpaper, you can place as many active content items on your screen as you prefer. (Depending on whether your computer was upgraded to Windows Me, you may see the old Internet Channel bar. To replace this old bar with your Favorites, simply delete the Channel folder in the \Windows\Favorites folder.)

FIGURE 14.4

Your Favorites list is now a channel bar.

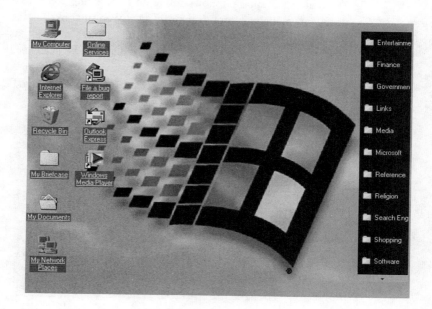

Your channel bar of favorite items will differ from that in Figure 14.4 because your Favorites list will be unique to your system.

You can enlarge the channel bar of your favorite Web sites by resizing with the mouse, or by clicking one of the two resizing buttons that appear when you point to the top edge of the bar.

3. Click any Favorites folder to see the contents of that folder.

4. If you click one of your Web page entries in the folder, Windows opens your Web browser and displays that page. (You cannot place active content on your desktop from your Favorites folders.)

5. Right-click on any item in your Favorites list and select the option labeled Make Available Offline. A wizard begins that walks you through the offline setup.

6. Click Next to start the wizard.

14

▼   7. The dialog box appears, shown in Figure 14.5, letting you determine how many levels deep you want content for. If your selected Web site links to others, as it surely will, you specify whether you want the other linked sites, or only your specific favorite site, to be made available. If you want the linked sites to be available, you must specify how many levels of links you want. Too many levels will require too much time and space to download. When grabbing content for offline viewing, be selective.

FIGURE 14.5

Determine how much of the Web site you want available.

8. You now must determine when Windows Me is to update the Web site. At the end of these steps, Windows will download the Web site to your disk so you can view the site, but that is only a snapshot picture of the Web site. The site will change, and you now must specify when Windows is to refresh the site with new content. You either specify a schedule, such as daily or weekly, or you can tell Windows that you only want to refresh the offline site with new content when you select Tools, Synchronize from the Internet Explorer menu as you view the page. At that time, Windows refreshes the site instead of doing so on a routine schedule.

9. Enter a password if the site requires one (most do not) and click Finish to download the first set of offline content.

▲ 10. You now can log off and read the site offline.

Summary

This hour described how to access push technology. Why should you search the Internet every time you want information? Let the Internet come to you!

You can request that Web information be sent directly to your desktop at the times you schedule. You might want to be notified by email if something changes, or you might want certain Internet information to always appear on your screen when you click your taskbar's Show Desktop button.

The channel subscription service that Internet Explorer offers provides you with specific content and a rich assortment of sites that place information in a minimized taskbar window or even on your Active Desktop. Many channel sites provide services that send active content to your PC as a screen saver to view when your PC is idle.

Q&A

Q Do I have to pay for push content that I subscribe to?

A At this time, push content is free. Many sites do throw in advertisements to defray the costs of the push material. Keep in mind, however, that as push content grows and more and more material is available, you might have to pay for some premium push content. If you don't have to pay to access a Web page, you don't have to pay to retrieve push content from that site.

Workshop

The quiz and exercise questions are designed to test your knowledge of the material covered in this hour. The answers are in Appendix C, "Answers to Quizzes."

Quiz

1. What is meant by push content?
2. Where does the selection of active desktop content reside?
3. Why do your Windows Me icons always appear, even when you display active desktop content?
4. What folder can you place in a bar on your desktop for quick access to Web sites?
5. When might you need offline content?

Exercises

1. Browse through Microsoft's active channel content on their Web site. Read through the details. You will be surprised at how much information is available to you as active content on your desktop.

2. Act as if you're going on a flight this morning, but want to read your favorite Web sites on the plane. Display your Favorites list on your laptop's Windows desktop and make several of your favorite and daily sites available for offline content. After they finish downloading (the download could take place while you pack for the trip if you have a modem-based Internet connection), the information will be available for you when you get in the air and power-on your laptop.

14

HOUR 15

Networking

This hour shows you ways to combine Windows Me and multiple PCs to develop a cost-effective, efficient, networked office in the small office or home office environment. The low prices and high power of today's PCs means that anyone can automate many areas of their small business that was not possible just a few years ago.

The material in this lesson focuses as much on computer hardware as Windows Me's networking interface. The nature of networking makes the understanding of hardware as important as the understanding of software. New technology makes PC networks an inexpensive way to pull the power of multiple PCs together into a single system. Whether in a home or small office, networked PCs help ensure file integrity and then enable you and people around you to share PC resources that they could not do without the network.

In this hour, you will

- Learn what it takes to network
- See your network hardware options
- Understand network speed options
- Master peer-to-peer networking
- Connect multiple networked computers to a single Internet connection

Networking Your Environment

Almost every home and office that has a PC has more than one PC. Perhaps you use a laptop on the road and a desktop at work. Perhaps you replaced an older PC with a more modern one and the older PC is relegated to the kids' room. One of the victims of today's low-priced, high-powered PCs are yesterday's PCs. They were too expensive to throw out, they aren't powerful enough to use as a serious business tool, and you've depreciated their costs so you cannot donate them to an organization for a tax break if they are written off.

You now can begin to use that second, slower PC in your home office. Such PCs used to be discarded but new advances in simple networking technology enables the home and small office user to take advantage of every computer. Although the slower machine might not be your primary computer, you can use it to access the other PC's files when you are in another room and put the slower machine back into operation once again.

The primary reasons why you will network PCs are to share a single printer, files, and possibly an Internet connection between them. Your office PC can be connected to a laser printer and the kitchen PC can, through the network, print documents to the laser upstairs. Of course, the printer must be turned on for the documents to print, but if it's not, Windows will hold the output until you can get there to turn on the printer.

Although the printer does not have to be on, your printer's PC must be connected and turned on to accept print commands from the network. Therefore, the machine that you designate as the file and printer server must be on or the network's PCs will be no better than standalone PCs. Unlike larger, more powerful, but more expensive networks, however, you don't have to designate a machine as a *network server* machine that nobody can use. In a home-based networking system described in this lesson, every PC on the network, including the file and printer servers, can also be used as additional PCs on the network. The networks described here are *peer-to-peer* networks, meaning that every machine is a usable machine and does not have to be designated as a reserved server for files and the printer.

Networking Hardware

A network used to require cabling between two or more computers. Most networks in use today still require cabling, but you have some new options that might eliminate the need to run cables. Right now, you can network PCs together using one or more of these three methods:

- Traditional wiring—Small wired networks are generally *ethernet*-based. Ethernet is a type of network that is simple to install and requires a *network hub* to which all network cables run to manage the traffic across the network (see Figure 15.1). The wiring, called *10BaseT wiring*, is similar to telephone cable, is flexible, and easy to run through walls and under carpet.

FIGURE 15.1

A hub routes network information to their proper destinations.

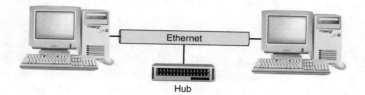

Ethernet

Hub

- RF (Radio Frequency) transmission—Each PC at each of these networks' stations includes an RF transmitter that transmits and receives network signals from other PCs. RF-based networks are traditionally slower than wired Ethernet but provide the obvious advantage of being wireless. RF networks are now beginning to show Ethernet performance but the units are extremely high, costing as much as five times the equivalent Ethernet-based network. Nevertheless, when you count the cost of professional wiring if you hire an electrician to run the wires in a wired network, the RF network is not so costly.

- Telephone and House Current Coat-riding networks—Low-cost, but slower-than-Ethernet networks now exist that you plug into your home or office's telephone or AC wiring, and the PCs will be communicating as soon as you tell Windows to share files and printers. The obvious ease of installation and setup makes these two kinds of networks attractive indeed. Some don't even require a network interface card or a hub! The drawback is their speed and lack of standards. These are the slowest networks you can get and suffice for temporary office setups but have some speed issues to resolve before they become the obvious choice.

The telephone-based networks promise not to interfere, in any way, with phone calls, telephone options such as call-waiting, or active modem connections. These networks use part of the wire's bandwidth left vacant by these other phone services so that your network will not conflict with anything happening on your telephone line.

When you install a network, each networked PC requires a *network interface card* (*NIC*) that you can insert into one of the empty PC slots. If you use a wire-based network, you'll run the wire from card-to-hub until all PCs are connected to the hub.

All the network options offer home-based packages that come with enough network interface cards, cables, and the hub (if required), to connect at least two PCs together right away. Computer stores sell individual parts of the network also so that you can add additional PCs to the network as needed. Buying a complete network has never been easier or less expensive; you can often come away with a two-machine network for less than $100.

> If you opt for an Ethernet wire-based network, still the most commonly purchased network because of its ease of use, lost cost, and high speed, get one that's rated at *10/100* Mbps, meaning that the network can transmit 100 megabits per second over a 10BaseT wire. Although you can save a few dollars by purchasing a slower network, you won't save *much* and the efficiency of the 10/100 speed is too much to sacrifice given today's multimedia environment.

If you use a laptop, you're not out of luck when it comes to networking hardware. All the hardware options are available to you because laptops have available a PC card-based network interface card that connects to networked PCs. When you work on the road and come back to your desktop, you only need to plug your laptop into its network cable and the laptop becomes another PC on the system. You will be able to transfer files back and forth without using diskettes.

After you assemble two or more networked PCs, you can keep all your name and address contact information on a single machine. When anyone in your house adds or changes a name and address, every other PC will instantly reflect that change because each machine will be accessing the same file. Your kids will also appreciate the networked files because they'll be able to play those cool, multiplayer, multimachine games!

Windows Me Helps You Network

More than ten years ago, managing a network of any size required a *Network Administrator*, one who was responsible for maintaining the network connections, adding users to the network, and setting up security, giving access to certain files and printers. Networks were extremely cumbersome to maintain. Although larger network systems still require extensive training and procedures to operate, the home-based PC boom of the past few years has turned the smaller segment of the networking market into a consumer-oriented technology segment.

15

One of the reasons home-based networks don't require more know-how to operate than they do today is because of Windows. Beginning with Windows 3.11 (called *Windows for Workgroups*), peer-to-peer networking became a reality instead of a difficult-to-deliver promise. More importantly, Windows 3.11 (which continued with Windows 95, Windows 98 and Windows Me) gave the industry a standard on which to build network hardware and write network software.

Each Windows network installation requires a slightly different setup. You'll have to read the documentation that comes with your network package, assuming that you purchased one of the all-in-one packages described in the previous section. These packages are designed to make the home or small office network as simple to install as possible, and you should have little trouble.

Keep in mind, however, that you will probably have to make some system settings although these settings should be described in your network's documentation. As an overview, the following To Do item explains the steps you can expect to make to get your network installed, set up, and running.

If you are following this hour's session to set up your network, read through the following To Do item's steps but do not follow them yet. The steps are useful for illustrating the process of networking setup. Windows Me can do some of the work for you with a special wizard. Following this To Do item is another To Do item that explains how to get network setup help with the new Windows Me wizard. Probably you'll use the wizard for your network setup but after reading through the following non-wizard steps, you will understand what the wizard is doing in the background and will be better prepared to understand how the network operates.

To Do: Setting Up a Network

1. Install the network interface card in your PC. Most are plug-and-play, and as long as you use Windows Me, your card should configure automatically the next time you start your PC and Windows begins. If you use a wireless network device that requires no card slot, or if you use a USB-based device or PC network card in a laptop, you don't even need to open your system unit to connect the device.

2. You might have to access your Start menu's Control Panel window to configure your network from the Network icon that you open. Figure 15.2 shows the Network window from which you might have to make settings. There is no way that this To Do item can describe the settings you must make. The settings are technical and confusing and differ for virtually each network system that exists. Your network card's documentation will describe exactly which settings you must make.

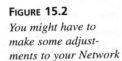

FIGURE 15.2

You might have to make some adjustments to your Network window's settings.

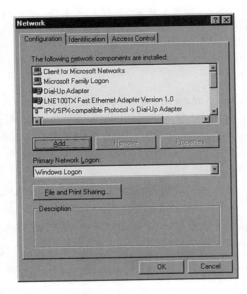

3. You now must designate which disk drives on each PC will be shared. In many cases, you'll share all the PC disks between the computers, but you can also designate only certain drives and printers to be shared if you don't want someone else to have access to a particular device. You must designate each PC's sharing capabilities from each individual machine.

    The sharing is a two-step process: You must set up the PC for overall sharing by clicking the button labeled File and Print Sharing on the Network window's tabbed Configuration page. From the dialog box that appears (see Figure 15.3), click one or both check boxes to indicate if you want this PC's files and printer to be shareable. Click OK to close the dialog box and click OK once again to close the Network window.

4. Start Windows Explorer or open the My Computer window so that you can access your PC's disks and printers.

5. Right-click over each drive you want to share and select Sharing from the pop-up menu. The Sharing property dialog box window opens.

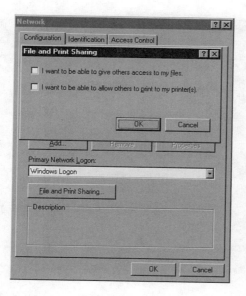

FIGURE 15.3

Specify printer and file sharing capabilities.

6. Assign a name to the resource you are sharing and specify how you want the sharing to take place. You have these sharing options:

   - Read-only—Any networked PC can only read files from this PC
   - Full—Any networked PC can read or write to this PC
   - Depends on Password—The user's password and profile, set up from the Control Panel's Users icon, determines whether the user has read-only or full access

   Figure 15.4 shows how you might designate one shared disk drive. All other PCs on the network will refer to this PC's shared drive as *Office-C*. Each PC's disk drive must have a network name because name clashes would occur if they were all accessed as *C:*.

7. Set up the PC's printer, if the PC has a printer, as shareable across the network in the same way you designate the disk drives. Printers do not have the read-only sharing option because they do not store files but only print. You can set up user passwords for particular printers, however.

8. After you complete the final PC's file and printer sharing specifications, your network is ready to use.

▼

Figure 15.4

You must tell Windows how to reference disk drives.

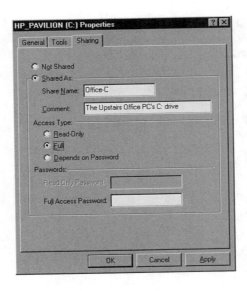

▲

To Do: Using the Home Networking Wizard to Set Up a Network

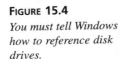

> If you are setting up a network for an office environment with multiple PCs, you might need to specify more networking options than the Home Networking Wizard defines. You will have to follow your networking hardware's instructions if the Home Networking Wizard seems to create an incomplete network for your needs. The primary advantage of the wizard is its capability to set up your network for Internet sharing.

1. Install your networking hardware by following the hardware's instructions. This includes your cables and NIC cards.
2. Close all open windows.
3. From the Windows Me desktop, open the My Network Places icon.
4. Select the Home Networking Wizard. The wizard will begin.
5. Click Next to display the Home Networking Wizard window shown in Figure 15.5. You have several options to choose from, the first of which will be the option you're most likely to select. If you want to share an Internet connection, you must

▼

specify whether the computer utilizes an always-on connection as would be the case for cable modems or DSL. If you use a phone modem, select the Dial-Up Adapter option listed in the center box.

15

FIGURE 15.5

Windows Me makes sharing an Internet connection simple.

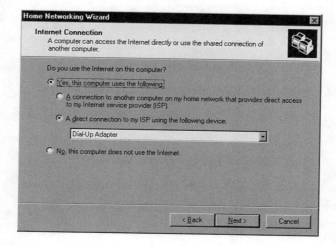

6. Click Next to continue the wizard. If you've chosen to share an Internet connection on this computer, the wizard needs to know how the other computers will connect to this one. Select the choice that determines how this machine connects to the network: Generally you'll have only one choice, which will be that of the computer's network card type (such as Ethernet).

7. Click Next to display the naming screen where you will name the computer that other networked computers reference this machine by. In addition, you must name a *workgroup* that acts as a subgroup on your network. All of your computers can be networked in the same system, but you can partition groups of subnetworks by name. Generally, for a home or small business network, all computers will share the same workgroup name. Windows Me prefers the workgroup name MSHOME, the default choice, and you should consider using MSHOME unless you want a more elaborate, subnetworked system.

8. Click Next to display the file and printer sharing window shown in Figure 15.6. The wizard gives you the option of sharing the My Documents folder. If you want to apply a password to this folder so that others on the network have access to the folder only if they know the password, click the Password button. (To share other folders, see the previous To Do item that explains how to use Windows Explorer to set up file sharing across disks and folders.) At the bottom of the window, select the printer (or printers) you want to share.

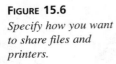

FIGURE 15.6
*Specify how you want
to share files and
printers.*

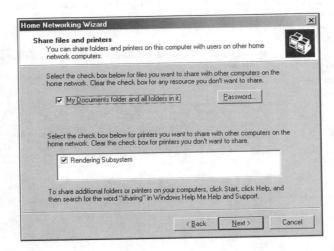

9. Click Next. To make network setup extremely simple for you, including Internet
sharing if you elected to do that, the wizard offers to create a startup disk that you
can take to all other machines on the network to set them up without your intervention. If you insert a diskette and create the startup disk, you only need to take that
disk to every other computer on the network and run the disk's program with the
diskette in drive A:. The wizard makes sure that all the other computers know this
computer's name, workgroup, sharing privileges, and access to the Internet. (To run
Setup.exe, select Start, Run and type **A:\Setup.exe** to start the program.)

Working with a Network

Using a network should be no different from using a standalone PC except that, instead
of selecting a printer connected to your PC when you print, or a disk in your system unit
when you access a file, you specify the printer or file on the other computer. When you
select File, Open in Any Windows Application, click the Look In drop-down text box to
locate the networked disk drive you want to access. To print to a network printer, select
File, Print as you normally do to prepare for printing and select the network printer from
the Printer dialog box's Name list. Windows prompts you for a password if one is
required to use the device.

If you ever disconnect one or more of the PCs from the network, reverse the file- and printer-sharing settings so that the PC is no longer designated for the network, or the computer will run more slowly than it has to. Remove the network card altogether if you don't want to use it, and your computer will also speed up because it will not continue to poll the network card looking for other computers.

15

Summary

This hour introduced you to the world of networking. Network technology has come a long way in power increases and cost decreases. The true winner in the network advances has been the small office and home-based PC users. Just a couple of years ago, consumer computers would not even carry networking equipment because of the network's place in the corporate world. At that time, the network's place meant that the network technology was expensive, difficult to use, hard to install, and costly to maintain.

All that's changed because with the low-cost PCs that have flooded the PC market in the past few years, the demand for connecting PCs together has increased as people buy second machines and laptops. Networks are popular for two reasons: users of multiple machines can share files and printers, and file integrity is maintained when only one disk keeps the data used by several PCs. Fortunately, Windows Me takes much of the mystery out of the software side to networking setup by providing you with the Home Networking Wizard that creates a diskette, which you take to the other computers on the network to make the computers communicate to each other the way you want them to do, including sharing an Internet connection.

Q&A

Q How does a network ensure file integrity?

A Consider what happens if you use the same program, such as Microsoft Outlook, on your kitchen PC as you use in your upstairs office. What if you record a new contact's name and phone number upstairs and then, two days later, you want to call from the downstairs PC. The second PC will not have the name. What do you do? You can walk upstairs to make the call, manually look up the name once again and type the information in the downstairs PC, or make a back up of your upstairs PC's PIM files and copy those files to your downstairs PC.

Neither of those solutions are elegant. As a matter of fact, they leave too much room for error. You might type the name and number incorrectly into one of the PCs. If you restore the one file on the other PC, you might overwrite information someone had just typed in the second PC! Without a network, your files can lose integrity and contain different information.

By utilizing a shared, networked-based disk drive, both PCs will use the same data file. You'll install the program to the shared disk drive and any PC on the network will then be able to use that program and access the shared file's information. If you make a change from one PC, and then walk to the other PC, that change will appear there as well.

Q If I build a new home, should I install network cabling if I think I'll network or will high-speed wireless be here soon?

A By all means, install the wiring. It appears that wireless network technology is getting better, faster, and less expensive every day, but the king of networks is the hard-wired system. As wireless speeds get better, wired speeds do too, so you still win if you have the wire.

The wire-based networks don't allow for as much freedom of machine placement as the wireless devices allow. Nevertheless, the low-cost of hard-wired networks makes them attractive alternatives for many years to come. When you install the wiring at the time you build your home, the added cost of the installation is negligible compared to the cost of having the cabling performed in an existing structure where sheetrock may have to be patched. Therefore, if you have any reason to believe you'll network your home, and technology is enabling more and more people to do just that, install the wire when the walls are still exposed.

Workshop

The quiz and exercise questions are designed to test your knowledge of the material covered in this hour. The answers are in Appendix C, "Answers to Quizzes."

Quiz

1. What is the difference between a local network and the Internet?

2. Which kind of physical network connection is easiest to install?

3. Which network connection generally provides the fastest connection speed?

4. *True or false*: If you have an Internet connection, all of the computers on the network can share the Internet connection.

5. What is a workgroup?

Exercises

1. Do you have multiple computers in your home or small office but still transfer files via *sneakernet*? (Sneakernet is the process of copying a file to a disk, high-capacity disk, or CD-ROM and walking the file to the computer on which you want to copy that file.) Go to your local computer store and look at the networking options available. Many are all-in-one solutions for a small networking system. For example, you can typically find all the hardware and cabling needed for a two-computer network system for under $100. Why are you waiting to network?

2. After you install your network hardware, run the Home Networking Wizard to set up the network's sharing of devices. Once installed on all of your networked computers, go to Windows Explorer and look at the drives available there. If you don't see a network drive, select My Network Places and you'll see the network drives there. You can reference those other computers' drives by name anytime you open or save a file just as you reference your own computer's disk drives by name, such as C: and D:, when you open or save files to them.

15

HOUR 16

Mail and Newsgroups with Outlook Express

The Internet Explorer portion of Windows Me includes a program called *Outlook Express* that manages both email and newsgroup information. By combining a newsgroup reader with email capabilities, you can manage more information easier than before.

Email plays as big or bigger role in today's communications than regular mail. Email's paperless aspect keeps your desk less cluttered, and email generally arrives at its destination within a few minutes to a few hours. Newsgroups offer a different kind of messaging center for messages you want to communicate publicly on a topic. You can post newsgroup topics, answers, and questions, as well as read responses from others interested in the same subject.

In this hour, you will

- Discover how Outlook Express enables you to view and send email messages
- Attach files to email messages you send

- Post and read newsgroup messages
- Set up Outlook Express for multiple accounts

The Email World

It is common for computer users to access more than one online service. Perhaps you work on the Internet but have two Internet accounts, one for personal use and one for business. Each morning you might log on to your business Internet account on your laptop to get incoming messages and send your outgoing Internet messages. The burden of managing email grows as more people sign up for more online services.

Wouldn't it be nice to tell your computer to send and receive all your email without any intervention on your part? The computer could store all received mail in a central location; you could then manage, sort, print, respond to, or delete from there. Outlook Express provides the one-stop answer.

Don't confuse Outlook Express with Microsoft Outlook that comes with Microsoft Office. Outlook Express is not the same program as Microsoft Outlook. Microsoft Outlook is more powerful than Outlook Express, but Outlook does not support newsgroups. Instead, Outlook is designed to use the Outlook Express newsreader or any other newsreader you specify.

Managing Email with Outlook Express

Outlook Express offers benefits over previous email programs because Outlook Express supports several formats within an email message. Although you could send text data, *binary data* (compressed data such as programs and graphics), sound files, and video as email in previous programs, Outlook Express enables you to store HTML code inside your message so that you can customize the look of your message. A message you send might look like a Web page. You can even send complete Web pages as email inside Outlook Express. If you embed a URL inside an email message, your message's recipient can click that URL and go straight to that site on the Web (as long as the recipient uses Outlook Express or some other email package that converts URLs to hyperlinks automatically).

Here are some of the additional features of Outlook Express's email capabilities:

- Send or receive email in plain, unformatted text to speed performance at the loss of seeing formatted messages.
- Attach files to your messages.

- Check spelling before you send a message (provided you have Microsoft Office installed).

- Reply to messages and forward messages to other recipients.

- Connect to Web-based email address search engines, such as BigFoot, to find people's addresses (see Hour 9, "Finding Files, Folders, and Friends," for more information on Web searching).

- Connect to the Windows Address Book program. Address Book is compatible with several other address programs, such as Office 2000's Outlook.

- Send and receive mail to and from multiple Internet accounts.

Setting Up Outlook Express

The following To Do item explains how to set up Outlook Express for use within Internet Explorer.

 If the wizard begins when you start Outlook Express the first time, you need to answer the wizard's prompts to set up your email account. Most of the online services, such as MSN, automatically set up Outlook Express, but if you see the wizard, you might need to contact your ISP to determine which settings are needed for Outlook Express to recognize your ISP-based email account.

To Do: Using Outlook Express and Internet Explorer Together

1. Start Internet Explorer and sign into your Internet account.

2. Select Tools, Internet Options and click the Programs tab to display the Internet Options dialog box, as shown in Figure 16.1.

3. Select Outlook Express from the second and third options labeled E-mail and Newsgroups, as Figure 16.1 shows.

4. Click OK to close the Internet Options dialog box. When you send or receive mail, Internet Explorer will now use Outlook Express as your email program.

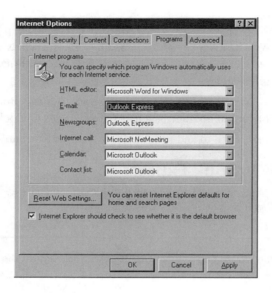

FIGURE 16.1

Make sure that Internet Explorer knows about Outlook Express.

Outlook Express is smart and recognizes whether you've already set up another email program before installing Windows. If you see an Import dialog box the first time you use Outlook Express to send or receive a message, Outlook Express offers to use your previous email program's messages and addresses, so you don't have to re-enter them. Follow the wizard to load any or all of your previous program's options.

After you've told Internet Explorer that you want to use Outlook Express as your email program, Internet Explorer remembers your setup and uses Outlook Express every time you send or receive email.

Sending Mail with Outlook Express

The following To Do item explains how to send various forms of email to recipients. Outlook Express has many options, but you can send email messages and files to others very easily without worrying too much about what else is under Outlook Express's hood.

To Do: Sending Email from Outlook Express

1. Start Internet Explorer and sign into your Internet account.

2. Click the toolbar's Mail button and select New Message from the menu that drops down. (You can also click the Windows taskbar's Outlook Express icon if you've displayed the Quick Launch toolbar.) The New Message dialog box opens, as shown in Figure 16.2.

FIGURE 16.2

You can now send a message to one or more recipients.

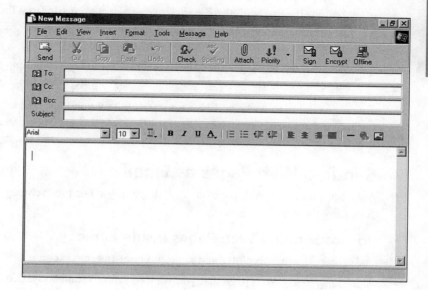

3. Enter your recipient's email address in the To field or click the To button to select the field. If you know the name under which you stored an email address in the Windows Address Book, you can type the name instead of the email address in the To field.

4. Use the Cc (Carbon copy) field to send copies of your message to another recipient. The recipient will know that the message was copied to him. If you enter an email address in the Bcc (Blind carbon copy) field, the To and Cc recipients will not know that the Bcc recipients got copies of the message. If you do not see the Bcc box, select View, All Headers.

5. Enter a subject line. Get in the habit of entering a subject so that your recipients can file your messages by subject.

6. Press the Tab or Shift+Tab key to move from field to field. When you type the message in the message area, the scrollbar appears to enable you to scroll through messages that don't fit inside the window completely. Use the formatting toolbar

▼   above the message area to apply formatting, color, and even numbered and bulleted
lists to your message. You must be careful, however, to make sure that your recipients have an email program capable of reading all the formatting that Outlook
Express can produce; unless you send plain text messages, your recipient might not
be able to read your message clearly without Outlook Express or a fully compatible email program.

7. If you want to attach one or more files to your message, click the Attach toolbar
   button (the one with the paper clip) and select your file from the Insert Attachment
   dialog box that appears. (The File, Attachment menu option also includes attach-
   ments.)

8. To send the message, click the Send button (the toolbar button with the flying
   ▲   envelope) and the message goes on its way toward the recipients.

Sending email messages and files requires only that you know the person's email address
or that you've stored the address in your Windows Address book. Attach files of any type
to your message and the recipient will receive the message and the files.

Sending Web Pages as Email

You can send entire Web pages or any file composed of the Web page's HTML code by
following the next To Do item.

To Do: Sending Web Pages Inside Email

1. Start Internet Explorer and sign into your Internet account.

2. Display the Web page that you want to send to somebody. (You can send the page
   to your own email account for a test.)

3. Click the toolbar's Mail button.

4. Select Send Page. If the Web page is complicated, it might be considered a read-
   only Web page that cannot be edited. If so, Internet Explorer displays a message
   telling you that your recipient might receive the message as an attached file or as
   a read-only file. In this case, if you are sending the page to yourself or to someone
   you know has Internet Explorer, send the page as a read-only page.

5. The email window opens so that you can select a recipient and add copies to others
   if you like. As you can see, the subject is supplied for you. You can see the Web
   page at the bottom of the window as shown in Figure 16.3. Now *that's* quite a
   ▼   fancy email message!

FIGURE 16.3

The recipient will see the Web page when viewing this email.

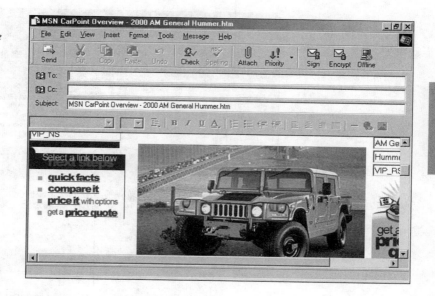

▲   6. Click the Send button to send the Web page.

> Remember that your recipient must also use an email program, such as Outlook Express, that can display HTML code, or the recipient will get a lot of garbage in the message. Your recipient will still be able to read the mail's text, but the email will be messed up because of all the HTML formatting codes that the recipient will see that are normally hidden. You can convert HTML pages to straight text from the Format menu.

Receiving Email

You can receive email that people send to you by following this To Do item.

To Do: Receiving Email in Outlook Express

1. Start Internet Explorer and sign into your Internet account.
2. Click the toolbar's Mail button.
3. Select Read Mail. The mail center window appears, as shown in Figure 16.4.

Folder list   Selected message

FIGURE 16.4
Check your email from
this window.

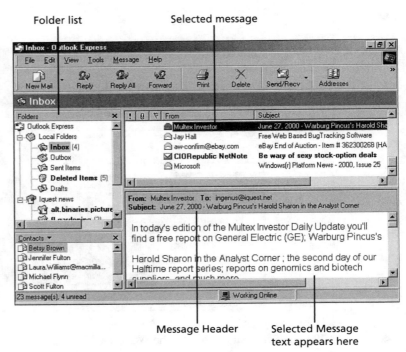

Message Header   Selected Message
text appears here

Email comes to your *Inbox* (the preview area) at regular intervals, but Outlook Express does not constantly check for new mail, or your Internet connection would slow down because of the mail check. Instead, it checks for new mail every 30 minutes. At any time, you can manually check for new mail and send any that has yet to be sent by clicking the toolbar's Send and Receive All button or by selecting from the Tools, Send and Receive menu option. You don't have to be signed onto the Internet to create or read email.

The Outbox area (you can click on the Folder list to see your Outbox contents) holds items that you've readied to send but that have not actually gone out yet. When your Outbox contains unsent mail, the icon changes to show mail in the Outbox. Your email contacts appear in the Contacts pane. Click the Contacts button to add new email addresses.

4. As you click on the headers in the Inbox, a preview appears for that message in the lower pane. (Drag the center bar up or down to make more or less room for the headers.) If you double-click on an Inbox item, a window opens so that you can view the message from a larger window without the other screen elements getting in the way.

5. Delete mail you do not want by selecting one or more message headers and dragging them to the Deleted Items icon. Deleted Items acts like the Windows Recycle Bin. Mail does not really go away until you delete items from the Deleted Items area by clicking on the Deleted Items icon and removing unwanted mail. You can also delete mail by clicking the mail item and pressing Delete.

6. You can easily reply to a message's author, or to the entire group if you are one of several who was sent mail, by clicking the Reply to Sender or Reply to All toolbar button. In addition, when reading email, you can compose a new message by clicking on the toolbar's New Message button.

Create new folders in the Folder list column so that you can organize your email the way you want it. Right-click over any item in the Folders list and select New Folder. For example, you might want to create a new folder that holds business correspondence and one for personal email. You can drag messages to either location to put mail with others that match the same purpose.

When you're in Outlook Express, click the Folder list's icon labeled Outlook Express to see the one-click Outlook Express window shown in Figure 16.5. From this window you can easily read and compose email, modify your Microsoft Address Book entries, locate people, and check newsgroups. (The next section describes newsgroup access.)

FIGURE 16.5

The Outlook Express folder shows this one-step usage screen.

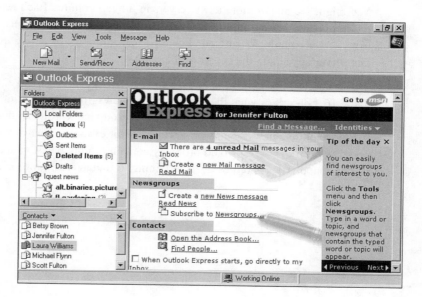

Using Newsgroups

In a way, a newsgroup acts like a combination of a slow email program and a community bulletin board. Newsgroups have little or nothing to do with the daily news. Newsgroups are thousands of lists, arranged by subject, that hold messages and files that you and others can post and read.

Suppose that you are interested in rollerblading and want to trade information you have with others who are interested in the sport. You could find one of the several newsgroups related to rollerblading and read the hundreds of messages and files posted to that newsgroup. Depending on the Internet service you use and the newsgroup filing rules, you might find messages months old or only from the past few days. Often, the larger newsgroups can keep only a limited number of days' worth of messages and files in the newsgroup.

This is how newsgroups act like slow email services: If someone has posted a question you know the answer to, you can post a reply. Your reply will be seen by all in the newsgroup who want to read the reply. There is no guarantee that the person who submitted the question will ever go back to the newsgroup to read the answer, but the postings are for anybody and everybody who is interested.

Each ISP provides access to a different number of the thousands and thousands of newsgroups in existence. To see newsgroups available to your service, click Internet Explorer's Mail button and select Read News. Although your ISP might give you access to thousands of newsgroups, subscribe just to those that interest you. The Internet Explorer Read News button displays the Newsgroups listing dialog box shown in Figure 16.6.

You might see one or more news servers in the left column. Each news server contains a different set of newsgroups. Your ISP determines the number of servers that appear in the news server column. When you click on a server, the list of newsgroups that reside on that server appears in the center of the window.

The newsgroups have strange names, such as `rec.pets.dogs` and `alt.algebra.help`. Table 16.1 describes what the more common newsgroup prefixes, the first part of the name, stand for. Somewhere else in the newsgroup name you can often glean more information about the newsgroup's primary topic; for example, a newsgroup named `rec.sport.skating.roller` would probably contain skating news, and `alt.autos.italian` would contain files and messages pertaining to Italian cars. (*i macchina l'italiani!*)

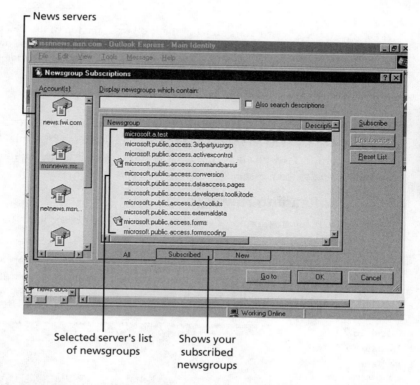

FIGURE 16.6
Select the newsgroups to which you want to subscribe.

News servers

Selected server's list of newsgroups

Shows your subscribed newsgroups

TABLE 16.1 Common Newsgroup Prefixes Describe the Nature of the Newsgroup

Prefix	Description
alt	Groups that allow for informal content and are not necessarily as widely distributed as the other newsgroups
biz	Business-related newsgroups
comp	Computer-related newsgroups
misc	Random newsgroups
rec	Recreational and sporting newsgroups
sci	Scientific newsgroups
soc	Social issue-related newsgroups
talk	Debate newsgroups

Scroll through the newsgroup list to find the newsgroups you want to see. When you find one or more newsgroups you want to see, subscribe to those newsgroups by double-clicking on the newsgroup name (or highlight the name and click Subscribe). If you click the Subscribe tab, you see the list of newsgroups to which you've subscribed. Click the OK button to close the Newsgroups window and prepare to read the news.

Enter a search topic in the text box at the top of the Newsgroups window to display newsgroups that contain that topic. As you type more of the topic to search for, the list below the textbox shrinks to include only those newsgroups that include the text you enter.

The following To Do item describes how you would read newsgroup messages and post new messages to the newsgroups. Keep in mind that a message might be a short note or an entire file. As with email, if a news posting contains a file, the file will come as an attachment to the message.

To Do: Reading Newsgroups

1. Start Internet Explorer and sign into your Internet account.

2. Click the toolbar's Mail button.

3. Select Read News. A list of your subscribed newsgroups appears, as shown in Figure 16.7. You might want to remove the Contacts list as well (using the View, Layout command) in order to view your newsgroup list more easily.

FIGURE 16.7

Your subscribed newsgroup messages appear when you first request newsgroup access.

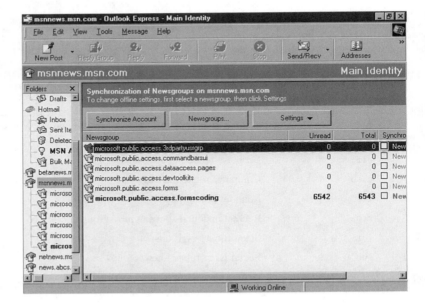

4. To read messages in a newsgroup, double-click that newsgroup name. Figure 16.8 appears showing the newsgroups in the upper window and the text for the selected newsgroup in the lower window. Some long messages take a while to arrive, and you won't see any of the message until the entire message downloads to your PC.

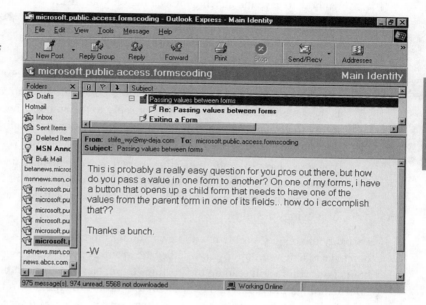

FIGURE 16.8
Scroll through the news message headers and see detail in the lower window.

16

If a message has a plus sign next to it, click the plus sign to open all related messages. The messages form a *thread*, meaning that they are related to each other. If someone posts a question, for example, and several people reply to that posting, all those related messages group under the first question's message, and you can see the replies only after you click the plus sign. The plus sign becomes a minus sign when you expand the newsgroup item so that you can collapse the item again.

> Some newsgroups are moderated better than others. You'll often find unrelated messages throughout all newsgroups that don't belong within that newsgroup. Some newsgroups are moderated by a staff that monitors and removes messages that do not pertain to the newsgroup subject.

5. Check the Size column to determine whether you can read the message in the lower window or whether you should open up a new window to view the message. If a message is over 2 or 3 kilobytes, you should probably double-click the message header to view the message inside a scrollable window. The window contains a menu that enables you to save the message in a file on your disk for later

▼ retrieval. If a message has an attachment, you must open the message in a separate window to save the attachment as a file on your disk.

After you read a message inside the preview pane, you can click another message header to view another message. If you view a message in a separate window, you can close the window to view a different message.

6. If you want to reply to a message, you have two options: reply to the group, in which case everybody who subscribes to the newsgroup can read your reply (which is the general idea of newsgroups), or reply to the author privately via email. The Reply to Group and Reply to Sender toolbar buttons accomplish these purposes. Each copies the original message at the bottom of your reply.

You don't have to reply to existing messages. You can also start a new message thread (related postings) by clicking the New Post button and typing a new message. Your message appears in the newsgroup as a new post and not part of a chain ▲ of previous postings.

Probably the biggest problem with newsgroups is the time you waste in them! You might hop over to a newsgroup to see whether the group contains an answer you need, and two hours later you're still reading the postings there. Newsgroups can provide a wealth of information on thousands and thousands of topics. Although the Web is great for organizing information into collections of pages, newsgroups are useful for the straight messages and files that people want to share with each other.

Summary

This hour explained how to use Outlook Express, Internet Explorer's email program and newsgroup manager. Email is a major part of the Internet user's life these days, and you'll appreciate Outlook Express's advanced support and email management simplicity.

If you want detailed information on a subject, you can search the Web for all kinds of data, but remember to look for related newsgroups as well. Whereas some Web sites are often consumer-related collections of merchandise and hype, newsgroups often contain thousands of messages from people such as you who have questions and answers for others with the same interest.

Q&A

Q How can I get email from my multiple Internet accounts?

A If you subscribe to multiple online services or to multiple ISPs, you can set up Outlook Express to send and retrieve email from all your Internet accounts. Select Tools, Accounts to display the Internet Accounts dialog box. Select Add, Mail and

follow the Wizard to add your accounts to the email. You will almost surely have to contact your ISP to get the Wizard's requested information. After you set up the accounts, Outlook Express will check each one when you request new mail.

Q I read a newsgroup message last month that I can no longer find in the newsgroup. How can I see old messages?

A Often you cannot. Each news server holds a limited number of messages. (Your news server has only so much disk space!) Often, Outlook Express downloads, at most, 300 messages at any one time. Sometimes the server will have more than 300 messages available. To request that Outlook Express retrieve additional messages, select Tools, Get Next 300 Headers. If more than 300 messages are available, Outlook Express will download up to 300 more. By the way, you can change the number of messages that Outlook Express downloads, from 1 to 1,000, by changing the number from the Tools, Options menu item on the Read tab page in the News section.

16

Workshop

The quiz and exercise questions are designed to test your knowledge of the material covered in this hour. The answers are in Appendix C, "Answers to Quizzes."

Quiz

1. *True or false*: Outlook Express supports only a single email account.
2. What is the purpose for the Bcc field?
3. How do you attach files to an email letter?
4. Where does your incoming email reside?
5. What is a newsgroup?

Exercises

1. Locate a Web page you want to send to a friend and send the page using the Outlook Express HTML support described in this hour's lesson.
2. What is your favorite hobby? Log onto the Internet, start Outlook Express, click on one of the newsgroup servers, and type your hobby name in the newsgroup list to see if any matching newsgroups appear. If so, read through the messages and make new friends with a similar interest to yours.

PART 5

An Evening with Extended Windows

Hour

HOUR 17

Exploring Your Hardware Interface

This hour shows how the Windows interface supports your hardware. Windows supports *Plug and Play*, a term that describes automatic installation of new hardware you add to your PC. Prior to Windows 95, you had to set jumper switches and make operating system settings. Often, hardware and software conflicts would occur, creating many hours of debugging headaches. With Plug and Play, you simply plug new hardware components (memory, disk drives, CD-ROM drives, and expansion boards) into your computer, and Windows immediately recognizes the change and sets everything up properly.

Plug and Play requires almost no thought when installing new hardware to your system. At least that's the theory. In reality, you might still encounter problems, as this hour explains. If Plug and Play does not perform as expected, Windows provides a hardware setup wizard that you can use to walk you through the new hardware's proper installation.

Windows has not only made it easier to change hardware on one system, but it also contains a program that aids you in changing entire machines. Many people work on multiple PCs. Perhaps you have a laptop and also a desktop computer. Perhaps you work both at home and at the office. Whatever your situation, the Windows Direct Cable Connection helps you transfer document files between machines without a network connection.

In this hour, you will

- Discover what Plug and Play is all about
- Learn which components must be in place for Plug and Play to work
- Learn how Plug and Play benefits both you and hardware companies
- Use the Hardware Wizard to add special hardware that requires more than Plug and Play
- Implement direct cable connection to make connecting two computers virtually trouble-free

Plug and Play

Despite the industry hype over Plug and Play, it does not always work. If you attempt to install an older board into your computer, Windows might not recognize the board, and you could have all kinds of hardware problems that take time to correct. Generally, devices currently billed as Plug and Play are fairly stable and install fairly well.

If your computer has one or more USB ports (*USB* stands for *Universal Serial Bus*), new USB generally works as well or better than the Plug and Play installations described here. The advantage to USB is that you don't have to power-off your computer to install new devices; simply plug the device's USB connector into your computer's USB port and Windows recognizes the device, prompts you for installation software if any is required, and you are ready to use the device. In spite of the advantages to USB, Plug and Play devices are still needed, such as graphics adapters that must plug directly into your computer's motherboard.

Things do not always go right when installing non–Plug and Play hardware. (New hardware that supports Plug and Play often has a seal with *PnP* on the box indicating its compatibility.) You often have to set certain hardware switches correctly. You might also have to move certain jumpers so that electrical lines on your new hardware flow properly to work with your specific computer. The new hardware can conflict with existing hardware in your machine. Most hardware devices, such as video and sound boards, often require new software support contained in small files called drivers that you must install and test.

Hardware designed before the invention of Plug and Play specifications is called *legacy hardware*.

Before Plug and Play can work in Windows, these two Plug and Play items must be in place:

- A Basic Input Output System (called the *BIOS*) in your computer's system unit that is compatible with Plug and Play. The computer manual's technical specifications or technical support should tell you whether the BIOS is compatible with Plug and Play. Fortunately, virtually all PCs sold since early 1996 have supported Plug and Play.

- A device to install that is compatible with Plug and Play

You are running Windows Me, which is compatible with Plug and Play. If you do not have the Plug and Play BIOS inside your computer (most computers made before 1994 have no form of Plug and Play compatibility at all), you have to help Windows with the installation process by answering some questions posed by a new hardware setup wizard. When you purchase new hardware in the future, try to purchase only hardware rated for Plug and Play compatibility.

17

One key in knowing whether the hardware is designed for Plug and Play is to make sure that the Windows logo appears on the new hardware's box or instructions. Before a hardware vendor can sell a product with the Windows logo, that product must offer some level of Plug and Play compatibility. If you have older hardware already installed under a version of Windows when you install Windows, you will not have to reinstall this hardware.

If you run Windows, own a computer with a Plug and Play BIOS, and purchase only Plug and Play hardware, the most you usually have to do is turn off the computer, install the hardware, and turn the computer back on. Everything should work fine after that.

Although most hardware sold today supports Plug and Play, some notable exceptions do not. For example, the Iomega Jaz and Zip high-capacity drives require several non–Plug and Play steps that you must go through to install these devices (the parallel port versions are simpler but are slower in their operation).

Plug and Play works both for newly installed hardware and for removed hardware. If you remove a sound card that you no longer want, or remove memory and replace that memory with a higher capacity memory, Plug and Play ought to recognize the removal and reconfigure the computer and operating system automatically. Again, Plug and Play is not always perfect and does not always operate as expected, but as long as you run a Plug-and-Play BIOS and install Plug and Play hardware, there should be little installation trouble ahead for you.

Windows Offers Hardware Help

If you install hardware and find that Windows does not properly recognize the change, double-click the Add New Hardware icon in the Control Panel window. (You might have to click the option labeled View All Control Panel Options to see the Add New Hardware icon.) Windows starts the Add New Hardware Wizard, shown in Figure 17.1, which helps walk you through the installation process.

FIGURE 17.1

The Add New Hardware Wizard helps you install non–Plug and Play hardware.

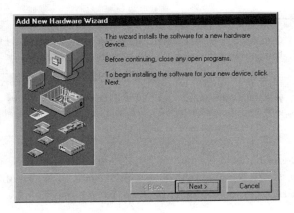

The wizard goes through a series of tests and attempts to detect the newly added hardware. Remember that Windows recognizes most Plug and Play hardware; that is, when you install a new graphics card, for example, and then restart Windows, Windows often recognizes the graphics card and configures itself for use with your new card. Nevertheless, Windows cannot automatically recognize all Plug and Play hardware.

After the Add New Hardware Wizard searches for Plug and Play hardware, you can have it search for non–Plug and Play hardware, or you can select the hardware from the list of vendors and products Windows offers. Of course, if your hardware is newer than Windows, Windows will not list your specific hardware.

> You can let the Add New Hardware Wizard search for the new hardware, and if the wizard does not recognize the hardware, you can select from the list of devices.

Be sure to read your new hardware's installation documentation thoroughly before you begin the installation. Often the new hardware comes with updated drivers that fix minor bugs and add features to drivers that Windows already includes. Therefore, instead of letting the Wizard search for the new device, and instead of selecting from the list of supported devices (shown in Figure 17.2), you use a disk or CD-ROM that comes with the new hardware to add the latest hardware support for the device to Windows. Therefore, you have to click the dialog box's Have Disk button and select the hardware's disk or CD-ROM location to complete the installation.

17

FIGURE 17.2

Select from the list of known hardware or use your hardware's own installation disk.

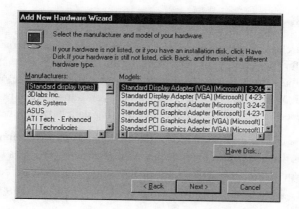

> If you add a new modem to a serial port or a printer to a parallel port, you should not run the Add New Hardware Wizard. The wizard works only for hardware you physically connect to the system unit, such as a disk drive or graphics card. If you plug a modem into an existing serial port, that serial port will already be installed, so you don't need to run Add New Hardware. You will, however, have to double-click the Control Panel's Modems icon and select your modem from the list of modems displayed if the modem does not automatically install thanks to Plug and Play.

If you have a laptop or desktop with a PC card (PC cards are sometimes called PCMCIA cards), you can plug PCMCIA cards directly into the laptop, changing a PC card hard disk to a PC card modem, and Windows will adjust itself automatically. Hour 18, "Using Windows on the Road," explains more about mobile computing and the hardware issues you'll encounter.

Additional Hardware Support

Windows uses a Registry and hardware tree to keep track of the current and changeable hardware configuration. The Registry is a central repository of all possible hardware information for your computer. The hardware tree is a collection of hardware configurations, taken from parts or all the Registry, for your computer. (In addition, your Registry holds software settings.)

Luckily, you don't have to know anything about the Registry because Windows keeps track of the details for you. If, however, you want to look at the hardware tree currently in place on your computer, you can display the Control Panel, double-click the System icon, and choose the Device Manager page. Windows displays the System Properties tabbed dialog box. The hardware tree shows the devices currently in use.

Setting Up a Second PC

When you purchase a second PC, such as a laptop or a second home PC, you'll probably want to transfer files from your current PC to the new one. For example, you might have data files on the current PC that you want to place on the new one. Windows supports a feature called Direct Cable Connection that lets you transfer files between computers without the need of a network and without moving data between the PCs via disk.

If you attach a high-speed parallel or serial cable between two computers, those computers can share files and printer resources with one another. This is a simple replacement for a more expensive and extensive network system such as described in Hour 15, "Networking." The cable connection is useful if you want only two computers to share resources.

The Direct Cable Connection option should be available in the Accessories, Communications menu. (If the Direct Cable Connection option is not installed, run the Windows Setup option from the Control Panel's Add/Remove Programs icon if you need to install Direct Cable Connection.) When you select Direct Cable Connection, Windows initiates the wizard shown in Figure 17.3. After answering the wizard's prompts, your two computers will be linked as the To Do steps explain next.

FIGURE 17.3

The Communications menu contains the Direct Cable Connection Wizard.

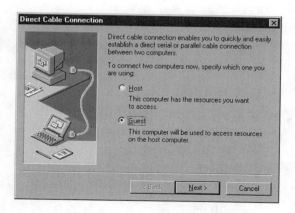

 The two computers connected using a direct cable connection must use the same type of port. Therefore, you must connect two parallel ports with a bidirectional parallel cable or two serial ports with a null-modem cable. You cannot connect a parallel port to a serial port.

17

To Do: Making a Direct Cable Connection

1. Connect your two computers with the cable.

2. Select the Start menu's Programs, Accessories, Communications, Direct Cable Connection option on both PCs to display the wizard's opening window, shown in Figure 17.3.

3. Select one PC as the host and one as the guest by clicking the appropriate options on the wizard's first page. The host is the PC from which you'll transfer the file (or files), and the guest receives those files. After you designate a host and guest, you cannot send information in the other direction without restarting the wizard.

4. Click the Next button to select the port on which you've connected the computers from the dialog box that appears in Figure 17.4. You'll have to select the port on each PC.

5. Click the Next button on both PCs so that the Finish button appears in the guest's window. The host dialog box will display a button labeled File and Print Sharing. Click this button to give access to both your files and printer from any guest PC that connects.

FIGURE 17.4

Tell the wizard which port the cable connects to.

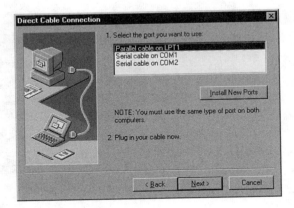

6. Click the host's File and Print Sharing button to specify whether you want to share files, your printer, or both. If you've never specified printer or file sharing, you might find that the host PC's wizard requires a system reboot to work after you've determined the file and printer sharing access. If so, you can restart the host PC's wizard and return to the final dialog box described in the next step without making a change on the waiting guest PC.

7. Click OK to return the host PC to the Direct Cable Connection Wizard.

8. If you want to require a password from the guest PC before allowing file or printer sharing (sometimes this is helpful when more than one person uses a computer connected to another's), click the Use Password Protection option and click Set Password to enter a password that the guest PC user will type to gain access.

9. Click Finish to make the connection. If the two PCs recognize each other, you've made the connection properly. Otherwise, you might have to check cable connections and rerun the wizard to ensure that all the options are set. (For example, you'll want to make sure that both PCs are not set as host or both as guest.)

10. The guest's Windows Explorer or My Computer window now holds an icon for the host PC, and you can transfer files from the host as easily as you can transfer from one of your disks to another. In addition, the guest's application programs can now print to the host printer because the host printer will be available from all File, Print dialog boxes.

The Direct Cable Connection provides a way for you to connect two computers to use the files and printer on one (the host) by the other (the guest). The Direct Cable Connection enables the guest computer to share the host's file and printer resources without requiring expensive and more elaborate networking hardware and software.

After you set up a host or guest PC, your subsequent use of Direct Cable Connection is easier. You then have to specify the dialog box settings only if you change computers or if you decide to change directions and switch between the host and guest when transferring files. Figure 17.5 shows the dialog box that appears when you start the host's Direct Cable Connection Wizard after you initially set up the connection.

FIGURE 17.5

Tell the wizard which port the cable connects to. The next time you use the cable connection, you don't have to specify a cable or port.

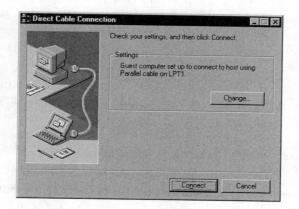

17

Summary

This hour got fairly technical during the discussion of hardware. An operating system must run through several operations before it can recognize and work with new hardware. Fortunately, the Plug and Play process makes such work slightly easier and sometimes trouble-free.

If you do not use 100% Plug and Play (or USB) hardware, the Add New Hardware Wizard will walk you through each installation and help make the hardware easier to install. Suppose, for example, you add an internal modem, but you cannot communicate with it. The Add New Hardware Wizard might realize that you have a new internal modem after running through its series of tests, but might not be able to determine exactly what kind of internal modem you have. You and the wizard together should be able to determine the proper configuration.

The Direct Cable Connection Wizard means that you'll be connecting more computers than ever before. You'll be able to transfer files and share printers easily from one to the other by attaching a cable between the parallel or serial ports of each machine.

Q&A

Q How do I know whether I have Plug and Play?

A You have Windows, which means that installing hardware ought to be easier than with previous operating systems and earlier versions of Windows. Perhaps the best way to see whether you have Plug and Play is to plug the next device you get for your computer into the computer, power on your machine, and see what happens. (Of course, you should read the new hardware's installation instructions to learn the correct way to install the device.)

If you turn on your computer and the computer responds to the new device properly, you have, for all intents and purposes, all the Plug and Play compatibility you need. You have Plug and Play, at least, for that one device. Just because Windows and your BIOS are compatible with Plug and Play, however, does not mean that the hardware you install will also be compatible with Plug and Play. Some hardware might be compatible with Plug and Play and some might not.

Q I don't want to buy and install a network in my house, but how do I easily connect my laptop to my desktop to share files between them?

A Use the Windows Direct Cable Connection. Connect a parallel or serial cable to both parallel or serial ports. Your laptop will be able to access the desktop's shared files. As simple as the Direct Cable Connection is, if your laptop contains an infrared port, you'll learn in Hour 18 how to share files between the laptop and another device without the need of wires.

Workshop

The quiz and exercise questions are designed to test your knowledge of the material covered in this hour. The answers are in Appendix C, "Answers to Quizzes."

Quiz

1. What is a legacy device?

2. What advantage does Plug and Play offer over legacy?

3. What further advantage does a Plug and Play USB device provide you?

4. What is a PC or PCMCIA card?

5. What kind of port, serial or parallel, do you need to use for the Direct Cable Connection feature?

Exercises

1. Open your Control Panel, display all the icons there, and open the System window. Click the Device Manager tab and look at all your installed hardware devices. Don't change anything unless you know exactly what to do. Close the System window when you're finished. You can learn a lot about your computer from the Control Panel's System window.

2. If you have a laptop, create a Direct Cable Connection between your desktop computer and your laptop. The next hour's lesson will explain how you can use Windows Me's Briefcase feature to transfer files over the Direct Cable Connection if you prefer not to use a network for file transfer.

17

Hour 18

Using Windows on the Road

This hour shows how Windows Me supports mobile computing environments. If you use a laptop, you'll appreciate the laptop features Microsoft included with Windows. Windows recognizes when you change a laptop's configuration using sort of a *Plug and Play on-the-fly* because you don't have to turn off your laptop when making common hardware changes, such as docking the laptop into a docking bay.

Perhaps you use a laptop while on the road and a desktop computer at the office or at home. If so, you need to transfer files easily between them and, at the same time, keep those files in synchronization so that you always work with the latest file version. Whatever your situation, the Windows *Briefcase* will help you synchronize your document files so they remain as current as possible.

The nature of laptop use is mobile computing. The cables you must plug in when connecting your laptop to a printer or to another PC make the laptop somewhat cumbersome when you want to communicate to another device. Fortunately, most of today's laptops come with infrared ports so that you can access other devices without cables.

In this hour, you will

- Learn why automatic configuration for mobile computing environments is so important
- Discover why the My Briefcase icon is one of the most important icons on the Windows desktop for users of both portable and desktop computers
- Watch as Windows detects common laptop hardware changes
- Use infrared connections to make communicating with peripherals and other computers simpler than using cables

Docking Your Laptop

The Microsoft programmers understood the need for mobile computing environments when they developed Windows. Mobile computing environments refer to those environments in which portable computers such as laptops are used. In the past few years, companies have begun developing *docking stations* for computer users who take a laptop with them on the road. Now they can come home and plug the laptop directly into a docking station. The docking station is a device that connects the laptop to a full-size color screen, printer, mouse, and keyboard. Therefore, the computer user uses the laptop on the road and then uses the laptop's system unit at home or in the office, with regular-size peripheral equipment.

> **Sitting at the Dock**
>
> Many devices known as docking stations are more accurately described as *port replicators* because they extend the laptop's expansion ports, such as the printer and serial port, to the docking station device on your desktop. Leaving all your peripherals plugged into the docking station is simpler than plugging each device into your laptop every time you arrive back at your desk. You only have to slide your laptop into the docking station to access those peripherals plugged into the docking station.

Figure 18.1 shows a laptop connected to a docking station. Windows can detect whether a computer is docked and make appropriate adjustments instantly and accordingly. When undocked, Windows can use the laptop's screen, and when docked, Windows can immediately adjust the screen to a larger and higher-resolution monitor.

FIGURE 18.1

*A docking station lets
you utilize full-size
desktop peripherals
from your laptop.*

Laptop docks
here.

Windows often can recognize that a computer has been docked, but most hardware does
not allow you to undock your PC without Windows knowing about the undocking. If
Windows does not recognize the fact that you've undocked, you can select Eject PC from
the Start menu, and Windows will know to reconfigure for the undocking and use the
laptop's own configuration. For example, if your laptop contains an internal modem, the
laptop, when undocked, will no longer be configured to use the docking station's modem.

When undocked, the Eject PC option does not appear on your Start menu.

Using PC Cards

For several years, laptops have supported PC cards (PC cards are sometimes called
PCMCIA cards), the small credit card–sized expansion peripherals that plug into the side
on your laptops. These cards enable you to add a modem, memory, networking capabilities,
and even another hard disk to your laptop.

Three card types exist:

- Type I—The original card soon replaced with Type II (Type I cards are no longer
  available)

- Type II—The most common PC card you can purchase today, primarily used for
  modems, memory, and networking

- Type III—A double-sized card used primarily for disk expansion (yes, you can fit
  several megabytes into the size of a couple of credit cards)

Most laptops in use today support two Type II (or Type I) cards at once, or one Type III
PC card, because of its double width.

The Control Panel includes an icon labeled PC card (PCMCIA) that contains the PC card
control you need as you work in Windows. When you select this Control Panel item,
Windows opens the PC card Properties dialog box shown in Figure 18.2.

18

FIGURE 18.2

The PC Card Properties dialog box enables you to control your PC card settings.

Figure 18.2 indicates that the laptop has one PC card socket (many have two) and that the socket is empty. The first option at the bottom of the dialog box determines whether the PC Card icon will appear on your taskbar, giving you quicker access to the PC Card Properties dialog box than going through the Control Panel. If selected, the second option warns you if you remove a PC card before you stop it. Although you can insert and remove most PC cards during the operation of Windows without stopping the card first, if you use a PC card with a hard disk, you must stop the card *before* removing it to ensure that all unwritten data is on the card's disk.

To start any card, simply insert the card into the appropriate PC card slot. Your PC can be on or off for this operation, one of the only times you can modify PC hardware with the power on. Windows senses the change, installs the modem support through Plug and Play, and adds the card to the list in the PC card Properties dialog box that will no longer be empty. To remove the card, eject the PC card from its slot and Windows reconfigures itself accordingly.

To stop a PC card before you eject it, open the Control Panel's PC Card Properties dialog box, click the PC card you want to stop, and click the Stop button. Windows then displays a dialog box telling you it's time to remove the card, and the PC Card icon is removed from your taskbar.

Clicking the Global Settings tab on the PC Properties dialog box opens the tabbed page shown in Figure 18.3. You should uncheck the Automatic selection option only if your PC card manual indicates the need to do so. You then can control the memory used by the PC card, as specified in your card owner's manual. The second option lets you enable and disable sound effects that occur when you insert and remove a PC card.

Figure 18.3

Control PC card memory and sound effects through the Global Settings.

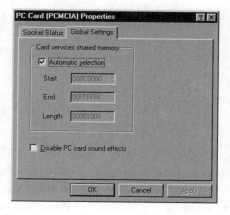

The PC Card Properties sound effects option has nothing to do with the sounds your modem makes when you initiate a phone call. The option controls a sound that Windows plays when you insert or remove a card.

Some PC cards are easy to eject—almost *too* easy! Therefore, by checking the sound effects option, you hear if you accidentally eject the PC card from its slot while your PC is in use.

18

The Windows Briefcase

When on the road, you want to work with the most up-to-date data files possible. Therefore, users often copy the latest files from their desktops to portable PCs before leaving on a trip. The direct cable connection, described at the end of the last section, is a great way to copy those files, as is a networked system. (Users also use diskettes and high-capacity disks, such as Zip disks, to transfer data between two computers.)

When they return, those users often have to reverse the process and copy their latest laptop data files over the ones on the desktops to refresh the desktop's files so that both computers stay in synchronization with each other. Until Windows, the only way to ensure that you were working with the latest data files was to look at the file date and time values and work with only the latest. At best, trying to maintain the latest files was a hassle and often caused confusion and errors as well.

The Briefcase application, sometimes called My Briefcase because of the Windows Me title beneath the application's icon, does all the nitty-gritty for you and synchronizes two computers that you have connected via a network or by cable. You may need to install the Briefcase application using Add/Remove Programs, Windows Setup in the Control Panel. When you open the My Briefcase icon, Windows displays the My Briefcase window.

> The Briefcase icon appears on the desktop and not on the Control Panel or within the Start menu so that you can drag files onto the Briefcase from Explorer or from an Open dialog box.

Briefcase acts just like a briefcase that you take between your office and home. Before leaving in the morning, you put important papers in your briefcase. In the Windows environment, before going on the road with your laptop, you should drag all data files that you want to work with to the Briefcase.

Unlike previous editions of Windows, Windows Me displays an introductory window when you first start the Briefcase program. The window provides an overview of the Briefcase operation.

Suppose that you copy two files to the Briefcase icon by dragging the files from Windows Explorer to the My Briefcase desktop icon. Figure 18.4 shows two files in the Briefcase window ready to be transferred to a laptop computer. Notice that the Update All toolbar button is available.

FIGURE 18.4

Two document files are in My Briefcase at the moment.

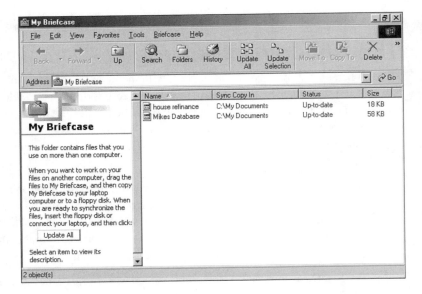

If you are using a floppy disk for the Briefcase intermediary storage media, move the My Briefcase icon to the floppy disk. You can display the floppy disk by displaying the Explorer window, or by opening the My Computer window and then dragging the My Briefcase icon to the floppy disk drive. You must have a formatted disk in the drive before you copy the desktop's My Briefcase icon there.

Insert the floppy disk into your laptop's disk drive. While on the road, you can work with those files in the Briefcase. If you save a Briefcase file to the laptop's hard disk, be sure to return the file to the laptop's Briefcase before you reconcile the files on your primary desktop computer later.

When you get back to the desktop, insert the floppy disk into the desktop's disk drive, drag the Briefcase back onto the desktop, and double-click the desktop's My Briefcase icon again. Select Briefcase, Update All (or click the toolbar button) or select only those files you want to update, and then select Briefcase, Update Selection (or click the toolbar button). A list of files that need updating appears. Click Update. Briefcase synchronizes the desktop's files by doing one of three things:

- If your desktop does not have one or more Briefcase files, the Briefcase application copies those files to the desktop computer.

- If your desktop already has those files on its disk, Briefcase transfers files from the Briefcase *only* if the Briefcase's files are newer than the desktop's.

- If your desktop already has one or more Briefcase files and the files are older than the Briefcase versions, the Briefcase application copies the newer versions over the old ones on the desktop.

If you want to update files using a direct cable connection, infrared connection (see the next section), or network instead of an intermediary floppy disk, make the physical connection first to the laptop with a direct cable or plug the laptop into your network. Then drag the files from the desktop computer to the laptop's My Briefcase icon. This sends the files to the Briefcase on the laptop. While on the road, work with the files inside the Briefcase icon. When you reconnect to the desktop or network, you can select the Briefcase, Update All menu command to bring the desktop up-to-date.

18

Going Wireless with Infrared

In the 1980s, IBM introduced the PCJr, a PC designed for home use and one that used an *infrared port* for its keyboard. (You cannot see infrared light, but infrared signals work well in remote-control devices such as television remotes.) The user was not encumbered by a wire on the keyboard; the user could lean back in the chair and point the keyboard in the general direction of the PC to use the PCJr.

IBM was years ahead of its time and years behind the market. The computer's sales bombed.

Today, the home computer market has not only grown, it's far surpassed anyone's expectations. With the integration of the television and PC, along with wireless keyboards and other peripherals, we can see that part of the PCJr's demise was because of bad timing.

Windows fully supports infrared devices. At the time of Windows's release, the most common device that uses infrared technology is the laptop PC. Infrared allows the laptop user to transfer files from one PC to another without the use of networks or even cables. As you saw in Hour 17, "Exploring Your Hardware Interface," Windows's Direct Cable Connection makes transferring files simple, but you can get even simpler if you use infrared transfer. Just point your laptop at your desktop, and Windows automatically senses the infrared devices and makes the connection you need.

 Many manufacturers are adding infrared ports to peripherals such as printers and networks. Forget about cables—just point your PC in the direction of your printer to begin printing!

Most infrared devices are truly Plug and Play. Turn on your printer and Windows configures itself for the printer, emitting a sound telling you that the infrared ports are communicating.

As with many Windows features, including the PC card support described in the previous section, an infrared icon appears on your taskbar when your PC or laptop is ready for infrared communications. If you do not see the icon, you can add it to your taskbar.

You must enable your infrared port before you can use it. This To Do item shows you how to let Windows know that you want the port enabled for use.

To Do: Enabling Your Infrared Port

1. Open the Start, Settings, Control Panel dialog box.

2. Display the full Control Panel window if you have only the commonly used Control Panel options showing.

3. Open the Wireless Link's window to display the Infrared Monitor dialog box. Figure 18.5 shows the dialog box that appears.

FIGURE 18.5

Enable your infrared device from the Wireless Link dialog box.

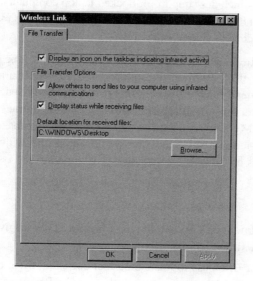

4. The choices you make determine how the infrared, wireless link operates. Check the top option to display the wireless link's icon on the taskbar that will indicate when your laptop sends or receives infrared instructions. Check the second option if you want to transfer files to your laptop via the wireless link. The final option shows the status of a wireless transfer during the operation.

5. When you click OK, your taskbar will show the infrared icon during a wireless transmission.

When you enable your infrared port, the icon will appear on your taskbar and your PC will be ready to search for another infrared device. Your PC sends out a signal every time interval that you specify in the Wireless Link dialog box, and the icon will show a second icon if another device comes within range.

Connecting another infrared device to your laptop is simple. Windows does all the configuration as long as you bring the second device within wireless range. You will have no need to hook cables between two PCs with infrared devices or between a PC and an

18

infrared printer. The infrared port is especially helpful for laptop users who want to use a wireless connection to transfer files between the PCs using the Direct Cable Connection Wizard.

Summary

This hour showed how laptop users can take advantage of Windows's special mobile support features. Windows includes support for docked laptop computers, so the configuration changes whenever you dock and undock. In addition, infrared ports make communicating between two infrared devices simple and wireless.

The easy interconnection possible in Windows means that you'll be connecting more computers than ever before. With those connections comes confusion, however. A desktop and laptop computers' files can get out of synchronization. Generally, you want to work with the latest version of a file, but comparing dates and times yourself is tedious and error-prone. The My Briefcase icon solves this problem by making the time and date comparisons for you and refreshing any laptop or desktop files which need it to make sure that both systems have the latest versions of document files.

Q&A

Q I often cross time zones and change my laptop accordingly. Will Briefcase be affected by the time changes?

A It is possible for Briefcase to make incorrect decisions when copying files using different time zones. You can do very little to make Briefcase happy when you move across time zones. The best thing you can do is resist the temptation to change the laptop's clock while on the road. Keep your laptop clock set the same as your desktop computer, so that when you return to the desktop, Briefcase will have no trouble reconciling your files.

Q I don't use a desktop PC, so do I need a docking station for my laptop?

A Actually, those without a desktop are the *best* candidates for a docking station. When on the road, you can use your laptop, and when you return to your desk, you can use the laptop's processor as your desktop PC. The docking station can connect to a full-screen monitor, keyboard, mouse, modem, and printer. To access these devices and to configure your laptop to use those devices, you only insert (*dock*) your laptop into the docking station, and Windows reconfigures itself for the new devices.

Workshop

The quiz and exercise questions are designed to test your knowledge of the material covered in this hour. The answers are in Appendix C, "Answers to Quizzes."

Quiz

1. Why would a laptop user need a docking station?

2. What common upgrade method, outside of using a docking station, do laptop users use to expand their laptop's options?

3. What utility program does Windows supply that helps you keep your laptop and desktop files in sync?

4. *True or false*: Users can use a floppy disk or a network to keep files up to date using My Briefcase.

5. *True or false*: Infrared signals are visible, but can only transmit of distances of up to 1.2 miles.

Exercises

1. If you have a laptop with a PC card, close all programs but keep Windows Me running. Eject the PC card. Windows Me displays a message warning you that you should stop any device you are about to eject. By first stopping a device, using the taskbar's Unplug or Eject Hardware icon, you ensure that you don't lose any data during a PC card, or even a USB's, ejection.

2. Try transferring files between two laptop computers that support the infrared transmission of data. If you can't locate a second laptop, see if your printer has an infrared port as many do. If so, print to the printer using the infrared connection. You might have to adjust your printer property settings so that the printer knows to look for the wireless transmission.

18

Hour 19

Performing Tune-Ups with the Update Manager

This hour shows you how Windows Me checks and updates itself. If you have Web access, you don't need to wait for a disk mailing or go to the store to get the latest Windows drivers and updates. You only click a menu option and Windows updates itself.

Not only can you be assured that you have the latest Windows support files, but also you can keep Windows running in tip-top shape. By fine-tuning your system's performance, a task that Windows considerably helps you with, Windows responds to your requests as soon as possible.

In this hour, you will

- Learn how Windows Me informs you of system updates
- Learn how you can delay the update's installation process
- Learn when Windows downloads update files from the Internet
- Update manually and bypass the automatic updates

As long as you have Internet access, you can request that Windows check the Microsoft Internet sites and update any Windows files that have changed, have been added, or have had bugs which have been corrected. The update site gives you full control over the update. You can

- View a list of files that are needed by your system to run the latest versions
- Read a description of each update to help you decide whether you need the update
- Submit problem reports that you experience
- Keep track of the updates you apply to your system

The Windows Update program updates your Windows Me operating system files to ensure that you have the latest and greatest system files available. Windows Update can be automatic. You don't have to initiate Windows Update although you can if you want.

If Windows realizes that an update is available for your installation, Windows pops up a message in your taskbar tray, as shown in Figure 19.1.

FIGURE 19.1

Windows automatically tells you when an update is available.

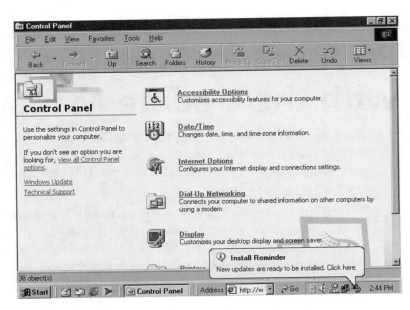

You can either ignore the message and continue working, or you can click the icon and elect to make the updates or change the way that Windows notifies you of updates.

To Do: Making an Update

1. When you see the message on your taskbar that informs you of a pending update, click the message's icon. The Updates dialog box appears asking if you want to install the update at that time.

2. Instead of installing the update, you can select the Remind Me Later button. Windows Me asks when you want to be reminded with the Remind Me Later dialog box shown in Figure 19.2.

FIGURE 19.2

You can delay the update.

3. Select from the 5 minutes to 24-hour range if you want to delay the update or click Cancel to start the update.

4. Click the Settings button. Windows Me displays the Automatic Updates settings dialog box shown in Figure 19.3. You can specify how you want to be reminded of the updates, or if you don't want to be reminded of them at all.

FIGURE 19.3

Specify how you want Windows to inform you of the updates.

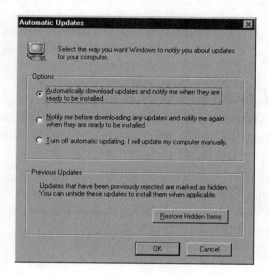

19

▼

▼ 5. After you change the way you want to be notified of subsequent updates, Windows applies the current update and exits back to the operating system as soon as you click the Install button to apply the update. If Windows already downloaded the update, the update installs. If Windows has not already downloaded the update, Windows must go online to grab the update and then install it.

The Hidden Updates button will, after you've worked through several Windows Updates, display those updates you chose to ignore previously. These hidden updates are still available for you to make when you click the Restore Hidden Items button. Suppose that you put off adding an update for your USB port system until you read whether the update cures your hardware problems or makes them worse. If you find that you need the update, you can unhide that update and apply the update at the current time.

▲

How the Updates Work

Where do the updates come from? You got a hint of that from the previous To Do list if you followed along. When you log onto the Internet, Windows Me, in the background, goes to the Microsoft Web site and looks to see if any updates are required for your particular combination of operating system components. If an update is available, Windows Me either downloads the update at that time and signals you with the taskbar message, or Windows tells you that the updates are available and asks if you want to install them. Windows notifies you in one of these two ways depending on how you set up Windows Update, not unlike the way you changed the settings in the previous To Do steps.

Updating Windows Yourself

If you don't want Windows to do any updating or file-retrieval automatically in preparation for an update, you can request that Windows Me not update itself until you take the action that directs Windows to locate updates that might be needed.

If you select the third option of the Automatic Updates dialog box, as you could have done at the end of the previous To Do task list, Windows waits until you select the Start menu's Windows Update option. Until then, Windows will not update your computer or download any updates until you request them.

If you select the Windows Update option from the Start menu, Windows always goes to the Internet to see if a current update is available, even if an update recently downloaded but has not been installed.

Often, Windows must restart your computer to complete the update process. Figure 19.4 shows the dialog box that appears when Windows completes the update and needs to restart your system. You should close all program windows before submitting to the system restart.

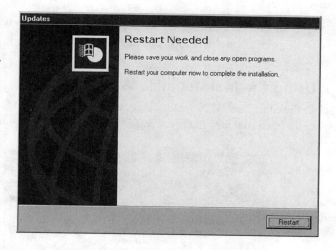

You don't have to wait for Windows to tell you that an update is available. You can routinely check to see if an upgrade is needed.

Select the Start menu's Windows Update option. Your computer connects to the Internet and enables you to select the appropriate update options that you need to make.

19

If you've turned off the automatic Windows Update check, you must perform the update manually and routinely, to ensure that you have the latest and most correct system files possible.

Fine-Tune Your System

You've been reading about ways to improve your system's performance throughout this 24-hour tutorial. In addition, subsequent hours describe other ways to increase system speed. For example, Hour 20, "Managing Your Hard Drive," explains several tools that improve your disk access.

In the earlier sections of this hour, you learned how to maintain the latest Windows drivers and components. As long as you're running the latest Windows version, you might as well keep your system in good shape by running the Maintenance Wizard, a program that routinely optimizes your system performance.

The Maintenance Wizard monitors the following system areas:

- Disk space
- Memory usage
- Program execution

The following To Do task shows you how to run the Maintenance Wizard. The wizard enables you to specify automatic tune-ups that your PC can perform on its own while you're away.

To Do: Using the Maintenance Wizard

1. Select the Start menu's Programs, Accessories, System Tools, Maintenance Wizard option to open the introductory wizard window shown in Figure 19.5.

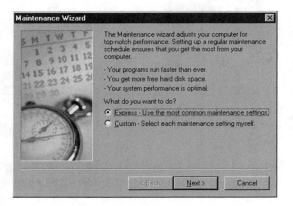

FIGURE 19.5

The opening Maintenance Wizard window describes the wizard's operation.

2. Select the Custom option and click Next to begin the wizard. The wizard gives a series of prompts, guiding you through the tune-up settings. For example, you are given the choice of changing the tune-up settings for later execution or performing a tune-up now. The Maintenance Wizard also enables you to customize the tune-up or follow preset settings that are common among most Windows users. First, select the time of day you want maintenance performed. Click Next.

3. If prompted, select any programs you no longer want Windows to automatically start whenever you boot your computer. Removing such programs helps speed up your computer restart time. Click Next.

4. Next you'll see a first screen that asks whether you want to optimize your hard disk. As you'll learn in Hour 20, you should optimize your hard disk about every month, and more often if you create and delete a lot of files. The wizard gives you the choice of optimizing on the wizard's completion, optimizing at a specific day and time (such as early morning before work), or bypassing the disk optimization

step. After you select the disk optimization you prefer, click Next to walk through the selections of a disk drive optimization routine and continue to look through the options available.

5. The Maintenance Wizard will regularly check your hard disk for errors if you select the option. As with any of the tune-up components, you can reschedule the hard disk scan's tune-up for a time different from the default time by clicking the Reschedule button. After you specify the disk scan time, click Next to continue with the tune-up.

6. The Delete Unnecessary Files window shown in Figure 19.6 is a welcome relief to many Windows users. During its operation, Windows creates several temporary files. Unfortunately, these temporary files often become permanent because of system problems and application programs that don't properly remove the files after using them.

FIGURE 19.6

The Maintenance Wizard safely removes files you no longer need.

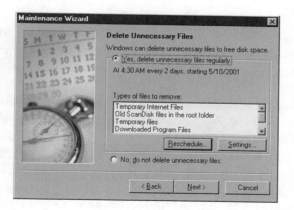

Some users of earlier versions of Windows could not safely remove temporary files because Windows could have been using them at the time of the deletion, causing a system crash. The Maintenance Wizard takes care of removing those temporary files that are still on your system but not being used anymore. In addition, the Maintenance Wizard removes backup files, unneeded system recovery files, and older files renamed during system upgrades.

7. When you eventually click Finish, the Maintenance Wizard goes dormant until the time comes to perform one or more of the maintenance items that you've chosen.

You can keep your Windows system in top-notch performance by scheduling regular maintenance tune-ups. You can schedule the tune-ups to begin any time of the day as long as your PC is turned on. You might want to schedule a tune-up once a week in the early morning hours before you get to work to ensure that your system runs efficiently during work.

19

You can always change the scheduled times you've set for Maintenance
Wizard items. When you run the Maintenance Wizard after setting up a
schedule once, Windows displays the dialog box shown in Figure 19.7 that
verifies whether you want to change a scheduling of programs or run one
or more of the wizard's programs immediately.

FIGURE 19.7

*The Maintenance
Wizard will ask you to
choose maintenance
settings.*

Summary

This hour described how you can keep Windows in top condition. The Windows Update
manager makes sure that you have the latest Windows files on your system. To guard
against possible application conflicts that sometimes occur with new Windows components,
Windows Update enables you to restore from previous updates you made that might now
be causing problems with older software you run. When you have the latest Windows
files, keep those files and your hardware running smoothly by scheduling regular system
tune-ups with the Maintenance Wizard.

Q&A

Q I don't leave my PC turned on when I'm away, so how can I schedule tune-ups?

A You cannot schedule tune-ups unless you plan to leave your PC on. Perhaps you
can schedule all your system tune-ups for the same day and leave your system on
that day only. You don't need to leave your monitor turned on for the tune-ups to
run. If you'd rather not leave your PC on, even for one 24-hour period, start the
tune-ups before you go to lunch and they should be complete or close to completion when you return. Remember that you can schedule tune-ups to begin as soon
as you quit the Maintenance Wizard.

Workshop

The quiz and exercise questions are designed to test your knowledge of the material
covered in this hour. The answers are in Appendix C, "Answers to Quizzes."

Quiz

1. How does Windows know when an update is needed?

2. How can you keep Windows from updating automatically?

3. What Windows program automatically runs programs for you?

4. How can the Maintenance Wizard help reclaim disk space for you?

5. *True or false*: The Maintenance Wizard runs the programs you set up as soon as you close the Maintenance Wizard window.

Exercises

1. If you have an Internet connection, perform a manual Windows Update now to make sure that you have the latest updates.

2. Set up the Maintenance Wizard to defragment your disk and delete unnecessary files every other morning at 5:00 am. Although you can leave your monitor turned off, you must leave your computer turned on and not in sleep state for the Maintenance Wizard to be able to work.

19

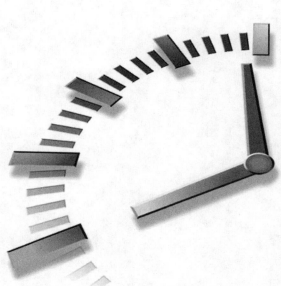

PART 6

Windows Safety at Nighttime

Hour

HOUR **20**

Managing Your Hard Drive

Everybody seems to need more disk space no matter how much one has. This hour shows you how to get more disk space and use your disk more efficiently with the Windows disk-related system utilities.

With ScanDisk, you can monitor your disk files and locate problems before they appear. In addition, Windows contains the *DriveSpace* technology that compresses disk space by as much as 30 percent or higher. DriveSpace compresses both hard disks and floppy disks.

In this hour, you will

- Learn why ScanDisk salvages disk files before you know you have problems
- Ensure that your disk is running efficiently by letting Disk Defragmenter clean up potential disk errors
- Learn how to squeeze more data onto your disk drive

Check the Disk

Windows supplies ScanDisk, which checks your disk drive for problems so that you can avoid future troubles. ScanDisk contains two levels of disk drive inspection: a standard scan and a thorough scan. The standard scan checks your disk files for errors. The thorough scan checks the files and performs a disk surface test to verify the integrity and safety of disk storage.

Run ScanDisk regularly (perhaps once or twice a week). As with most Windows programs, you can multitask ScanDisk while running another program. ScanDisk checks only disk drives, not CD-ROM drives. ScanDisk is simple to run as the following To Do item shows.

To Do: Checking a Disk with ScanDisk

1. Display the Start menu and select Programs, Accessories, System Tools, ScanDisk. Windows displays the ScanDisk window shown in Figure 20.1.

FIGURE 20.1

The opening ScanDisk window for analyzing your disk drives.

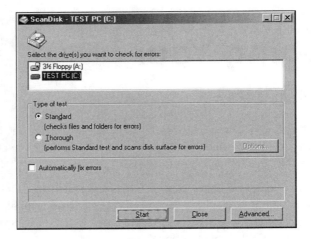

2. The Standard option is initially checked by default. To perform a standard ScanDisk, press Enter to choose the Start command button now. ScanDisk begins its chore of checking your files. Its window displays a moving graphics bar to show how much time remains in each ScanDisk step, as well as a description of each step in the process.

If ScanDisk finds a problem and you've checked the option labeled Automatically fix errors, it attempts to fix any problems it finds using default repair tools. (You can change the way ScanDisk repairs the disk by pushing the Advanced command button described toward the end of this task.)

3. When ScanDisk finishes, you will see a results window.

   The most important line in the results window is the number of bad sectors. Rarely will the number be anything but zero. If bad sectors appear, ScanDisk attempts to repair them and reports the results. Press Enter to close the results window.

4. Click the Advanced command button. ScanDisk displays the ScanDisk Advanced Options dialog box shown in Figure 20.2. The default values are usually fine, but if you understand disk drive technology and file storage details, you might want to change an option. Click the OK command button to close the dialog box.

FIGURE 20.2

*The advanced
ScanDisk options that
you control.*

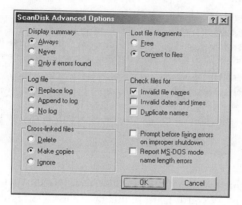

5. Click the Thorough option and click the Start command button to perform a thorough ScanDisk check. The thorough scan performs a more intense disk check than the standard scan, but it can take up to two hours to finish, depending on your disk speed and size. You see the results dialog box when ScanDisk finishes.

ScanDisk does *not* run well while you work on other programs in another window. Close all programs before you start ScanDisk. If you want to perform a ScanDisk check on a disk drive that you share over a network, you must turn off sharing for that drive before ScanDisk will be able to check the drive. To turn off the sharing of your disk, right-click over the desktop's My Network Places icon, select Properties and click the File and Print Sharing button. You then must uncheck the first option and click OK twice to turn off file sharing before running ScanDisk. A message might appear telling you that you must reboot your PC before the changes take effect and before you run ScanDisk.

20

Fill In the Holes

Disk Defragmenter fills empty gaps on your disks. As you add and delete files, the deleted space leaves free holes around the disk. Over time, your disk response time will slow down as you add or delete document files to and from the disk drive.

Pick Up the Pieces

Windows can store large files on a fragmented disk as long as there is enough free fragmented space to hold the file. Windows stores the files in linked chunks across the disk drive, filling in fragments and linking them.

A large file is stored as one continuous file if enough space exists to do so. But often, Windows tries to reuse fragment space left over from a deleted file. Over time, the number of these file fragments can grow considerably and slow down your PC when you access a file that's fragmented.

Disk access slows down on a fragmented disk drive because Windows must jump to each file fragment when retrieving a file. If you run Disk Defragmenter often enough (once or twice a month for the average user ought to be enough), Windows keeps the fragments to a minimum and, thus, increases the disk access speed.

This following To Do item walks you through an example that demonstrates how to defragment a disk drive. As you'll learn in this task, Disk Defragmenter not only closes empty disk gaps but also rearranges your disk drive so that often-used programs run faster.

To Do: Correcting Disk Fragmentation

1. Display the Start menu and select Programs, Accessories, System Tools, Disk Defragmenter. Windows displays an opening window that enables you to select the drive to defragment.

2. Click the Settings button and the Disk Defragmenter Settings dialog box appears, as shown in Figure 20.3. The dialog box enables you to decide whether you want the program to rearrange your files by selecting your most-used files and putting them at the beginning of your file space for faster access. Disk Defragmenter scans your disk during the defragment process and looks for common files and recently accessed programs to place in the early spaces of your disk. Click Next and the program tells you to quit all running programs. Press Alt+Tab to change to another running program that you can quit before returning to defragment the disk. Click Next when you've closed all open programs.

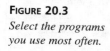

FIGURE 20.3

Select the programs you use most often.

In addition, if you select the option labeled Check the Drive for Errors, Disk Defragmenter checks your files and folders for storage errors before starting to defragment. If errors are found, the Disk Defragmenter stops until you fix them using the ScanDisk program. If not, Disk Defragmenter displays a list box window similar to the one in Figure 20.3. From the Disk Defragmenter Settings dialog box, you can elect to keep these settings for all subsequent defragmentation that you perform or keep the settings for the current defragment only.

3. Disk Defragmenter places the programs you use most often in an efficient disk location so that those programs start faster than the others. Click on one or more programs to select them before clicking Next. If you don't see a program you run frequently, click Other to select one not in the list.

4. Disk Defragmenter then starts each selected program, one at a time, and asks that you close the program after its startup. Disk Defragmenter is able to learn the program and its ancillary files when you do this. After you close all open programs, Disk Defragmenter issues a final wizard window.

5. Click the Finish button to move to the disk-selection process.

6. Select the disk drive you want to defragment. When you do, Disk Defragmenter begins the defragmentation process. In addition to putting your often-used programs in a quick-launch location, Disk Defragmenter also removes the gaps from your disk drive.

7. Click OK to start the defrag process. Windows can multitask while defragmenting your disk space, so you can run other programs while Disk Defragmenter runs. At any point during the defragmentation, you can pause Disk Defragmenter or cancel the process. If the drive is not fragmented, Disk Defragmenter tells you so and asks whether you want to run Disk Defragmenter anyway.

20

> Be careful that you don't work in another window while defragmenting your disk drive. Disk Defragmenter will not be able to defragment your disk, and will keep attempting a restart, until you close all other running programs.

▲   8. When finished, click Yes to close the application.

Running DriveSpace

DriveSpace compresses drives and is easy to run. You need to run DriveSpace only once because after compressing the disk drive, the disk stays compressed. You also can reverse the DriveSpace compression if you want to, as long as you have enough space on the uncompressed disk drive to hold all your files.

After you compress a drive, Windows and your computer act as if you've got more disk space. The free disk statistics show the extra drive space, and all programs access the disk as if the disk were originally designed to have the extra space.

The following example explains how to compress a disk drive using DriveSpace. The disk will be a floppy disk. After you've compressed a floppy disk drive, you will more fully understand the process and can then compress a hard disk.

When compressing a disk drive, DriveSpace adds a logical disk drive to your system, called the *host drive*. DriveSpace names the new host drive H, or some other name that falls far down anyone's list of disk drives, so that you'll be able to determine which drive is a host drive and which drive is from your list of real disk drives. The host drive will be uncompressed, and you will never work with the host drive. DriveSpace and Windows use the host drive to hold descriptive information about the compressed drive. All you really need to know about the new host drive is that the host is not an actual drive on your system, and Windows uses the host drive to support the DriveSpace compression scheme. All open dialog boxes you see, as well as the My Computer window, will display the host drive now that you've compressed.

To Do: Compressing Disks Using DriveSpace

1. Display the Start menu and select Programs, Accessories, System Tools, DriveSpace. Windows displays the DriveSpace window. (If DriveSpace is not listed on the menu, you can install it with the Windows Setup tab in the Add/Remove Programs dialog box.)

2. Insert a formatted disk in the disk drive. The disk can have data on it. The disk, however, should contain about 30% free space. Before you can compress a disk, the disk should contain some free space so that DriveSpace can write some temporary files during the compression process. If the drive does not have enough free space, DriveSpace will tell you before starting the actual compression so that you can free some space.

3. Select the floppy disk drive from the list of drives.

4. Select Drive, Compress. DriveSpace analyzes the disk and displays the Compress a Drive dialog box

> If you want to decompress a compressed drive, you repeat these steps and choose Drive, Uncompress instead of Drive, Compress.

5. Click the Options command button. Windows displays the Compression Options dialog box that describes the host drive's name (you can select a different name if you want to) and free space (usually there will be no free space). Click the OK command button to close the Compression Options dialog box and return to the Compress a Drive dialog box.

6. Click the Start command button to initiate the drive compression. Before compressing, DriveSpace gives you one last chance to cancel the compression. DriveSpace also offers the option of backing up your files. Although there rarely will be a problem during the compression, it is possible that a power failure during the compression could interrupt the process and cause DriveSpace to corrupt the disk drive (so that the drive would need reformatting). By backing up the drive, you ensure that you can return to an uncompressed drive if needed.

7. When the compression begins, DriveSpace checks the disk for errors and then compresses the disk. The compression can take a while. After finishing, DriveSpace displays a completion dialog box. Close the dialog box and look at My Computer's properties for the compressed drive to see how much disk space you gained.

After you compress a disk drive, Windows recognizes the compressed drive and stores up to 100% more data on that drive. There will actually be a second disk added to your drive letters, called the host disk, but you can ignore the host disk because DriveSpace uses the it to store data tables used for accessing the compressed drive.

20

> If you want to format a compressed disk, you must run DriveSpace and select Drive, Format. The Explorer Format command will not format compressed disks. The disk stays compressed during the formatting procedure.

> After you compress a drive, you can change the amount of compression by running the Compression Agent program found in the System Tools folder.

Summary

This hour described Windows's disk utilities. Backup enables you to back up, restore, and compare backups to their original files. This is the most full-featured backup program that Microsoft has offered. You can create backup jobs that quickly initiate specific backup descriptions.

If you have disk trouble, run ScanDisk to see whether the problem goes away. Defragmenter eliminates the empty holes in your drive so that your disk access runs at top-notch performance.

For added space, DriveSpace can almost double your disk drive space. By compressing your files and the free file space, you effectively squeeze more data into the same amount of disk space. You can compress both your hard disk drives and floppy disk drives.

Q&A

Q How often should I defragment and compress my hard disk?

A You should defragment every week or so. Depending on the amount of file accessing you do, you might need to defragment more or less often. If you notice your disk speed slowing down a bit, you'll find that defragmenting speeds the access process somewhat.

Compress your disk drive (or each floppy disk) only once. After the compression, the drive stays compressed. Unless you uncompress the drive, Windows always recognizes the compressed drive.

Workshop

The quiz and exercise questions are designed to test your knowledge of the material covered in this hour. The answers are in Appendix C, "Answers to Quizzes."

Quiz

1. What is the difference between ScanDisk and Disk Defragmenter?

2. *True or false*: ScanDisk can fix some disk errors.

3. *True or false*: If you run ScanDisk regularly, you'll never have to defragment your disk.

4. Why does your hard disk access speed improve when you regularly use Disk Defragmenter?

5. What is a host drive?

Exercises

1. Nobody backs up the first time until they have to because they lost data and don't want the same thing to happen again. At least that's the industry rumor. You can buck the trend now by backing up without needing to and before a problem actually occurs. The practice is good and you will create a backup set that you can easily reuse regularly to keep your data safe. Back up your entire C: drive to your backup device using Windows Backup.

2. Add ScanDisk to your start-up Windows Me Start menu folder. Windows Me will then run ScanDisk every time you start your computer. Although ScanDisk will take a few minutes to run, your hard disk will be more reliable as you use your PC.

20

HOUR 21

Using the Advanced System Tools

Windows Me works well but, like a well-made automobile, sometimes gets overloaded with work and gets sluggish. (Nobody wants a sluggish operating system.) When your operating system slows down, your entire computer system slows down because the operating system controls everything else that happens. Windows provides system programs that enable you to monitor Windows Me's performance and determine where bottlenecks reside.

Periodically, you can schedule Windows programs to keep your system running smoothly even when you're not at the PC. By updating your system files, backing up, and scheduling system checking programs to run when you're away, you can help ensure that your system runs in top condition and that you don't have to remember to run important tasks.

In this hour, you will

- Learn what system resources are critical for good system performance
- Check system resources
- Learn why technical support can use your system snapshot to correct problems

- Schedule tasks to run when you're away from your PC
- Manage your scheduled tasks
- Learn when to use System Restore

Check Your System

Windows contains two programs, *System Monitor* and *System Resource Meter*, that monitor your system resources. These applications are advanced; many Windows users never run the programs, but they can give insight into problems that might slow down your system.

System Monitor tracks these three items:

- The *file system*—Comprised of disk access statistics
- The *kernel*—Comprised of the CPU's activity, as well as some multitasking activities
- The *memory manager*—Comprised of the various segments of memory that Windows tracks

System Monitor graphically displays one or more of these items and continuously updates the graph to show how your system is being used. You can start the System Monitor and go about your regular Windows work. If the system begins to slow and you want an idea as to which parts of the system are getting the most use, click on the System Monitor on the toolbar to have an idea of your machine's current workload.

When you run the Resource Meter, its program puts a Resource Meter icon next to the taskbar's clock. You can click the icon to obtain statistics on these items:

- *System resources*, which describe the system's resource use percentage (the lower value of the other two kinds of specific resources, User and GDI)
- *User resources*, which describe your resource use percentage
- *GDI* (*graphics device interface*), which describes your graphics resource use percentage

You can see these values if you rest your cursor over the Resource Meter on the taskbar. The following To Do demonstrates how you can use the System Monitor and Resource Meter to check the efficiency of your computer system.

To Do: Checking Resources

1. Display the Start menu's Programs, Accessories, System Tools menu. If you do not see the System Tools menu on the Accessories menu, your Windows Me personalized menu settings are keeping the System Tools menu from showing. Click the Accessories menu's down arrow to display the rest of its options and to select from the System Tools menu.

2. Click the System Monitor menu item. (If you don't see it, you have to install the System Monitor option from the Control Panel's Add/Remove Programs Windows Setup option.) Windows displays the System Monitor window. Start another program or two. Click the taskbar to return to the System Monitor graph every so often. As you will see, System Monitor updates its graph, and eventually the graph will fill the window, as shown in Figure 21.1.

FIGURE 21.1

The System Monitor screen updates regularly to show your resources.

3. Your System Monitor screen might be blank or display only the kernel information. Select Edit, Add Item or click the far-left button on the toolbar to add additional system resources to the graphs. Click the File System in the left window and highlight every option inside the right window to request that System Monitor update all the file system statistics. To highlight multiple items, hold Ctrl while clicking each item. To highlight all items in the list, select the first item, then hold both the Shift and the Ctrl key while selecting the last item and Windows will highlight all items in the list. Click OK.

4. Select Edit, Add Item again to add all the detail items for the Memory Manager. When you click OK, the System Monitor displays several small graphs. Watch the graphs for a moment as they update after they check the resources being analyzed. Your System Monitor window can get full, as Figure 21.2 shows.

21

FIGURE 21.2

The System Monitor can display statistics for several items.

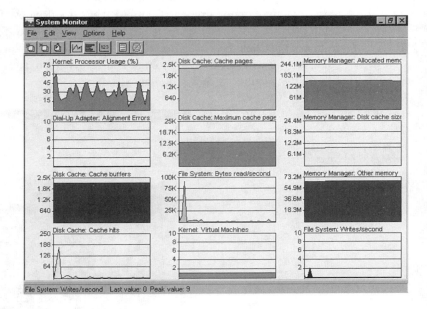

Click over any of the small graphs. System Monitor describes what the graph means in the status bar at the bottom of the System Monitor window.

5. Select File, Exit to close the System Monitor so you can start the Resource Meter.

6. Display the Start menu and select the Programs, Accessories, System Tools menu once again.

7. Click the Resource Meter menu item. The first time you start the Resource Meter in each power-up session, Windows displays an opening description dialog box. Read the dialog box and press Enter to close the dialog box.

8. Windows displays the Resource Meter icon next to the taskbar clock.

9. Right-click on the Resource Meter icon and select Details. Windows displays a graph showing the current resource usage statistics for the three Resource Meter measurements, as shown in Figure 21.3.

    As you work in Windows, you can check the Resource Meter graphs as often as you want to make sure that you don't get close to running out of resources.

10. Right-click the Resource Meter icon and select Exit to unload the Resource Meter.

FIGURE 21.3

The Resource Meter window available from the taskbar.

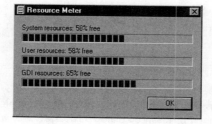

If you run graphics- and processor-intensive programs, you can run System Monitor and Resource Meter to see how much load you are placing on Windows and the hardware. If starting a collection of programs often causes your system to slow down or freeze, monitor your system's resources to see which ones are running low right before the problem begins. You can then begin to locate a solution (such as purchasing more RAM or a faster CPU).

> If you use a networked PC, you might see more than the three resource items described in this section. In addition, these meters themselves use some of your system's resources.

Dr. Watson, Come Right Away

Although you won't find it on the Windows menus, a program called Dr. Watson can help you trace severe problems that occur when you run some programs. When you start Dr. Watson, it sits in the background (a new taskbar icon appears) and waits for a problem.

Although Windows Me is more stable than previous Windows versions, problems can still occur. If your system freezes and you've started Dr. Watson, Dr. Watson will record all pertinent system information right before the error occurred. In other words, if your system freezes or displays a serious system error, you can restart your PC and read the log file that Dr. Watson will have created right before the problem occurred. (Dr. Watson is not foolproof; some system crashes and freezes escape it, but it handles most common situations.)

Dr. Watson's log file will describe the error and often will suggest corrected action you can use to keep the problem from reappearing. If you cannot fix the problem, you can contact Microsoft's Technical Support staff on its Web site (www.microsoft.com) or by calling Microsoft's voice support number. The support staff will use Dr. Watson's log to diagnose and correct the problem.

21

Unlike the programs on your Start menu, Dr. Watson does not appear on the typical Windows menu. Therefore, you must start Dr. Watson from the Start menu's Run command as the following To Do illustrates.

You can load Dr. Watson every time you start your PC by selecting the Start menu's Settings, Taskbar and Start menu option and selecting Add from the Start Menu Programs Advanced dialog box page. Type **\windows\drwatson. exe** for the command line-prompt, click Next, select the StartUp group, click Next, and type **Dr. Watson** for the shortcut name. When you click Finish, Windows adds Dr. Watson to your StartUp group. All programs that appear in the StartUp menu group begin automatically when you start Windows.

To Do: Starting and Using Dr. Watson

1. Display the Start menu's Run command.

2. At the Run prompt, type **Drwatson** and click OK to start the system program. After a brief pause, the Dr. Watson icon appears on the taskbar.

3. Right-click over the Dr. Watson icon and select Dr. Watson to force a snapshot log even though an error has not occurred. The log is created based on your current system information.

Dr. Watson creates a listing of your PC's system information at a single instant in time, hence the term snapshot. Dr. Watson's log shows up to ten of the most recent system snapshots taken because of errors or in response to your request.

4. Although you triggered Dr. Watson when no error occurred, it still recorded a detailed view of your system, just as it would do if a problem *did* trigger its execution. Select View, Advanced View to display the full view of snapshot pages.

5. Click System to display the system snapshot shown in Figure 21.4. All this information can come in handy if support personnel need to know the kind of system that you run.

6. Click the rest of the tabs to see the detailed information Dr. Watson determined about your system at the time of the snapshot.

7. Select File, Save and enter a filename if you want to save the current snapshot to your disk. (Right-clicking over the Dr. Watson icon and selecting Open Log File enables you to open the file whenever you need to.)

FIGURE 21.4
*Dr. Watson records
all your system's
information.*

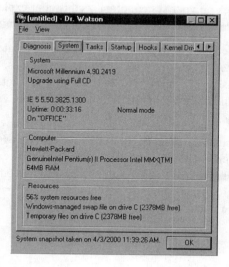

If installing a particular software program seems to cause a freeze-up problem, force a system snapshot before you install the program and then let Dr.
Watson record another snapshot upon attempting the install. The software's
support staff may be able to use the before-and-after Dr. Watson snapshots
to determine the problem.

8. Select View, Options to display the Dr. Watson Options dialog box. You can determine how many logs to save, the folder Dr. Watson uses to save the log files, the
number of disassembly instructions (these let the support staff re-create the problem from an operating system level), and the default view that Dr. Watson automatically displays when you first display a log. (You can access this Options dialog
box by right-clicking over Dr. Watson's taskbar icon and selecting Options.)

9. Select File, Exit Dr. Watson to close the program.

Scheduling System Tasks

Throughout this 24-hour tutorial, you've seen numerous tools that enable you to manage
your Windows system and fine-tune its work environment. Hour 19, "Performing Tune-
Ups with the Update Manager," explains how to update your system to the latest files and
download Windows corrections and upgrades when Microsoft releases them. You saw
that, with the Maintenance Wizard, you can let your PC fine-tune your disk drives while
you're away. Hour 20, "Managing Your Hard Drive," discusses how disk drive tools keep

21

your disk drives running at their most efficient state. In addition, proper system procedures require that you back up your system often, as this hour explains. To restore your system to its latest and greatest state in case of system failure requires recent backups.

A Windows program called Task Scheduler enables you to schedule these system programs (as well as any other program) to run at preset time periods. You can defragment and back up your hard disk every morning at 4:00 a.m. if you want. You can log into the Internet and retrieve email before work, during lunch, and before you leave work.

When you designate Task Scheduler to run when you start Windows, Task Scheduler waits in the background until the time comes to run one of its programs. If you're using your PC when the program runs, you won't be bothered. If, however, a program that you schedule tries to use a data file that you are editing, the Task Scheduler program will be unable to function and will display an error or shut down (as long as the program does not interfere with any you're currently running, which might be the case if they share the same data files).

> One of Task Scheduler's strengths is its scheduling capabilities. You don't have to designate a specific day that a Task Scheduler program runs. Instead, you can specify that Task Scheduler runs a program (or a group of programs) daily, weekly, monthly, or when certain events take place, such as when you start or shut down your PC.

Scheduling Task Scheduler is simple. After you set it up, you can easily modify the times or dates your scheduled programs run. In addition, you can easily add and remove scheduled programs as the following To Do demonstrates:

To Do: Working with Task Scheduler

1. Select the Start menu's Programs, Accessories, System Tools, Scheduled Tasks program. Figure 21.5 shows a typical Task Scheduler window. If your taskbar shows the Scheduled Tasks icon, you can double-click that icon to more quickly open the Scheduled Tasks program. (Even when you start Task Scheduler for the first time, the Task Scheduler window contains some entries.)

2. Double-click the first entry, called Add Scheduled Task. The Scheduled Task Wizard begins, which enables you to set up a scheduled program. Click Next to see the list of wizard programs shown in Figure 21.6.

FIGURE 21.5
These programs will run at preset times.

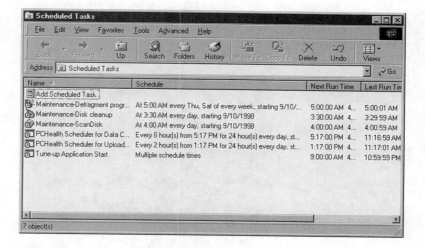

FIGURE 21.6
The Scheduled Task Wizard gives you a list of common programs to schedule.

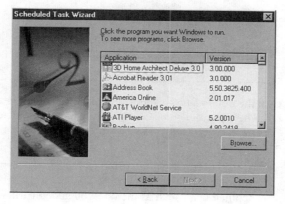

If the program you want to schedule does not appear in the list, click the Browse button to select a program from the folders that appear.

3. Walk through the wizard and set up Resource Meter to run weekly. The final wizard dialog box gives you the option of setting up program options available for most programs you schedule. For example, you can set up the scheduled task to stop after running for a certain period of time in some cases. This dialog box appears once you select the check box labeled, Open advanced properties for this task when I click Finish.

4. To change a scheduled task's scheduled time, open that task (by double-clicking or single-clicking if you've set up the single-click option) to display a dialog box that enables you to change the scheduled properties. Click on the Schedule tab to display

21

the Schedule page shown in Figure 21.7 and make any change you want to make. As you can see, Windows gives you total control over a task's schedule, even letting you omit weekend days from the schedule. Close the Resource Meter window.

FIGURE 21.7

Change the schedule for a task to suit your requirements for the program.

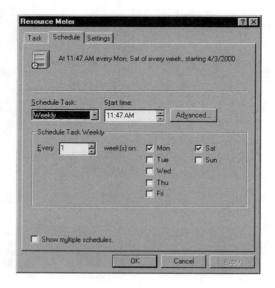

> Click the option labeled Show Multiple Schedules to receive a drop-down list box where you can enter two or more separate schedules for the same task. For example, you might want to run the same program daily before work and at noon.

5. To delete a scheduled task, such as the one you added earlier, select the task and click the toolbar's Delete button. Task Scheduler sends the scheduled task to the Recycle Bin where you can retrieve the task, if you change your mind, until you empty the Recycle Bin.

6. To turn off an individual scheduled task without removing the task, open the task (by clicking or double-clicking on the task's entry) and uncheck the Enabled option. The task remains in the task list, but idle, until you check Enabled or until you remove the task from the list.

7. You can temporarily turn off all scheduled tasks without having to change each one individually by selecting Advanced, Stop Using Task Scheduler.

> If you select Advanced, Pause Task Scheduler, Task Scheduler stops until you
> select Advanced, Continue Task Scheduler or until you subsequently reboot
> your PC.

Suppose that you want to run a special disk-checking utility program that you bor-
rowed from a friend. You can temporarily pause your scheduled tasks that might
include a disk scan, run the disk-checking utility program, and then resume your
scheduled tasks.

8. Select File, Close to terminate your Task Scheduler session.

The Task Scheduler program can be there when you cannot be there. Defragment and
back up your disk in the middle of the night so that your system isn't slowed during the
day by those routine operations. Schedule certain programs to run when you start or shut
down Windows. Task Scheduler gives you complete control over your scheduled tasks.

Using System Restore

New with Windows Me, the System Restore system tool enables you to restore your computer system back to a previous state. Perhaps you are installing a new program or piece
of hardware such as a second hard disk. If the installation goes smoothly, you won't need
to revert back to the original system state. If, however, a problem occurs, the Windows
Me's System Restore feature enables you to return to the exact state of the computer
before you performed the installation. Even better, you can undo and redo the restore
process so that you can go back and forth between previous system states until you locate
the one that works best or that enables you to determine the cause of any problems you
might be having.

The System Restore program keeps track of all system changes you make as the result of
adding hardware or software or when you change settings. When you want to restore a
particular computer state, you have three ways to do so:

1. Restore back to a particular event, such as the installation of a new hard disk.

2. Restore back to a system checkpoint. Windows Me automatically saves system
   checkpoints throughout the day and keeps a rolling two-weeks' worth at any time.
   If you are unsure of an event that caused your current system problem, you can
   keep restoring back to previous system checkpoints until your computer begins to
   behave normally once again.

3. Restore back to a particular date.

21

If you want to restore several iterations at one time, you can do so. System Restore is intelligent enough to know what not to restore, however. System Restore will not change any data files you've saved into the My Documents folder, which is a folder often used for data files by many programs on the market today. In addition, if System Restore runs across a data file that it recognizes, such as a database file, and that file is not inside the My Documents folder, system restore will leave that data file alone.

> If you want to keep System Restore from changing a particular file but the file is not a registered data file, temporarily move the file to your My Documents folder before starting the System Restore process.

To use the System Restore tool, follow these To Do steps:

To Do: Restoring a System to Its Previous State

1. Select the Start menu's Programs, Accessories, System Tools, System Restore option. Windows opens the System Restore program window as shown in Figure 21.8.

2. Select Restore My Computer to an Earlier Time and click Next to continue the restore process.

FIGURE 21.8

Use the System Restore program to revert back to a previous Windows state.

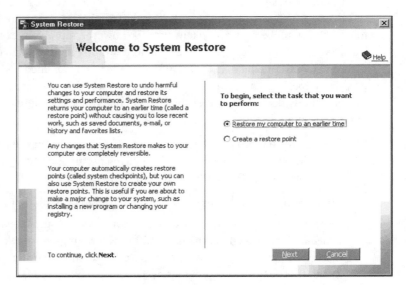

3. System Restore displays a calendar with all possible system restore dates bold-faced. When you click one of the days, the System Restore program displays all the checkpoints performed that day, even those triggered by events such as a hardware change, in the right window.

4. Click on a checkpoint to select that checkpoint for the restore.

5. Click Next to see a message window telling you information related to the restore. For example, the System Restore program might have restored a few additional states if you've installed other hardware or software between the checkpoint you chose and now. You're reminded to close all programs before proceeding.

6. When you click on Next, Windows Me begins the process. Sometimes a restore can take a few minutes to appear and you might see your computer rebooting one or more times. Eventually, your PC will resume the exact state it was in at the point of the restore's checkpoint. The only exception might be data files you've created between that point and now that will still be intact.

7. Click OK to close the System Restore window.

When you restore, Windows restores your system as it was at the time of the checkpoint. Therefore, if you've scheduled backups, changed your Start menu, and made other system changes, you will lose those changes.

Summary

This hour described several system tools you can run to manage and monitor your disk, memory, and other system resources. System Monitor and Resource Meter work passively to display statistics about your memory, disk, and system usage. Windows handles resources better than previous versions of Windows, but these tools give you two additional ways to monitor the usage.

Dr. Watson gives you a perfect snapshot of your system, either when you request the snapshot or when trouble occurs. The Dr. Watson program records vital system information when system errors cause your system to shut down, so technical support people can diagnose the problem better. Sometimes, Dr. Watson's log files offer suggestions you can try to eliminate the problem.

You don't have to remember to run routine tasks because the Task Scheduler program runs them for you. You control all aspects of all automated programs that you schedule so that important system check-up and fine-tuning take place when you're not using your PC.

The System Restore helps cure many ills. If your system is working fine one day but erratically the next, run System Restore and revert your system back to a previous time when things ran well.

21

Q&A

Q Should I use Dr. Watson, the System Resource Meter, or the System Monitor when a certain program keeps causing my PC to freeze up?

A Use all three! If you can duplicate the problem consistently, System Monitor and System Resource Meter can help you locate resource problems before they occur. You might be running out of memory right before you attempt to start a program that pushes your memory limits over the edge. Dr. Watson is the program that helps you trace problems which have already occurred. When your system freezes, you can be assured that Dr. Watson recorded all your system's information right before the crash so that you or a technical support representative can eliminate the problem.

Q Does my PC have to be turned on for scheduled programs to run?

A Yes, but you can keep your monitor turned off to save money. The monitor consumes the majority of power in a typical PC system, so you can turn off your monitor when you're not using the PC but leave your PC running so that you won't have to restart your PC the next time you need to use the computer. If you have a laser printer, you should turn it off as well because laser printers also consume a lot of power.

Workshop

The quiz and exercise questions are designed to test your knowledge of the material covered in this hour. The answers are in Appendix C, "Answers to Quizzes."

Quiz

1. Which program, System Monitor or Resource Meter, stays on your taskbar and monitors the memory, disk, and timing of your PC?
2. How can you use the System Monitor to determine if your PC needs more RAM?
3. Why does Dr. Watson provide the option of taking a system snapshot?
4. Which system program enables you to revert your computer back to a previous time?
5. What is the difference between Dr. Watson and System Restore?

Exercises

1. Run Resource Meter to place the meter on your taskbar. After you work on your computer for a few hours, double-click the Resource Meter's taskbar icon to see how your computer resources are holding up. If memory or disk usage falls below

30%, you should close your open programs and restart Windows Me. Doing so will help prevent your system from freezing up as it can do when resources run low.

2. The next time you want to install a program, try System Restore for the practice. Install the program and then run System Restore to revert your PC back to its pre-install state. You should see no traces of the program. System Restore is better than an uninstallation routine because System Restore not only uninstalls software but also ensures that Windows Me is untouched by any of the software's stray programs which sometimes stick around long after you've attempted to uninstall the program.

21

HOUR 22

Using Multimedia and Sound

A few years ago, an industry consortium of software and hardware developers led by Microsoft developed a multimedia standard that opened the door for today's wealth of multimedia hardware and software. To use multimedia at its full potential, your operating system must support multimedia, and Windows does just that, as you will see in this hour.

In this hour, you will

- Learn how AutoPlay eliminates the CD-ROM startup command
- Master the Windows Media Player program
- Learn why Windows keeps tabs on the Windows Media Manager

Introducing the Windows Media Player

Beginning with Windows Me, a Windows multimedia player takes charge of virtually every aspect of your computer's sound and video. Consider just some of the multimedia-based capabilities of the Windows Media Player:

- Plays audio CDs
- Copies audio CDs
- Organizes your entire library of audio and video files
- Generates *play lists*, lists of your favorite songs no matter what their source
- Plays Internet-based video and sound, including the *de facto* standard format of digital audio, *MP3*
- Supports *streaming video* and *streaming audio*, the process of playing video and sound clips from the Internet as they download to your computer from the Internet instead of having to wait for the entire clip to download before playing
- Downloads music on your computer to a portable music player, such as an MP3 player
- Automatically self-upgrades the Windows Media Player when an update is available on the Internet

Throughout the following sections, the Windows Media Player takes center stage. Instead of a comprehensive study of every aspect of the Windows Media Player, this hour focuses on the top tasks users generally want to perform with the Windows Media Player. The Windows Media Player is only a means to an end; the program is much less important than the software, the *media*, that you play.

Playing with AutoPlay

AutoPlay is one of the Windows multimedia capabilities. If you've ever played a game or an audio CD in your computer's CD-ROM drive, you'll appreciate AutoPlay very much indeed. AutoPlay automatically inspects your audio CD or CD-ROM as soon as you place it in the computer's CD-ROM drive. AutoPlay then does one of three things:

- Starts the installation on your CD-ROM if you've yet to install the program
- Begins the CD-ROM's program if the program is installed
- Starts the audio CD player if it is an audio CD

Microsoft knows that putting a CD-ROM (or audio CD) into your CD-ROM drive almost always means that you want to do something with that CD-ROM. Of course, you might be inserting the CD-ROM in the drive for later use, but that's rare; most of the time when you insert a CD-ROM, you're ready to do something with it right away.

> If you insert a CD-ROM but want to bypass the AutoPlay feature (perhaps you want to access the CD-ROM later but insert the disc now), press Shift as you insert the CD-ROM. Keep holding Shift until the CD-ROM light goes out. Windows will not start AutoPlay.

22

To Do: Using AutoPlay to Play Music from a CD

1. Find an audio CD that contains music you like to hear.

2. Place the CD in the CD-ROM drive and close the door or push the CD-ROM drive's insert button to close the CD-ROM drive.

3. Windows immediately recognizes that you've inserted the CD into the CD-ROM and begins playing the music. Figure 22.1 shows the Windows Media Player when the first song begins.

FIGURE 22.1

The Windows Media Player plays the CD and displays the CD's information.

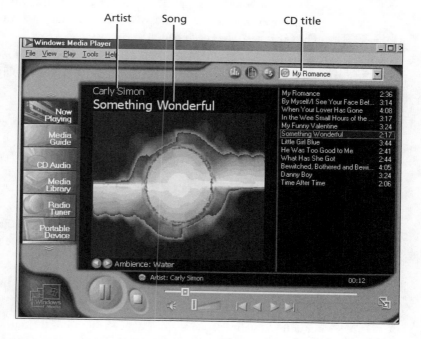

4. Windows Media Player immediately loads and, if you have Internet access, goes to the Internet to look for the CD's artist, title, and song list! Windows Media Player scans your CD, looks for unique identifying information, and searches the Internet where the majority of song lists are stored for the majority of CDs published in the

▼ world. This magnificent database of audio tracks puts the song list on your computer so that you can later store the CD, or individual selections from the CD, to
your hard disk, and you never have to enter the track or artist information. Some
CDs will download with art that might appear in the center of the Windows Media
Player as the CD plays.

> After Windows Me downloads an audio CD's track information, Windows
> Media Player never has to search the Internet a second time for that CD. The
> information stores on your computer for subsequent reference and quicker
> access if you ever play the CD again.

The Windows Media Player acts like a physical CD player that you can control by
clicking the buttons. It displays Play, Pause, Stop, Eject, Previous, and Next track
buttons, Previous and Forward time buttons, and volume and mute controls. (Move
the cursor over the buttons on the Windows Media Player's window to see a pop-up
help box that describes each button.)

5. Click the Pause button. Click the Play button. Press Alt+K to move the cursor to
the drop-down list box and click the down arrow button to play a different track
on the CD.

▲ 6. Click OK to close the window and eject the CD.

Changing the Look of the Windows Media Player

You have full control over the look of the Windows Media Player's window. For example,
if you click the button in the lower-right corner, the Windows Media Player shrinks to a
more compact size, or expands back to full size if the compact size was already in effect.

After you shrink the Windows Media Player to a smaller size, you can click either control on the bottom or right edge of the Windows Media Player to display an equalizer and
song play list for the current CD, as shown in Figure 22.2.

You can drag the equalizer controls to change the tones of the music. In addition, double-
click over any song to play that song in the play list.

Besides changing the size of the Windows Media Player, you can change the entire look
of the Windows Media Player's screen. A *skin* is a name for Windows Media Player
theme and you can select a skin to match your musical play list's mood.

FIGURE 22.2

The Windows Media Player provides you with an equalizer and access to all the CD's songs by title.

To Do: Changing the Windows Media Player's Skin

▼ To Do

1. Maximize the Windows Media Player window if you've made it compact.

2. Click the down arrow beneath the Portable Device button to display the Skin Chooser button. Depending on your Windows Media Player composition, the Skin Chooser button might already be displayed.

3. Click the Skin Chooser button to display a list of available skins. As you click each skin, a preview of that skin appears in the window.

4. Select a skin and click Apply Skin. Your Windows Media Player takes on the look of that skin, such as the new skin shown in Figure 22.3. All the Windows Media Player controls appear on the new skin, but the player takes on the theme of the skin.

▲

The skins only appear when you change the Windows Media Player's size to compact. You can download additional skins from the Internet at the Windows Media Player's site available when you click More Skins in the skin list window.

FIGURE 22.3

The Windows Media Player skins can dramatically change the player's theme.

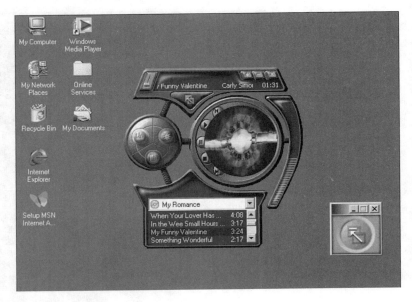

The Media Guide

The Windows Media Player offers online access to a special Internet site devoted to the Windows Media Player and the types of multimedia that the Windows Media Player can play.

Figure 22.4 shows the Windows Media Player's Media Guide. a screen such as this appears, assuming that you have Internet access, when you click the Media Guide button. Microsoft calls the Media Guide a daily online multimedia newspaper that contains news, gossip, and media that relate to the Windows Media Player.

CD Audio Extras

The button labeled CD Audio tells you much about the CD you are currently playing, assuming that you let the Windows Media Player go to the Internet to download information about the audio CD. When you click CD Audio, a list of songs, or more accurately, a list of the tracks on the CD appear, along with information such as the song's time, artist, and album information.

But click on the Album Details button and more appears, as Figure 22.5 shows. The picture of the CD's case appears as well as information on the artist and music company when you click the appropriate links.

You can even record tracks and the entire CD from the CD Audio window.

FIGURE 22.4

Check out the Media Player window daily for multimedia news.

22

FIGURE 22.5

The CD Audio window gives you more information, often in a multimedia format, than the CD case could ever hope to.

To Do: Recording CD Tracks

1. Click Back to move from the Album Details window back to the regular CD Audio window, unless you are already at the song list inside the CD Audio window.

2. Click to check or uncheck every track you want to record.

3. Click Copy Music on the CD Audio window and the tracks you've selected will record, along with the track information such as title and artist. The music plays and is recorded to the My Music folder located in the Windows\All Users\Documents folder. To organize your files, the Windows Media Player creates a folder for the artist, with all albums you've recorded for that artist in their own subfolders, and individual files inside those folders named with the actual track names. Windows Media Player stores the track files in the default Windows Media Player format with the filename extension of .WMA.

> You can change options related to the Windows Media Player, such as the default folder for storing the recorded music, in the Tools, Options menu.

4. You can open any music you've stored, and select as many songs as you want by holding Ctrl while clicking on the tracks, after selecting File, Open from the Windows Media Player menu.

The Media Library and Playlists

To make access to your media files easier, you'll want to visit the Media Library button on the Windows Media Player that produces a tree-structured hierarchy of all your multimedia files, sorted by title, artist, album, or genre. The Media Manager, a database of multimedia content, keeps tabs on your Media Library of files so that when you perform a search, you'll quickly locate a multimedia file because the Media Manager won't waste time looking where multimedia files are not located.

If you click the New Playlist button, you can name a new *playlist*, a list of tracks from one or more albums in your music library on your disk. Perhaps you want to create a playlist of your party favorites. Even though the Windows Media Player recorded CDs by artist, album, and track, your playlists can contain any track from any album on your disk.

A Radio in Your PC!

You don't have a radio inside your PC, even though the Windows Media Player includes a button that reads, Radio Tuner. Instead of a radio inside your PC, you've got something better: a radio for the entire world.

When you click the Radio Tuner, the Windows Media Player logs onto the Internet and connects you with Microsoft's Radio Tuner Web page, offering you numerous online broadcasts that begin playing in a streaming audio format as soon as you select them. Unlike a real radio, you can listen to what you want when you want.

Downloading to a Portable Player

When you click the Portable Device button, the Windows Media Player screen changes to the two-pane Music to Copy and Music On Device screen shown in Figure 22.6. Connect your portable music device to your computer (the device must be able to be plugged digitally into your computer and cannot be an analog music device such as a cassette player that has no digital computer connection), select songs from the drop-down list under Music to Copy, and either drag the songs to the right window or double-click them to send them to the right window, which represents your target portable music device. The space left on your portable device, as you copy music, updates to let you know how much room is left.

FIGURE 22.6

Select the music you want to download to your portable player.

What About Video?

So far, most of this hour's lesson has focused on audio playback and recording. Yet, your computer richly supports the playback of video, as you well know by now. What about video files?

It turns out that little changes between the way you manage video and the way you manage audio files. Use the File, Open option to open a video file as opposed to an audio file, and the Windows Media Player plays the file as you see in Figure 22.7.

Windows Media Player supports the most common video formats, including those listed in Table 22.1. You won't run across a common video format that Windows Media Player does not support. When you click on a video file on the Web, the Windows Media Player will start automatically and play that video clip.

Other kinds of media players can interfere with Windows Media Player's capability to start automatically. For example, if you have the RealNetworks RealPlayer software installed, RealPlayer might take over the playback of Internet video.

FIGURE 22.7

The controls remain the same when you play video, even if you play streaming video from the Internet.

TABLE 22.1 The Windows Media Player Supports These Media File Types

File Format	Extension
CD Audio	`.cda`
Intel Video	`.ivf`
Mac AIFF	`.aif, .aifc,` and `.aiff`
Microsoft media files	`.asf, .asx, .avi, .wav, .wax, .wma, .wmv, .wvx`
MPEG	`.mpeg, .mp3, .m1v, .mp2, .mp3, .mpa, .mpe, .mpv2, .mp2v, .m3u, .pls`
MIDI	`.mid, .midi, .rmi`
UNIX	`.au, .snd`

22

Summary

This hour described how Windows contains integrated multimedia in its windowed multi-tasking environment. The multimedia capabilities of Windows are advanced and provide for smooth video and sound. The Windows Media Player takes charge of your computer's multimedia content and plays, records, and manages your multimedia files and physical CDs.

Audio is only part of the multimedia glitz. Full-motion video capabilities enable viewing of video clips by using the Windows Media Player. Depending on the speed of your computer hardware, the video is smooth and provides playback of digital files on your disk as well as digital video you download from the Internet.

Q&A

Q What's the purpose of the speaker icon on my taskbar?

A The speaker icon provides a volume control that's available at all times during your Windows operation. When you double-click the speaker, a multilevel volume control panel opens from which you can adjust the volume of several different types of sound, including your PC's microphone recording level.

Q Why are there so many kinds of sounds (CD, Wave, FM synthesis, and MIDI)?

A The different sounds produce different qualities of audio. Your hardware and software determine the kinds of sound that come out of your computer's speakers. Luckily, you probably won't have to worry about the different sounds because Windows recognizes most sound sources and selects the proper playing software accordingly.

Workshop

The quiz and exercise questions are designed to test your knowledge of the material covered in this hour. The answers are in Appendix C, "Answers to Quizzes."

Quiz

1. How can you insert an audio CD in your computer and keep the CD from playing automatically?
2. Where does the Windows Media Player get artist and track information for the CDs you insert?
3. What is a skin?
4. What is a playlist?
5. What do you use to play video clips?

Exercises

1. Log onto the Internet. Locate one of your most obscure CDs, perhaps one you bought at a second-hand shop that contains the best of the early 1950s Frank Sinatra titles. Almost surely, the online database of CD titles will locate that CD and download all the track information to your computer. The database is vast. Although you won't find every CD, and although the CD's information does not always match your expectations, the database is very accurate.
2. Search the Windows Media Player's radio section and play some stations. You have your choice of music or talk 24 hours a day.

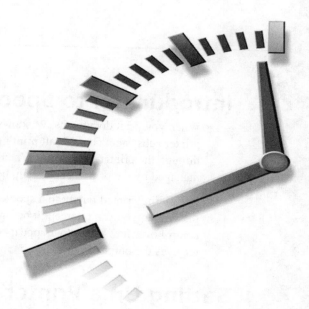

HOUR 23

Understanding Printing and Fonts

This hour explains the printing options available to you as a Windows Me user. The printer is one of those devices that you don't want to think a lot about; you want to print a document and a few moments later, grab the resulting printed output from the printer. You can better manage your printer's output with this hour's information.

When you work with documents, the availability of fonts is important so that you have the richness that fonts provide. This hour explains how to work with fonts inside Windows. With ample fonts, you can view more documents accurately.

In this hour, you will

- Use the Add Printers Wizard to set up new printers
- Work with Print dialog boxes to route output to a printer
- Manage the Print job window's list of printed documents
- Master the Fonts window
- Add and remove fonts in Windows

Introduction to Spooled Printing

When you print documents, Windows automatically starts the printer subsystem. The printer subsystem controls all printing from within Windows. Windows *spools* output through the printer subsystem. When spooled, the print job first goes to a disk file, managed by the printer subsystem, before being sent directly to the printer.

By routing printed output to a spooled disk file instead of sending the output directly to the printer, you can intercept it before that output goes to paper. You therefore have more control over how the output appears on the printer. You also can select which printer receives the output in case there is more than one printer connected to your computer.

Setting Up a Printer

If you add a printer to your system, remove a printer from your system, or set up Windows to use a printer for the first time, you'll have to inform Windows. But that's not always a problem because Windows offers Plug and Play as well as gives you the *Add Printer Wizard* to help you each step of the way.

Turn off your PC before you plug a new printer into your PC's parallel printer port. When you turn your PC on once again, Windows might recognize, through Plug and Play, that you've added a new printer and perform one of the following tasks:

- Automatically recognize the printer and install the drivers for you
- Recognize that you've changed the hardware and start the Add New Printer wizard so that you can select the new printer
- Not realize that you added a printer and you'll have to run the Add Printer Wizard yourself

A special Printers folder available from the Start, Settings menu contains all information about your computer's printer hardware. If you have yet to set up a printer, and Plug and Play failed to install the printer, you will have to open the Printers folder and walk through the Add Printer Wizard so that Windows knows exactly what printer to use.

Windows needs to know how to format the printed output that you want. Almost every printer supports different combinations of print functions, and almost every printer requires unique *print codes* that determine how the printer interprets specific characters and character-formatting options. The Add Printer Wizard configures the necessary details and asks you appropriate questions that determine how printed output eventually appears.

If you use a network and you need to set up a network printer in Windows, use the Network Neighborhood window to open the network printer; you can browse the network to find the printer. Then set up the printer following the instructions that appear on the screen.

▼ To Do

To Do: Using the Add Printer Wizard

1. Connect your printer to your computer using a printer cable. Most printers connect to the computer's *parallel port*.

2. Click the Start button to display the Start menu.

3. Select Settings, Printers to open the Printers window shown in Figure 23.1.

FIGURE 23.1

The Printers window controls the setup and operation of printers.

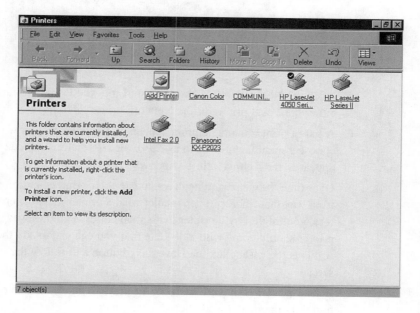

If you have not yet set up any printer, you will see only the Add Printer icon in the Printers window.

The Printers window provides access to all your printer subsystem capabilities. It is from the Printers window that you can manage and rearrange print jobs you've started from Windows applications.

▼   4. The Printers window contains the icon, labeled Add Printer, that starts the Add
        Printer Wizard. If you haven't set up a printer yet, you should open the Add Printer
        icon now. When you open it, you will see the first screen of the Add Printer Wizard
        shown in Figure 23.2.

FIGURE 23.2

*The Add Printer Wizard
walks you through the
setup of a new printer.*

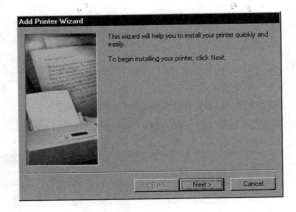

5. Click the Next command button to start the Add Printer Wizard's operation. Select
    either the Local printer or the Network printer option.

6. A list of printer manufacturers appears in the left scrolling window. When you
    choose a manufacturer, such as *Epson* or *HP*, that manufacturer's printer models
    appear in the right scrolling window.

    Over time, printer manufacturers update their printers and offer new models. There
    is no way that Microsoft can predict what a printer manufacturer will do next. There-
    fore, you might buy a printer that's made after Windows was written. If so, the
    printer should come with a diskette that you can use to add the printer to Windows.
    If this is the case, click the Have Disk button and follow the instructions on the
    screen.

    If your printer *is* in the list, find your printer's model on the right of the dialog box,
    highlight the model, and click the Next button.

7. The wizard next needs information about the port that your printer is plugged into.
    Select the location of your printer.

    Most of the time, you'll click Next to select the default value of the parallel printer
    port. Perhaps before doing so, you should click the Configure Port command but-
    ton. The Configure Port dialog box contains two options. The first option deter-
    mines if the spooling should apply to MS-DOS programs in addition to Windows
▼   programs. The second option determines if you want the printer subsystem to

▼ check the port before printing, to make sure that the port is ready for data. Unless you are using special printer hardware that requires extra control, you'll want to leave both these options checked and click the OK command button to return to the wizard.

Select the port where your computer is connected and click the Next command button now.

8. When you see the screen shown in Figure 23.3, you can enter the name you want to use for the printer when selecting among printers within Windows. If you like the default name, don't change it. If you want a different name, such as Joe's Printer (in case you're setting up a network printer), type the new name. If this is the only printer you are setting up, select Yes when the wizard asks about this being the default printer. (If this is the first printer you've installed, Windows makes it the default printer.) Windows will then use the printer automatically every time you print something. If you are setting up a secondary printer, select No.

FIGURE 23.3

You must tell Windows how to refer to the printer.

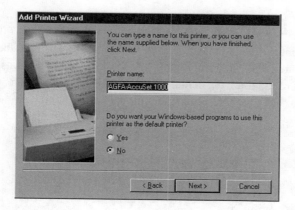

9. Click the Next command button to move to the next wizard screen.

10. If you click Yes on the next wizard screen, Windows will print a test page on the printer. (Be sure that your printer is turned on and that it has paper.) By printing a test page, you ensure that Windows properly recognizes the printer. Click the Finish command button to complete the wizard.

11. After Windows completes the printer setup, a new icon with your printer's name ▲ appears in the Printers window.

When running the Add Printer Wizard, you specify which printer Windows should use for the default printer. (The default printer might appear with a check mark next to it in the Printers window depending on your Windows installation.) Of course, any time you print documents, you can select a printer that differs from the default printer if you want output to go to a secondary printer source. You can also change the default printer by right-clicking over the printer you want to set as the default printer and selecting the Set As Default command from the right-click menu.

> If you use your computer for accounting or personal finance, you might have a laser printer for reports and a color ink-jet printer for color banners. The default printer should be the printer that you print to most often. If your laser printer is the default printer, you'll have to route output, using the Print dialog box explained in the next section, back to the default check printer when you want to print checks.

The Print Dialog Box

When you print from an application such as WordPad, you'll see the Print dialog box shown in Figure 23.4. The Print dialog box contains several options from which you can choose. Most of the time, the default option values are appropriate, so you'll simply press Enter to select the OK command button when printing.

FIGURE 23.4

The Print dialog box controls the way a print job is routed.

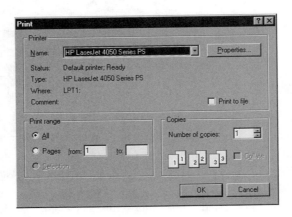

The Print dialog box contains a drop-down list box of every printer you've added to Windows. The default printer will be the printer you've chosen using the Add Printer Wizard's final screen. To change the default printer to another printer so that Windows automatically routes output to it when you print (unless you select another printer at printing time), right click the printer's icon from within the Printers dialog box in My Computer and choose Set as Default.

> You can route the printer's output to a file by clicking the Print-to-file option. If you want output to go to a physical printer as soon as possible, as is most often the case, leave this option unchecked. By printing to the file, you can print the file at a later time.

23

The Print range will be All if you want to print all pages. For example, if you are printing 20 pages from a word processor, the All option sends all 20 pages to the printer. If you select the Pages option, you can enter a starting page number and ending page number to print only a portion of the document.

The Copies section determines how many copies you want to print. The default is one copy, but you can request an additional number of copies. If you enter a number greater than 1, check the Collate option if you want the pages collated (you usually do). If you highlight part of the text before beginning the print process, you can click the Selection option button to print only the selected text.

For special print jobs, you can click the Properties command button to display a printer Properties dialog box. Each printer model supports a different set of options so each printer's Properties dialog box contains different options as well. In the Properties dialog box, you specify the type of paper in the printer's paper tray, the *orientation* (the direction the printed output appears on the paper), and the printer resolution (the higher the printer resolution, the better your output looks, but the longer the printer takes to print a single page), among other options that your printer might support.

Keep in mind that the output goes to the print spooler and *not* directly to the printer. The next section explains how you can manage the print spooler.

> Some print jobs take a while to send their output to the spool file and, subsequently, to the printer. The taskbar displays a printer icon to the left of the clock during the printing process. If you rest the cursor over the printer icon, Windows displays a roving help box that describes how many jobs are in line to print. If you open the print icon, Windows displays the list of all print jobs (the next section describes the window of print jobs). If you right-click over the icon, Windows gives you the choice of displaying a window containing a list of all print jobs or the print jobs for specific printers that are queued up waiting for printed output.

Explorer and Open dialog boxes all display documents, as you've seen already through-out this book. If you want to print a document, such as a bitmap graphic document file, a text document file, or a word processing document file, the right-click menu contains a Print command that automatically prints the selected document (or documents) that you right-click over. The right-click does *not* produce the Print dialog box described in this section; rather, Windows automatically and instantly prints one copy of the document on the primary default printer.

There's yet one more way to print documents that works well in some situations. If you have the My Computer window open or if you are using Windows Explorer, you can print any printable document by dragging it to any printer icon inside the Printers window. Windows automatically begins printing the document that you drag to the printer icon.

Managing Print Jobs

When you print documents, Windows formats the output into the format required by the default printer and then sends that output to a spool file. When the output completes, the printer subsystem routes the output to the actual printer, as long as it is connected and turned on.

Suppose that you want to print several documents to your printer in succession. Although today's printers are fairly fast, the computer's disk drives and memory are much faster than the relative speed of printers. Therefore, you can end up sending several documents to the printer before the first document even finishes printing on paper.

After printing one or more documents, go to the Printer window and open the printer icon that matches the printer you've routed all your output to. A scrolling list of print jobs, such as the one shown in Figure 23.5, appears inside the window.

FIGURE 23.5

You can see all the print jobs spooled up, waiting to print.

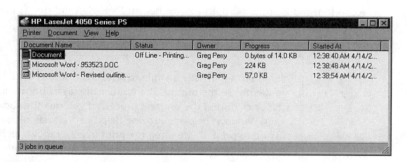

Each line in the window describes one print job. If you've printed three documents, all three documents appear inside the window. The Progress column shows how far along your print job is by telling you how many pages of the print job have completed. The remaining print jobs on the list are awaiting their turn to print.

If you want to change the order of the print jobs in the *queue* (another name for the list of print jobs), you can drag a print job to the top or bottom. Dragging a print job around in the list changes priority for that print job. For example, your boss might be waiting over your shoulder for a report. If you had several jobs you had sent to print before your boss showed up, you could move the boss's print job to the top of the list so that it would print next.

Right-clicking over a print job gives you the option of pausing a print job (putting it on hold until you resume the job) or canceling the print job altogether.

Deferred Printing

There might be times when you'll print documents but *not* want those documents to appear on a printer! Often people carry a laptop with them but not a printer. Even if you don't have a printer with you, you might create expense reports and other documents that you want to print as soon as you get back to your office.

Instead of keeping track of each document you want to print later, you can go ahead and issue a *deferred printing* request. When you do this, Windows spools the document or documents to a file on your disk drive. The printer subsystem will not attempt to send the spooled data to a printer just yet. When you later attach a printer to your PC, you can release the deferred printing request and Windows begins printing the saved print jobs.

Ordinarily, if you were to print a document to a printer but you had no printer attached to your computer, Windows would issue the error message shown in Figure 23.6. Although Windows can spool the output properly and set up a print job for the output, Windows cannot finish the job because of a lack of a printer, and so the dialog box lets you know about the problem.

FIGURE 23.6

Windows cannot print if a printer is not attached to your PC.

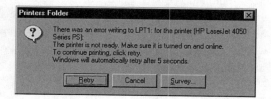

If you do have a printer attached to your computer but you get the error dialog box shown in Figure 23.6, you probably forgot to turn on the printer or put the printer *online* so that it can accept output. You can correct the problem and click Retry to restart the printing. If you do not click Retry, Windows will automatically retry printing every five seconds.

If you want to defer printing for another time, open the Printers folder and click over the icon that matches the printer you want to store print jobs for. After you highlight the icon, select File, Use Printer Offline. When you return to your office or plug a printer into the printer port, you can repeat this process to uncheck the Use Printer Offline option. As soon as you set the printer icon back to its normal online status, Windows will begin printing to that printer.

> If your printer icon's File menu does not have a Use Printer Offline option, you can select Pause Printing to achieve the same delayed printing effect. The actual printing will begin when you click Pause Printing once more to turn off the pause. The Use Printer Offline option is available only on certain laptop and networked computer configurations.

Fonts Have Style

Because of the design of documents, the way that Windows displays documents is critical to your viewing of them. The documents must be easy to read. If Windows doesn't automatically display a document in a form that provides for easy viewing, you'll have to change the way the document appears. Perhaps the simplest way to make a document easier to read, no matter what tool you use to view those documents, is by changing the document's font. A font is the typeface Windows uses to display a character. If you see two letter A's on the screen and one is larger, more slanted, bolder, fancier, or more scripted, you are looking at two different fonts.

Fonts from the same *font family* contain the same typeface (they look alike) but they come in standard formatting versions such as italicized, boldfaced, and underlined text. Therefore, an italicized font named *Courier* and a boldfaced font named *Courier* both belong to the same font family, even though they look different because of the italicized version of the one and the boldface of the other. A font named *Algerian* and a font named *Symbol*, however, would belong to two different font families; not only do they look different, but they also come in various styles.

Fonts and Typefaces

Before computers were invented, printer experts stored collections of typefaces in their shops. Each typeface contained every letter, number, and special character the printer would need for printed documents. Therefore, the printer might have 50 typefaces in his inventory with each of those typefaces containing the same letters, numbers, and special characters but each having a different appearance or size.

Windows also contains a collection of typefaces, and those typefaces are stored as fonts on the hard disk. If you want to use a special typeface for a title, you must make sure that Windows contains the typeface in its font collection. If not, you will have to purchase the font and add that font to your system. Software dealers sell numerous font collections. Several fonts come with Windows and with the programs that you use, so you might not even need additional fonts.

The Control Panel contains an icon labeled Fonts from which you can manage, add, and delete fonts from Windows's collection of fonts. When you open the Control Panel's Fonts icon, Windows opens the Fonts window shown in Figure 23.7. The following To Do item explains how to manage fonts from the Fonts window.

FIGURE 23.7

The Fonts window displays your fonts.

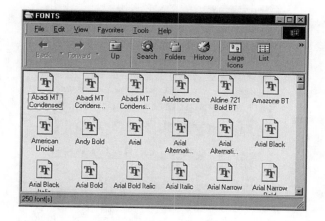

To Do: Working in the Fonts Window

1. Open the Control Panel.

2. Open the Fonts icon. Windows opens the Fonts window.

   Each icon inside the Fonts window contains information about one specific font on your system. Some fonts are *scaleable,* which means that Windows can display the fonts in one of several different sizes.

> Font sizes are measured in *points*. A font that is 12 points high is 1/6 inch high, and a font that is 72 points is one inch high.

▼   3. Open any of the icons inside the Fonts window. Windows immediately displays a preview of that font, as shown in Figure 23.8. When you want to create a special letter or flier with a fancy font, you can preview all of the fonts by opening each one until you find one you like. When you find a font, you can select it from your word processor to enter the text using that font.

FIGURE 23.8

Get a preview before selecting a font.

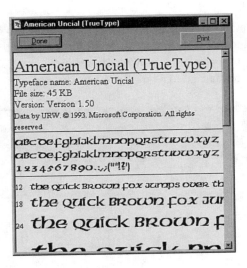

Many fancy fonts are available to you. Don't go overboard, though. Your message is always more important than the font you use. Make your font's style fit the message, and don't mix more than two or three fonts on a single page. Too many different fonts on a single page make the page look cluttered.

4. If you click the Print command button, Windows prints the preview of the font. If you click Done (do so now), Windows closes the font's preview window.

5. Another way to gather information about certain kinds of fonts is to right-click over a font and select Properties from the menu that appears. The Font Properties dialog box will appear.

The font icons with the letters *TT* are *TrueType* fonts. A TrueType font is a scaleable font that Windows prints using 32-bit technology so it will look as close to typeset characters as possible. The remaining fonts, with the letter A or another icon, refer to screen and printer fonts of more limited size ranges than TrueType fonts normally can provide.

▼

Some users prefer to work only with TrueType fonts because of the rich look associated with them and their scaleability. If you want to view only TrueType fonts in the Fonts window, select Tools, Folder Options and click the TrueType tab. Click the screen's option to display only TrueType fonts.

6. Choose View, List Fonts By Similarity from the menu. Windows searches through your fonts looking for all other fonts that are similar to the font you choose from the drop-down list box and displays the result of that search. Some fonts are very similar, some are somewhat similar, and some are not similar at all.

7. Choose View, Large Icons to return to the icon view.

8. Check or uncheck View, Hide Variations (Bold, Italic, and so on) depending on whether you want to see variations within font families. If the command is unchecked, Windows displays a different icon for each font variation within the same family.

9. When you purchase new fonts, you cannot simply copy those fonts to a directory and expect Windows to know that the fonts are there. When you want to add fonts, you'll probably obtain those fonts on a CD-ROM, diskette, or downloaded to your hard disk from the Internet. Insert the diskette or CD-ROM (or make sure that you know where the file is located on your hard disk) and select File, Install New Font. Windows displays the Add Fonts dialog box.

   Select the drive with the new fonts inside the Drives list box, and Windows displays a list of fonts from that drive in the upper window. Click on the font you want to install (hold Ctrl and click more than one font if you want to install several fonts) and click the OK command button to install the font to the Windows folder named Fonts.

▲ 10. Close the Fonts window.

After you install fonts, they will immediately be available to all your Windows applications.

Windows provides a single location, the Fonts window, where you can view and manage all the fonts on your system. Because of the graphical and document-centered design of Windows, your collection and selection of fonts is vital to making your documents as easy to read as possible.

Removing Fonts

Fonts take up a lot of disk space and slow down the start up of Windows. If your disk space is a premium and if you have lots of fonts you rarely or never use, you can follow the steps in this To Do item to remove some of the fonts. Often, today's word processing and desktop publishing programs add lots of fonts to your system and you might not need as many as you have at hand.

▼ To Do: Removing Fonts from Windows

1. Open the Control Panel.
2. Open the Fonts icon.
3. Scroll to the font you want to delete.
4. Click the font you want to delete; Windows highlights the font. If you hold the Ctrl key while you click, you can select more than one font to delete. By selecting several at once, you can remove the fonts with one task instead of removing each one individually.
5. Right-click over any highlighted font to display the menu.
6. Select Delete.
7. Click the Yes button to confirm the removal.

▲

Remove unwanted fonts if you want to save disk space and make your fonts more manageable. The Control Panel's Fonts entry lets you easily select and remove fonts.

Summary

This hour explored the printer options you have with Windows. Before using a printer for the first time, you must set up the printer using the Add Printer Wizard available inside the Printers folder. Windows supports several hundred makes and models of printers so you stand a very good chance of finding your printer on the list.

The Fonts window contains a centralized location from which you can manage all the fonts used by Windows. When you purchase new fonts, you'll add those fonts using the Fonts window.

Workshop

The quiz and exercise questions are designed to test your knowledge of the material covered in this hour. The answers are in Appendix C, "Answers to Quizzes."

Quiz

1. Where does Windows Me initially send all printed output?

2. If you plug in a new printer but Plug and Play does not properly detect the printer, what must you run to install the printer?

3. If you have two or more printers attached to your computer, how can you direct output to a specific one?

4. *True or false*: If you issue print commands to print ten documents in a row, you can change the order in which the documents print as long as you make the change to the documents that are still waiting to print.

5. What fonts are considered to be the best Windows fonts?

Exercises

1. Print a document that's at least ten pages and when the printer icon appears in your taskbar, double-click the icon. Watch how Windows updates the status of the print job as each page prints. If you leave this window open and print more documents, those documents will appear in the window.

2. Open your Fonts dialog window and look through the fonts you have installed on your Windows system. Notice the variety. Print samples of both TrueType and non-TrueType to see if you can tell the difference. On some systems, the non-TrueType fonts are similar, but often the non-TrueType fonts are not as superior as the TrueType fonts.

23

HOUR 24

Advanced Windows Tips

You've worked hard to master Windows! You've already mastered the basics, so now you're ready to move up to the level of *Windows guru*. This hour teaches several practical tips that you are ready for now that you understand the ins and outs of Windows.

Because of the nature of tips, you won't find step-by-step tasks in this hour. Instead, this hour presents its Windows tips in several categories. For example, if you are comfortable with Windows's interface, you can now turn to this hour's first section for some advanced tips that will help you manage the desktop.

In this hour, you will

- Learn desktop tips that help you more quickly manage Windows
- Create a startup disk for safety
- Use Internet Explorer shortcuts that save you online time
- Learn where to look for Outlook Express shortcuts
- Improve your computing efficiency when on the road with a laptop

Windows Desktop Tips

When you master this section's desktop tips, you'll more quickly select programs and manage your desktop.

Rearrange Start Menu Items

If you don't like the location of a menu item on one of your Start menus, drag the item to another location. When you've opened one of the Start menus, such as the Programs, Accessories menu, you can click and drag any menu item to another menu.

Suppose that you use Notepad a lot to edit text files and want to place the Notepad program at the top of your Start menu so that you don't have to traverse all the way over to the Accessories menu. Open the Accessories menu and drag the Notepad option to your Start menu. You'll notice two things:

- The menu option's name does not drag, but the mouse cursor displays a box showing the movement.
- You cannot drop the item onto the lower section of the Start menu (the section with the Settings and Programs options). The cursor turns into the international Don't symbol as you drag the Notepad over the Start menu's lower portion.

When you release your mouse button, the menu option will appear on the Start menu.

> The menu item does not move. Instead, the item appears in both places. If you want to move an option instead of copying the option, you must delete the menu item from its original menu location.

Deleting Menu Items

To remove a menu item, drag the item to the Recycle Bin. If you change your mind about removing the item, you can restore it from the Recycle Bin up until the time you empty the Recycle Bin.

> You can move menu options and send them to the Recycle Bin because the Start menu contains shortcuts to programs. A shortcut is just a pointer to a program, not the program's filename. So when you drag a shortcut from one location to another, the pointer moves but not the file itself.
>
> You can drag a menu item to your desktop. Then, if you want to launch that program, you need only open the desktop's icon. You won't have to use the Start menu every time you start the program.

If you want to rearrange more than one or two items from your Start menu, consider selecting the Start menu's Settings, Taskbar and Start Menu option, clicking the Advanced tab, and then clicking the Advanced button to display the Explorer menu shown in Figure 24.1. You can also press your keyboard's Window key and, while still holding the key, press E before letting up on both to start Explorer. The two panes enable you to move and rearrange entire menu groups. The click-and-drag approach to menu management works well if you need to move or remove only a few menu items because you can select only one item at a time.

Click a menu
group to see
its contents
in the right
panel.

24

FIGURE 24.1

The Start Menu Explorer window enables you to perform advanced menu editing.

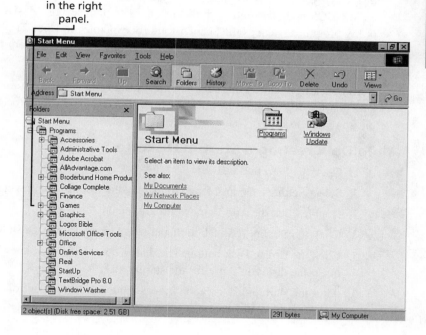

Right-Click Menu Options

When you right-click over a Start menu option, Windows displays a pop-up menu. You can delete or rename menu items with the pop-up menu as well as view the item's properties. The Properties option describes the menu option and its underlying file information.

Make a Startup Diskette

During the course of using Windows, you will add hardware and software. Windows makes adding such components relatively easy, but in some cases, problems might occur. Perhaps you receive a bad installation disk, or a hardware conflict arises that freezes up Windows.

By making a *startup disk*, you can safely get your computer started and access your hard disk when you otherwise cannot start your machine. The startup disk is little more than an MS-DOS boot disk, although the disk does contain several MS-DOS and Windows utility programs (such as the ScanDisk utility explained in Hour 21, "Using the Advanced System Tools") that can help you locate disk and memory troubles that can cause boot problems.

Before making a startup diskette, you must locate a high-density formatted disk. Make sure that the disk contains no data you need because the startup process overwrites all data on your disk.

To Do: Creating a Startup Diskette

1. Click the Start button.
2. Select Settings, Control Panel to display the Control Panel window.
3. Double-click the Add/Remove Program icon.
4. Click the Startup Disk tab to display the Startup Disk page shown in Figure 24.2.
5. Click the Create Disk button. The dialog box will let you know when you need to insert the disk you'll use for the startup disk.
6. After the startup disk creation process ends, close the Control Panel and put away the startup disk in a safe place.

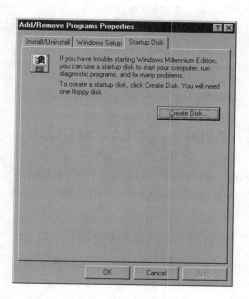

FIGURE 24.2

Create a startup disk for emergencies.

When you create a startup disk, you'll have a disk in case of emergencies. If you find that you cannot access your hard disk or boot your computer because your system files are corrupt, you'll be able to regain hard disk access by inserting the startup disk and rebooting your computer. The startup disk will not be able to cure any problems, but you will have system access once again so that you can begin tracing the difficulties.

Don't Wait for a Disaster!

Most people back up regularly...after they've had a disaster! Don't wait. Master Hour 20, "Managing Your Hard Drive," and back up your system. The Windows Backup program is adequate but includes few bells and whistles, such as full support for recordable CD drives. For a more complete backup program, consider going to your local software dealer and search through the many inexpensive programs on the shelves for one that looks as though it will suit your needs and hardware the best. Your disk drives are mechanical and will break down over time. Don't wait to make your first backup or you'll regret the first time your disk has a problem.

Software is available that not only makes a backup of every file on your system, but also actually makes a disk drive image of your hard disk. From that saved image, you can restore your computer to its exact configuration if you ever have a disk breakdown. Look for products such as DriveImage (their Web site is www.powerquest.com for more information) if you want to make an image of your disk for backup storage.

Make Yourself More Comfortable

What's the most important component in your PC system? It's not your system unit. It's not your CPU. It's not how fast Windows performs. It's not your hard disk. It's not your printer. Your most important component is the very chair you sit in. The smarter PC users spend more money on their chair than on their operating systems.

If you spend an hour or more a day at your PC, run, don't walk, to your local office furniture store and check out their desk chair selection. If you've never paid much attention, you'll be shocked at how many kinds of chairs that you find. Your back, arms, shoulders, and wrists (not to mention the body part on which you sit), deserve far better than the average chair most people place in front of their computer. You'll be more productive, work more accurately, and you'll take care of your body.

The better desk chairs provide separate controls for the arm rests, back and lumbar support, and height. Make sure that you can adjust these components easily *while sitting in the chair*. Look for a chair on wheels that roll easily so that you can move between your PC and writing area.

Start Windows Explorer Quickly

If your keyboard is a Windows keyboard—that is, your keyboard has a key with the flying Windows logo that displays the Start menu when you press it—you can press the Windows key along with the letter E to start Windows Explorer. (This is not Internet Explorer but the Windows Explorer program you use to traverse disks, folders, and files.)

Adjust the Toolbar in Any Window

You can right-click over any Windows window's toolbar to display a menu of toolbar options, as shown in Figure 24.3, that determines how the toolbar appears.

The toolbar's
pop-up menu

FIGURE 24.3

*The pop-up menus give
you control over a
menu option.*

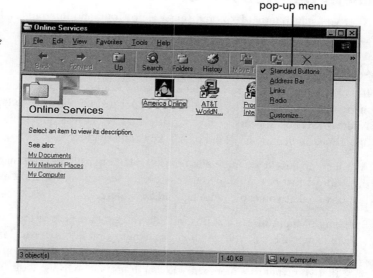

24

You can display or hide any of the following on your toolbar:

- **Standard Buttons**—Displays the toolbar buttons using the icon-based standard.

- **Address Bar**—Displays the Web Address text box in which you can type a Web URL or any pathname to a folder you want to work in.

- **Links**—Displays hyperlink buttons (they appear next to the address bar if you display the address bar) that quickly point the window to a Web or folder location. You can drag other shortcuts to the links to add your own buttons, and you can also right-click over a link button to change its property or rename the button.

- **Radio**—Actually adds an Internet-based radio station guide and volume control to your window toolbar. Listen while you work!

- **Customize**—Enables you to add or remove buttons on the toolbar.

Internet Explorer Tips

If you load Internet Explorer and the Web view, Internet Explorer becomes such an important part of the Windows interface that you find yourself using it more and more when you upgrade to Windows. Therefore, the more shortcuts you learn about Internet Explorer, the more efficient and effective you are with the Internet Explorer program interface.

Learn the Web As You Use It

After you start Internet Explorer, select Help, Tour, and Internet Explorer starts an interactive Web tutorial that teaches you about the Web.

Quickly Enter Web Addresses

If you often type URLs in Internet Explorer's Address text box, you'll find yourself having to click the Address box first to place your text cursor there to type an address. The Address text box appears to have no shortcut key because no letter in the label Address is underlined indicating any kind of Alt+key combination.

Although no Alt+key combination exists, Internet Explorer does map a shortcut key to the Address text box. When you press F4, the text cursor instantly moves to the Address text box so that you can enter a new address there.

Speaking of the Address text box, all addresses that appear in the Address text box have a small icon to the left. You can drag that icon to your desktop, email message, or anywhere else you want to place that address for later reference. If, for example, you visit a Web page that you want to remember, you can drag its icon to the toolbar's link buttons to create a new link button (assuming that you've turned on the toolbar links, as previously described in the section "Adjust the Toolbar in Any Window").

Set Up Internet Explorer Security

When you select Tools, Internet Options, Internet Explorer displays a dialog box that enables you to adjust Internet settings. Click the Security tab to display the dialog box shown in Figure 24.4. The four options in the center of the box determine how secure you want to be with your Web browsing.

A high security level protects your PC from incoming information that could possibly contain virus-laden files. A virus is a computer file that destroys other files. The problem with this high security level, however, is that you often access secure sites and want to purchase something or give other information, and Internet Explorer will not let you send that information. You can always lower your security level when you know that a site is secure.

FIGURE 24.4

Select the security with which you feel most comfortable.

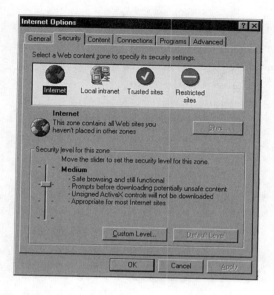

Keep More History for Faster Access

The General tab of the Tools, Internet Options dialog box enables you to enter a value that determines the number of history days to keep track of. As you traverse the Web, Internet Explorer saves each Web page that you visit in a history area. By adjusting the value in the option labeled Days to Keep Pages in History, you can make Internet Explorer keep more pages in case you return to recently visited pages.

> The more days of history you keep, the less disk space you will have. Some Web pages consume a lot of disk space.

Take a Look at Advanced Internet Explorer Options

Select Internet Explorer's Tools, Internet Options menu and click the Advanced tab to display the customization list shown in Figure 24.5. Each item in the list describes a different aspect of Internet Explorer that you can control, from browsing tasks to toolbar information.

FIGURE 24.5

*You can completely
customize Internet
Explorer.*

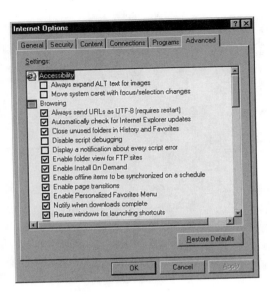

It pays to return to this dialog box every month or two. As you use the Internet in different ways, and as you develop procedures you routinely follow, set options that help Internet Explorer work the way you do.

Change Your Home Page

If you begin traversing to a particular site, such as your company's Web page, as soon as you sign into the Web, you might want to make that page your home page so your browser automatically displays that page when you first start. Instead of using the Internet Options dialog box to change your start page, drag the Address text box icon to the Home button to change your browser's home (start) page. The next time you start your browser, the page will appear as soon as you sign into the Internet.

Disconnect Quickly

To disconnect your Internet dial-up connection, whether or not you are using Internet Explorer, double-click the taskbar's Web icon next to the clock to display a small connection dialog box window. (The Web icon might show two PCs connected by a wire or a different symbol, depending on your Internet connection.) Select Disconnect and Windows immediately signs off from your Internet provider.

Outlook Express Tips

You'll often work in Outlook Express because of the prevalence of email in today's online world. You can make Outlook Express more enjoyable by utilizing some of the following tips.

Compress Files

If you store many sent and retrieved email messages or subscribe to a lot of newsgroups, your disk space can fill up fast. To help, you can reduce the amount of space consumed by messages and newsgroup files by selecting Tools, Options, and clicking the Maintenance tab. When you click the Compact Messages in the Background option, Outlook Express compresses your message and file space.

If you click Delete Read Message Bodies in Newsgroups, Outlook Express removes the message bodies but retains all message headers (descriptions) so that you'll know which messages you've already read. (Outlook Express places a read icon next to your read messages as long as you've saved the headers.)

If you click Delete news messages x days after being downloaded, you save the most space because Outlook Express removes all newsgroup messages and files from your disk after the given time period; but you have to download those newsgroup messages and files if you ever need them again. Reset performs a clean up that deletes both message headers and bodies.

Clean Up Your Deleted Folder

Like files that you delete to the Recycle Bin from within Windows Explorer, email messages that you delete from your Inbox and Outbox don't really go away but go to your Deleted Items folder. If you want to free space completely of unwanted, old email messages, routinely open your Deleted Items folder and delete the messages from there. You have to confirm the delete because Outlook Express knows that the files are truly gone when you delete them from the Deleted Items folder.

If you decide not to delete one or more messages from the Deleted Items folder, you can drag messages from the Deleted Items folder to any other folder at the left of the Outlook Express screen. Feel free to create new folders, from the File menu or by right-clicking over the list of folders, if you want to create an organized set of folders. You can create a folder for your business correspondence and one for your personal correspondence. You then can keep your Inbox, Outbox, and Deleted Items folders free from messages that should appear in other folders.

24

Create a Personal Signature

You cannot sign your email with your handwriting, but Outlook Express's signature feature is the next-best thing. An email signature is text that appears at the end of your email. Your signature might be just your name, or you might want to close all correspondence with your name, address, and phone number.

You can choose not to enclose your signature with certain email messages.

Outlook Express enables you to add a signature to your email messages, your newsgroup postings, or both. To create the signature, select Tools, Options and click the Signatures tab. Click New, then add your signature, as shown in Figure 24.6.

FIGURE 24.6

Create a signature for the bottom of your messages and postings.

Your signature can come from text you type at the Text option or from a text file on disk that you select at the File option.

Check Email Often

If you receive lots of email throughout the day, select Tools, Options and decrease the time that Outlook Express waits before checking for new email. If you read your email only once or twice a day, you might want to check for new email less often than the 30-minute default so that your system runs more efficiently when you don't want email. You must have Outlook Express running before it can check for new email.

Outlook Express emits a sound if you get email. When you hear the sound, it's time to check the Outlook Express Inbox for new messages. Check or uncheck the option on the Options General page that reads Play Sound When New Messages Arrive to request or cancel the new message sound. (Open the Control Panel's Sounds icon to change the sound that plays when you get a new message.)

Printing Tips

Windows adds advanced printer support that enables you to manage the documents you send to the printer. As you probably know, you can begin printing a second (or more) document even before the first one finishes printing. Windows stores the output in memory and on disk until all the documents are on the paper. Have you ever printed two or three long documents and then wished you could cancel the first one? You can, as the next tip shows.

24

Manage Printer Jobs

As soon as you print, Windows sends the output to the print queue. The *print queue* is a temporary file that resides partially in memory and partially on disk. The print queue holds the document or documents that you've sent to the printer but have not finished printing yet.

From the time you issue a print command until the time the document is completely printed, Windows displays a printer icon on your taskbar. If you double-click that icon, the printer window appears.

The printer window tells you which jobs are printing and their status, including the number of pages printed for the current job. If you change your mind and want to cancel a job that's started or one that has yet to start, right-click over the job's name and select Cancel printing.

Rearrange print jobs when you want to move a more important job up in the queue. Drag a job up or down to change its priority and printing order.

Cancel All Print Jobs Easily

Select the printer window's Printer, Purge Print Documents option to remove all jobs from the print queue.

Multiple Users Should Print Separator Pages

If you share a networked printer with others in an office setting, make sure that you've specified a separator page for your networked printer. A separator page prints before or after every print job. If several people print at the same time, the separator pages help you determine where one print job begins and ends.

The separator page can contain text, but if you select a large graphic image (the image must end in the graphic file extension .wmf), you can more easily locate the separator page when sorting through a list of printed output.

Miscellaneous Tips

Although Windows offers hundreds of shortcuts and tips that you'll run across as you use Windows, your 24 hours is about up, and the day must end. The following sections round out the final Windows tips offered here.

Save the Scraps

Suppose that you work within a word processor and want to copy a paragraph or two from the word processor to several different programs over the next few days. The Windows clipboard will hold data only as long you don't replace the clipboard with additional contents or until you shut down Windows.

You can create a *scrap,* a portion of a data file, by dragging selected text and data from an application to your desktop. When you release the data, a scrap icon appears on the desktop. Keep in mind that a scrap is not a complete document but only text you've selected and copied to the desktop.

The scrap stays on your desktop until you delete it. Therefore, as long as the scrap remains on your desktop, you can copy to any file.

Stop a Copy or Move

Sometimes you begin a copy or move operation with your mouse by dragging something from one location to another, and you realize that you want to cancel the copy or move. Press Esc to cancel the current copy or move in process.

Laptop Security

If you use a laptop, you can help get your laptop back if you lose it. Right now, before you forget, tape your business card to the bottom of your laptop. If you leave the laptop in an airport or hotel, the finder of your PC will be able to contact you to return the laptop.

Sure, if a thief steals your laptop with a business card, he will know who to thank! The thief won't return the laptop. It's the honest finder of your laptop who will act on the business card as long as you've put one there.

Delay On-the-Road Printing

Without a laptop printer, you cannot get a hardcopy (a printout) of your data. You can, however, print all your data to an offline printer. When you print to an offline printer, you appear to print but your laptop stores the printing for later.

To convert your laptop to offline printing, open your Control Panel's Printers folder and select File, Use Printer Offline to check the offline printing option. All subsequent printing goes to the disk. You can print as much as you want, and Windows stores the output for when you eventually connect a printer to your laptop. When you get back to the office, plug a printer into your laptop, select Printers File, Use Printer Offline again, and the laptop will print every file you sent to the printer while on the road.

Print to a Hotel Fax

When you create something with your laptop while you're on the road, you probably won't have your printer with you. Although you can back up your files to a diskette, you might feel better if you print your data. You'll then have the printed hardcopy in case something happens to your diskette. If you don't have a printer, fax your document to the hotel fax machine. You will, in a few seconds, have a printout of your document.

> If you want to back up your files and you have a laptop modem, email your files to yourself! When you get home you can download the mail or ignore it if your laptop files made it home safely.

Purchase a Desktop Infrared Transmitter

If you transfer files between your desktop and laptop more than once a week, you'll soon tire of the cable connection that you have to make. If you use a network, plug the network cable into your laptop's PC card slot, perhaps also removing your PC card hard disk or modem first and inserting the network PC card. If you use a Direct Cable Connection or network, you might have to unplug your desktop's printer or modem before you can cable the desktop to your laptop.

An infrared device frees you from the cables. People who use an infrared transmitter to transfer files between their laptop and desktop are more likely to keep their files up to date than users who must mess with cables.

Summary

This hour wrapped up your 24-hour tutorial with some tips that help you streamline your work. As you work more with Windows, you'll find many other tips that lighten your workload. Windows itself is there to help you, not to hinder you. As you've learned throughout this 24-hour tutorial, Windows often provides several ways to accomplish the same purpose. Although Windows Me is powerful, it tries not to get in your way; instead, it is there to help you get your work done faster.

Q&A

Because of the nature of this hour's material, questions and answers aren't necessary.

Appendixes

APPENDIX **A**

Aid via the Accessibility Options

This appendix describes the Windows Me tools that provide help for users with special needs. The Windows accessibility options change the behavior of the keyboard, screen, and speakers so that they operate differently from their default behaviors. Microsoft designed Windows Me so that everybody can take advantage of the new operating environment.

The Accessibility Wizard

Windows includes an Accessibility menu on the Programs, Accessories menu that contains the following options:

- Accessibility Wizard
- Microsoft Magnifier
- Onscreen Keyboard

If you don't see the Accessibility menu, open the Windows Control Panel, select Add/Remove Programs, click the Windows Setup tab, and install the full Accessibility option.

The Accessibility Wizard is a front-end, question-and-answer wizard that guides you through various *accessibility options* available in Windows. The accessibility options provide different approaches to various Windows activities that you will perform. For example, you might be unable to distinguish between certain screen colors or you might be limited in what you can do with a mouse. The Windows accessibility options provide alternative methods for triggering and responding to various Windows tasks.

The Microsoft Magnifier is a program that magnifies part of your Windows screen. As you move your mouse around the screen, the magnified viewer updates to show you a magnified view of your mouse cursor's area.

The onscreen keyboard enables users to enter keystrokes by clicking the mouse or other input device over the keys that appear on an onscreen keyboard that appears when the user displays the onscreen keyboard.

Microsoft updates accessibility information related to their products and informs you of other accessibility products that are available on the following Web page: http://www.microsoft.com/enable/.

Run the Accessibility Wizard so that you will know what Windows might be able to help you with. Although you can set any of the accessibility options without the wizard, the wizard is simpler to use when setting the options you require. To run the wizard, follow these steps:

1. Select the Start menu's Programs, Accessories, Accessibility, Accessibility Wizard option to see the opening window.

2. Click Next to display the wizard's opening dialog box shown in Figure A.1.

3. Click the various options that you want help with (each option has a hotkey, so you can use your keyboard to add a check mark next to any option). The options you select determine the screens that next appear.

4. Click the Next button to move to the next wizard screen. The screen offers help on one of the options you selected. For example, if items are too small for you to read in Windows, a wizard screen enables you to adjust the size of common window

elements, such as window titles and menu options. If you cannot hear response sounds that Windows provides at various times (such as occurs when an error dialog box appears), a screen appears that enables you to substitute flashing warnings when a sound would otherwise occur. Other screens might appear, such as the one in Figure A.2, that show a mouse cursor selection window where you can choose a more readable mouse cursor.

FIGURE A.1

The Accessibility Wizard helps you designate special Windows options.

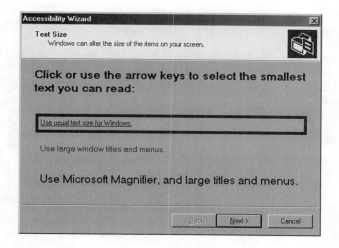

FIGURE A.2

Select a mouse cursor that you can best see.

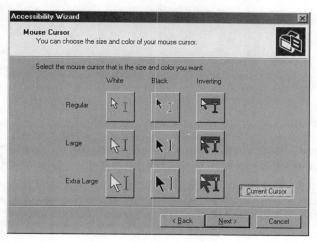

5. After you complete the wizard, setting the options you prefer, Windows takes on the accessibility attributes you selected. At any point, you can run the wizard to adjust, change, or remove any settings. In addition, you can adjust the settings from your Control Panel.

6. If you have trouble reading text on your screen, you might want to try Microsoft Magnifier. Although the Microsoft Magnifier program consumes some of your screen space to show a magnified area, text is much more readable than on the standard Windows screen. Select the Start menu's Programs, Accessories, Accessibility, Magnifier option to start the Microsoft Magnifier program. Figure A.3 shows the resulting screen.

Magnified screen moves
with your cursor

FIGURE A.3

As you move your cursor around the lower half of your screen, the magnified upper half gives you a better view of the details.

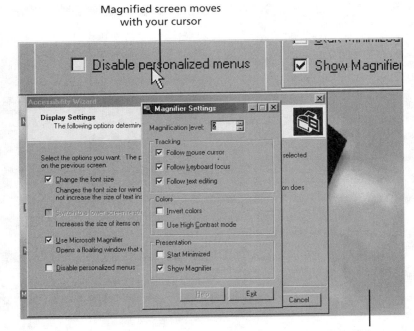

Normal srceen
appears here

7. Adjust the options in the settings box to control the elements Windows magnifies. Perhaps you just want to magnify the area of the screen where the mouse cursor moves. Perhaps you want to magnify areas where you enter text. You can turn off the display of the new Windows Me personalized menus from the Accessibility Wizard. You soon will find the appropriate settings that give you the view you need to more effectively use Windows.

You can adjust the magnified and unmagnified portions of the screen by dragging the dividing line up or down.

8. Click the Exit button to terminate Microsoft Magnifier. You regain the full screen, and the screen elements return to their normal size.

The Accessibility menu option gives you access to the Windows accessibility options by using the Accessibility Wizard. The Accessibility Wizard guides you through a series of wizard screens to which you respond to set Windows accessibility settings. In addition, the Microsoft Magnifier program enlarges elements of your screen as you move the mouse cursor to make viewing easier.

All the Accessibility Wizard's screens control the Windows accessibility options. You have more control over individual options if you access them through the Control Panel, as described in the following section. Although the Accessibility Wizard is simpler to use when setting up your initial accessibility options, you can control the settings in more detail via the Control Panel, as explained next.

The Accessibility Options

After you install the accessibility options, you can access the individual options from your Control Panel. The Control Panel's Accessibility Options tabbed dialog box contains settings for the accessibility options that you can set up for your Windows environment. All the accessibility options are available from this dialog box. You can set any or all of the accessibility options from the Accessibility Options tabbed dialog box.

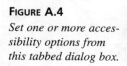

Figure A.4 shows the Control Panel's Accessibility Options dialog box.

FIGURE A.4

Set one or more accessibility options from this tabbed dialog box.

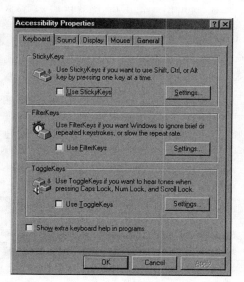

Table A.1 contains a list of every accessibility option available in Windows. From the Accessibility Options dialog box, you can set one or more of these options and remove options you decide later that you no longer want.

TABLE A.1   The Numerous Accessibility Options Help You Control Your Computer

Option	Description
Accessibility reset	When the computer sits idle for a preset period of time, the accessibility options revert to their default state.
Accessibility status	A graphical display of icons that describes which accessibility indicator options are turned on at any given time.
Customizable	You can change the mouse pointer to make the mouse cursor pointer easier to see.
FilterKeys	The group of keystroke aids that include RepeatKeys.
High-contrast	By changing the Windows color scheme to a different color scheme set, you can make the screen's color contrast more obvious and discernible for people with impaired vision.
High-contrast mode	In addition to offering adjustable, high-contrast color schemes, Windows can also ensure that applications adjust themselves to display the highest possible contrast so that visually impaired users can distinguish between background and foreground screen elements.
MouseKeys	Enables you to simulate mouse movements and clicks by using the keyboard.
RepeatKeys	Users can turn on or off the repetition of keys so that holding down a key does not necessarily repeat that keystroke.
SerialKeys	Enables the user to use a non-keyboard input device.
ShowSounds	Provides visual feedback on the screen when applications produce sounds.
SlowKeys	Windows can disregard keystrokes that are not held down for a preset time period. This aids users who often accidentally press keys.
SoundSentry	Sends a visual clue when Windows beeps the speaker (in the case of warning and error message dialog boxes).
StickyKeys	Enables the user to press the *modifier* keys (the Shift, Ctrl, or Alt keys) individually instead of having to press them by using combined keystrokes. Therefore, the user can press Alt, let up on Alt, and then press C instead of combining the two for Alt+C.
ToggleKeys	Sounds a noise on the speaker when the user presses the CapsLock, NumLock, or ScrollLock keys to make them active.

The Onscreen Keyboard

The onscreen keyboard, shown in Figure A.5, appears when you select the Start menu's Programs, Accessories, Accessibility, On-Screen Keyboard. After you display the onscreen keyboard, you must click on your application's window to activate that window. The onscreen keyboard works with any open window on your screen as long as you first activate, or highlight, that window by clicking somewhere in the window or on the window's title bar. When you activate the window that is to receive the keystrokes, you then can click the onscreen keyboard keys to simulate typing those keys on the actual keyboard. When you finish with the onscreen keyboard, click the onscreen keyboard's Close button to eliminate it.

FIGURE A.5

Type keystrokes by clicking keys on the screen.

A

APPENDIX B

GLOSSARY

accelerator key   A key found on a menu (usually a function key used in conjunction with the Alt key, such as Alt+F4) that enables you initiate a menu command from the keyboard without first having to display the menu.

Active Desktop   The Web-based desktop you can create for Windows Me that contains active content direct from the Internet.

anchor position   The starting coordinate pair of lines and other geometric shapes.

animated cursors   Cursors that display movement during the cursor's display, such as a cursor showing a picture of a running horse or a playing piano.

applets   Small programs, embedded in Web pages that come to your PC, that give life to Web pages by making the pages interactive.

AutoPlay   The Windows Me feature that starts the loading and execution of CD-ROMs as soon as you place the CD-ROM in your computer's CD-ROM drive.

backup job   A description that contains a list of files, folders, and drives you want to back up.

binary data   Compressed data, such as programs and graphics, as opposed to text files.

BIOS   Basic Input Output System. The system unit's ROM-based code that handles I/O devices.

Briefcase   The Windows application that synchronizes the document files from two computers so that you can always have the most up-to-date files.

browser   Software that searches for, loads, and displays Web pages. Browsers display the text, graphics, sound, and even video that appear on modern Web pages.

burn-in   Characters left on older computer monitors begin to burn into the monitor, leaving their outlines even after the monitor's power is turned off.

byte   One character of storage.

cascade   The effect of neatly stacking all open windows on the screen so that each window's title bar appears.

channels   Specific areas of Web content you can subscribe to.

Channel Definition Format (CDF)   Enables existing HTML-based Web pages to incorporate push content.

chat   An online keyboard-based conversation you have with others in the chat room you've selected.

chat room   An area of interest where people can meet to discuss a particular topic. Different online services offer an assortment of chat room topics.

check box   A Windows Me control, which appears next to each item in a list, that you use to select one or more items from the list.

command button   A Windows Me control that appears and acts like a push button on the screen.

compression   The process of squeezing your disk drive so that almost 100% more data fits on a disk.

context-sensitive   The process Windows Me uses to respond to what you're doing.

Control Panel   A folder window within the My Computer window that enables you to change your computer's system settings.

coordinate   A point position on the screen defined by a coordinate pair.

coordinate pair   A pair of numbers in which the first represents the number of drawing points from the left edge of the drawing area of an image, and the second represents the number of drawing points from the top edge of the drawing area. In Paint, the coordinates appear on the status bar.

criteria   Search instructions that help you target information you need.

cross-referenced help topic   Green underlined text inside Help dialog boxes that display definitions when you click them.

cursor   A pointing device, such as the arrow that represents the mouse pointer location and the insert bar that represents the Windows Me text location. The cursor moves across the screen as you type or move the mouse.

desktop   The Windows Me screen and background.

dialog box   A window containing text and one or more screen controls that you use to issue instructions to Windows Me.

differential backup   A backup of only the files that have changed since the most recent backup. Also called an incremental backup.

direct cable connection   The connection between two computers with a cable attached to both parallel or serial ports.

disassembly instructions   Low-level instructions that describe a program's commands for the operating system.

disk operating system   The program inside memory that controls all the hardware and software interactions.

DLL file   A dynamic link library file. A shared routine used by more than one program.

docking station   A device into which you can insert some laptop computers, which instantly connects the laptop to a full-size screen, keyboard, mouse, and printer.

Dr. Watson   A system program that records system information when your PC freezes up.

drivers   Software files that often accompany hardware to tell the computer how to control the hardware when you install it.

DriveSpace   The Windows utility program that condenses the disk space so that more data fits on a disk drive.

drop-down list box   A list of choices that opens when you click the down arrow to the right of the list box.

B

email   Electronic mail service that enables you to transfer files and messages to others who have an online account.

Energy Star   A name applied to monitors that comply with environmental guidelines that limit the use of continuous power applied to your monitor.

Ethernet   A high-speed network connection.

Explorer   A powerful file-listing application that gives you both high-level and detailed descriptions of your computer system and the files on the system.

FAT (File Allocation Table)   Describes the layout of your hard disk's files and folders. FAT16 is older 16-bit technology, and FAT32 adds better support for today's large hard disks.

FilterKeys   The group of keystroke aids that includes RepeatKeys and BounceKeys.

flat-rate pricing plan   An ISP payment plan in which you get unlimited usage for the same monthly rate.

focus   The highlighted command button or control in a dialog box that Windows Me automatically selects when you press Enter.

folder   A special icon that contains other icons that are displayed when you double-click the folder icon; a grouping of related files stored under the same subdirectory.

font   A specific typestyle. Fonts have names that distinguish them from one another. Some fonts are fancy, and others are plain.

GDI   *Graphics device interface* consisting of your graphics resources.

guest   The computer that uses files and printer resources, accessed by cable, in the Direct Cable Connection Wizard.

hardcopy   Another name for printed output.

hardware tree   A collection of hardware configurations, taken from parts or all of the Registry, that your computer might require.

header   The Inbox's one-line display that shows incoming message's sender, subject, and date received.

home page   A Web site's foundational page from which all other pages connect. Often, your browser's starting page will be the home page of a Web site such as Microsoft's home page.

host   The computer that supplies the file and printer resources shared by guest computers in using the Direct Cable Connection.

host drive   A logical new drive that DriveSpace creates to hold compression information.

hotkey   The combination of an Alt keypress combined with another key that selects command buttons. The key you press with Alt is displayed with an underlined letter.

hot links (Also called links and hypertext links)   Web page items with descriptions that you can click to display other Web pages. Often, a Web page will contain several links to other sites that contain related information.

hot spot   A link you can click to see another HTML-based Web page.

HTML   *Hypertext Markup Language* is the language behind all Web pages that formats the page to look and respond the way it does.

icons   Small pictures that represent commands and programs in Windows Me.

imaging   The Windows accessory program that enables you to view and manage photographic image files.

Inbox   The Outlook Express folder that holds your incoming email.

incremental backup   See differential backup.

information overload   Confusion that occurs when too much information passes by you, as with the Internet, without proper search tools to filter out unwanted material.

infrared   Invisible light that works well for transmitting between digital devices, such as television remote controls and infrared peripherals.

installation routine   The steps needed to add programs to your PC so that they interact properly with the Windows Me environment.

Internet   A collection of networked computer systems that you can dial in to by using a modem that contains a vast assortment of information.

Internet Explorer   The Web-browsing software that Microsoft provides with Windows.

Internet Phone   A program that enables you and another to speak to each other over your Internet connection.

I/O   Input and output.

ISP   Stands for Internet service provider; the company that you use to connect to the Internet. An example of an ISP is America Online.

Java   A language that programmers use to create Web page applets.

kernel   The internal native operating system that controls the hardware and software interaction.

B

legacy   Older hardware that was designed before engineers invented the Plug-and-Play specification.

log on   The process that enables you to gain access to a networked computer.

mailing lists   Services organized by topic that you can subscribe to and receive free (usually) messages and files for the topics that interest you.

Maintenance Wizard   A Windows program that routinely monitors your system and makes changes that improve system performance.

media   The types of storage on which you store and back up data. Examples of media are a disk, a tape, and paper.

Memory Manager   Controls the various segments of memory that Windows tracks.

Microsoft Outlook   A program that comes with Microsoft Office that keeps track of contacts, to-do lists, phone calls, messages, faxes, and your appointment calendar.

mobile computing environment   The computer environment that includes laptop computers and desktop docking stations for the laptops.

modem   A device that enables your computer to communicate with other computers over the telephone.

modifier keys   The Alt, Ctrl, and Shift keys.

MouseKeys   Enables you to simulate mouse movements and clicks by using the keyboard's numeric keypad.

multitasking   The process of a computer that is running more than one program at the same time.

Mutually exclusive   Two or more Windows controls, such as option buttons, are mutually exclusive if you can set only one option at a time.

network   One or more computers that share files or hardware resources by means of a cable or wireless connection.

newsgroups   Areas of the Internet, organized by topic, that contain files and messages you can read and send.

offline printing   The process of printing to a disk file when no printer is attached to your PC.

opening a window   The process of starting a program in a window or double-clicking an icon to display a window.

option buttons   A Windows 98 control that appears next to each item in a list that you use to select one and only one item from the list.

Outbox   The Outlook Express folder that holds your outgoing email that has yet to be sent. After Outlook Express sends the message, the Sent Items folder holds a copy of the message.

Outlook Express   A Windows integrated address book and email system that handles email messages and gives you access to Internet newsgroups.

PCMCIA Cards   Also called PC cards. Small credit card-sized I/O cards that add functionality, such as modems and memory, to laptops and to some desktops.

pixel   Stands for picture element. A pixel is the smallest addressable dot on your screen.

Plug and Play   The feature that detects and automatically configures the operating system to match new hardware that you install in your computer system.

point   A measurement of 1/72 of an inch (72 points equals one inch). Most computer onscreen and printed text measures from 9–12 points in size.

Print Preview   A full-screen representation of how your document will look when you print the document.

print queue   A combination of memory and disk space that temporarily holds printed output until the printing completes.

push content   Information you've requested to be sent to your Web browser.

push technology   Web content sent directly to your PC.

Readme file   A file with last-minute changes, notes, tips, and warnings about the software you're about to install. Often a software vendor puts notes in the Readme file that didn't make it into the printed owner's manual.

read-only Web page   A Web page that contains frames and other advanced HTML code that cannot be changed.

reboot   The process of restarting your computer through the keyboard (by pressing Alt+Ctrl+Delete).

registered   A file is registered when you've associated an application with that file's extension.

Registry   A central repository of all possible information for your hardware.

B

RepeatKeys   Users can turn the repetition of keys on or off so that holding down a key does not necessarily repeat that keystroke.

running total   The calculator maintains a constant display. For example, if the display contains the value 87 and you press the plus sign and then press 5, the calculator adds the 5 to the 87 and produces the sum of 92.

ScanDisk   A program that monitors your disk for errors.

scientific calculator   A Windows calculator that supports trigonometric, scientific, and number-conversion operations.

scrap   A part of a data document you place on the Windows desktop.

screen saver   A program that waits in the background and executes only if you stop using your computer for a while. The screen saver either blanks your screen or displays moving text and graphics. Screen savers have, in the past, helped eliminate burn-in problems.

scrollbars   Windows Me controlling tools that enable you to view a window's contents more fully.

search engine   A Web-based program that looks for Internet information for you.

secure connection   An online connection with controls in place to protect the current transaction.

Sent Items folder   The Outlook Express folder that holds all messages that have been sent over the Internet from you.

separator page   A page that contains text or graphics that prints between print jobs.

SerialKeys   Enables the user to use a non-keyboard input device.

shortcut   A link (the shortcut) to a file item that takes the place of a copy and saves disk storage.

shortcut key   An underlined letter on a menu that you can combine with the Alt key to issue a menu command.

ShowSounds   Provides visual feedback on the screen when applications produce sounds.

signature   A text message that follows the email and newsgroup postings you send.

site   The location of a Web page or set of related Web pages.

SlowKeys   Windows can disregard keystrokes that are not held down for a preset time period. This aids users who often accidentally press keys.

SoundSentry Sends a visual clue when Windows beeps the speaker (in the case of warning or error message dialog boxes).

standard calculator A Windows calculator that performs common mathematical operations.

Start button The button at the left of the taskbar that displays the Windows Me cascading menu of choices. When you click the Start button, the Windows Me Start menu appears.

Start menu A Windows Me system and program menu that appears when you click the taskbar's Start button.

startup disk A disk you create from the Control Panel so that you can start your computer when your hard disk's system files get corrupted because of a hardware or software problem.

Startup logo The image you see when Windows loads.

status bar A message area at the bottom of a window that updates to show you what is happening at any given moment.

StickyKeys Enables the user to press the Shift, Alt, or Ctrl keys individually instead of having to press them with their combined keystrokes.

System Administrator The person in charge of assigning usernames and setting up new users on networked environments.

System File Checker A Windows utility program that guards against DLL file problems.

system menu A menu available on all windows that enables you to move and resize windows with the keyboard.

System Monitor A Windows program that graphically illustrates your computer's resources as you use the computer.

system resources The amount of CPU, memory, and disk space utilization consumed by Windows and the applications you are running.

T1 connection A high-speed constant Internet connection available to people who work in companies that install T1 lines.

Task Scheduler A program that runs other programs at given time periods.

taskbar The bar at the bottom of a Windows Me screen where running program icons appear along with the system clock.

B

taskbar properties menu   The menu that appears when you click the right mouse button over an empty spot on the taskbar. You can control the performance and appearance of the taskbar and Windows Me through the taskbar properties menu.

thread   A set of postings that go together, such as a question and the answer replies.

thumbnail sketch   A small representation that shows the overall layout without showing a lot of detail.

tiling   The effect of placing all open windows on the screen so that the body of each window appears next to, above, or below the other windows.

ToggleKeys   Sounds a high noise on the speaker if the CapsLock, NumLock, or ScrollLock keys are activated and a low noise when these keys are deactivated.

tool box   Paint's collection of drawing, coloring, and painting tools.

toolbar   A strip of buttons across a window that offers one-button access to common commands and tasks.

toolbar handle control   A toolbar control that lets you move areas of a toolbar left or right to make room for the items you need to see.

ToolTips   Pop-up messages that describe buttons under the mouse cursor.

TrueType   A Windows type of font that renders well in the Windows environment.

uninstallation   The process of removing installed programs from the Windows Me environment.

URL   The address of an Internet Web site. URL is an acronym for *uniform resource locator.*

user profile   The customized interface and file-access rules set up for each networked user.

utility program   A program that helps you interact with Windows Me more efficiently or effectively, as opposed to application programs that you run to do your work.

virus   A computer file that destroys other files.

wallpaper   The background graphics that appear on the Windows Me desktop.

Web   A system for formatting Internet information into readable and manageable pages of text, graphics, video, and sound.

wildcard character   A character that represents one or more characters in file and folder names.

Windows Media Player   The Windows application that plays video clips.

Windows Update   A program that automatically checks your Windows system files against an online database to ensure that they match the latest release.

wizard   A step-by-step process that leads you through the execution of a Windows Me task. Many Windows Me programs, such as Microsoft Word for Windows, include specific wizards.

WWW (Stands for Wide World Web)   See Web.

B

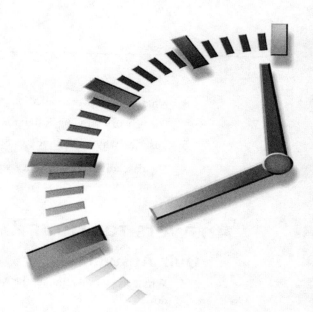

Appendix C

Answers to Quizzes

Answers for Hour 1

Quiz Answers

1. Why is the Windows screen called the *desktop*?

   The Windows desktop often mimics the way your own desktop might appear, with overlapping items that you work with.

2. *True or false*: Windows Me helps you locate files on the Internet.

   True. Although Windows Me is controlling your own machine, Windows often blurs the distinction between the files on your own disk and those online.

3. What is the difference between moving and dragging your mouse?

   When you move your mouse, the mouse pointer (also called the mouse cursor) moves; but when you drag, you point to an object on the screen, click, and hold your mouse, and then move the mouse which, in turn, drags the object along with the mouse pointer.

4. What is the artwork called on your Windows desktop?

The artwork on your desktop is called wallpaper.

5. Describe why your Windows Start menu cascades.

The cascading effect enables you to view several layers of the Windows start menu at one time.

Answers for Hour 2

Quiz Answers

1. Why can you manipulate the My Computer window as you do most other windows?

One of the strengths of Windows Millennium is its consistency. Once you learn how to manage one window, most others manage in a similar fashion.

2. What is the difference between closing and minimizing a window?

When you close a window, it goes away completely from the desktop; when you minimize a window, the window disappears from the screen but the window contents, such as a program or a data window such as My Computer, remains open and ready for use.

3. *True or false*: When you minimize a window, its taskbar button goes away.

False. The taskbar always displays a button for each active window, minimized and maximized. Only when you close a window does its button go away.

4. How does a toolbar differ from a window menu?

A window menu contains commands from which you can select; a toolbar holds buttons you click to perform tasks.

5. How do you change the size of a toolbar?

Change the size of toolbars by dragging the toolbar sliders left or right.

Answers for Hour 3

Quiz Answers

1. Which option enables you to keep the taskbar off the screen until you're ready to use the taskbar?

The Auto Hide taskbar option keeps the taskbar out of site until you point to the edge of the screen that holds the taskbar.

2. What happens when you right-click over a blank area of the taskbar?

The taskbar's Properties menu appears from which you can change the taskbar's look and actions.

3. What are the two ways to change your PC's date and time?

Double-click the time on the taskbar or right-click the taskbar and select Adjust Date/Time to display the Date/Time Properties dialog box.

4. What does it mean to *tile* windows?

Tiling windows refers to the way you organize several open windows on your screen.

5. Name one way that Window Me's single-click feature mimics Web browsing.

The Windows Me's single-click features enable you to select items, meaning that you can open windows and start programs, with a single mouse click instead of a double-click.

Answers for Hour 4

Quiz Answers

1. What are some of the items you can manage from the My Computer window?

The My Computer window enables you to manage many hardware and software settings, as well as networking and dial-up networking options.

2. Why does Windows Me offer multiple views of the same window?

Depending on the window's contents, you might need to see the items differently. For example, you might want to see a detailed view to learn the date and time that you created a file, or you might prefer to use icons to locate types of files that you want to work with.

3. How can you tell if a folder is shared?

A shared folder's icon appears with a hand holding the folder.

4. If you need to modify the way your mouse behaves, where would you go?

The Control Panel contains a Mouse icon with which you can specify your mouse's behavior.

5. Why do you need a startup disk?

When Windows Me will not start properly, or when you suspect a bad hard disk problem, the startup disk often enables your computer to start at a state in which you or another computer expert can diagnose and possibly repair the problem.

C

Answers for Hour 5

Quiz Answers

1. How does the new Windows Me thumbnail view display lists of files?

   The thumbnail view shows not only the file names and icons, but also shows a small version of the first page of the actual file contents for graphics and Web files.

2. *True or false*: You should start Internet Explorer to manage your computer's drives, folders, and files.

   False. Use Windows Explorer to manage disk elements.

3. Why would you want to display filename extensions in Windows Explorer?

   The extensions show up in all of Windows file listings when you display the extensions in Windows Explorer.

4. How can you rearrange Start menu entries with your mouse only?

   Use your mouse to drag any Start menu item to a new location on the menu.

5. How can you tell at a glance that an icon represents a shortcut and not a file?

   The shortcut's icon includes a small arrow that indicates the shortcut.

Answers for Hour 6

Quiz Answers

1. What two kinds of help does Windows Me provide?

   Windows Me offers local and online help.

2. In what ways does the Windows Me help system mimic an Internet Web browser?

   You can move back and forth between topics, displayed as Web pages, inside the help system by clicking the Back and Next buttons.

3. What is a hot spot?

   A hot spot is a link to another entry or to a program. You activate a hot spot by clicking the hot spot with your mouse.

4. If you know exactly which Windows Me topic you need help with, which is the fastest way to go directly to that topic's help information?

   Display the help system and click Index to locate specific topics.

5. *True or false*: Programs compatible with Windows Me must use the same help system format as Windows Me uses.

False. Many programs that you'll use do not use a help system that mimics the Windows Me help system. However, over time, more programs released will use help systems that mimic the one in Windows Me.

Answers for Hour 7

Quiz Answers

1. Where are HTML files often used?

   HTML files appear on the Internet.

2. *True or false*: Without a screen saver, characters can burn themselves into your monitor.

   False. Today's screens do not have the burn-in problems of older monitors.

3. What does Energy Star monitor?

   Energy Star monitors the screen and helps you save money on electricity by turning off your screen after a period of non-use.

4. How can a password-protected screen saver help secure your system?

   By protecting your screen saver with a password, you can leave your computer for a while and after the screen saver begins, your password is required to shut down the screen saver and use the computer.

5. Name two ways the Display Properties Appearance tab helps you see your Windows work better.

   The Appearance tab's dialog page enables you to activate more contrasting colors and increase the size of common Windows elements.

Answers for Hour 8

Quiz Answers

1. What Windows Control Panel option helps you install and uninstall application programs?

   The Add/Remove Programs option helps you install and uninstall applications.

C

2. What happens if you insert an application program's CD-ROM in your PC's CD-ROM drive and the application is not already installed?

   The application's installation routine usually begins automatically. If it does not, go to the Install/Uninstall tab and click Install to begin the process.

3. From where can you modify the Windows installation options?

   You can change the installed options of Windows from the Windows Setup page on the Add/Remove Programs dialog box.

4. What are some ways to uninstall application programs?

   You can use the Add/Remove Programs dialog box, select the uninstall option on the application's menu if such an option exists. You can purchase uninstallation utility programs that help you uninstall some applications, and you can manually delete files related to the program as a last resort.

5. Why would you never want to uninstall Windows Me?

   Actually, you will want to uninstall Windows Me but only when you replace Windows Me with a new version of the operating system. Until then, you might want to change Windows Me options from the Windows Setup page of the Add/Remove programs dialog box. If you dislike Windows Me and decide that you want to return to Window 98, you can uninstall Windows Me using that option in the Add/Remove Program dialog box.

Answers for Hour 9

Quiz Answers

1. Where are some of the areas Windows Me looks for data?

   Windows Me looks for data on your computer, computers networked to yours, and the Internet.

2. What is a wildcard character?

   A wildcard character is a character that stands for zero, one, or more other characters. The wildcard acts as a placeholder in searches.

3. What is the difference between the * and the ? wildcard characters?

   The * can substitute for multiple characters in the search target but the ? can substitute only for single characters.

4. *True or false*: You can execute any found programs from within the search window.

   True. A common way to execute programs buried somewhere on your disk is to make Search locate the program on one of your PC's hard disks and then execute the program from the search window.

5. What is a search engine?

A search engine is an Internet-based program that locates information over the Internet. Each search engine has its own personality and traits. You might try two or three search engines for some searches looking for a particular piece of information.

Answers for Hour 10

Quiz Answers

1. What are the two kinds of calculators available in Windows Me?

The Windows Me calculator contains a standard and a scientific calculator.

2. How does WordPad differ from Notepad and from major word processors such as Microsoft Word?

WordPad offers more powerful text-editing features than Notepad but does not contain the same rich assortment of features you find in Word, such as an outliner or spell checker.

3. A common type size is the size of *pica,* which is 12 points. What is the actual height, in inches, of pica?

Pica is 1/6th of an inch because a pica is 12 points and 72 points are an inch high.

4. How can you center text in WordPad?

The WordPad toolbar offers buttons with which you can center text. You can also use the Format, Paragraph menu.

5. How can you draw perfect squares in Paint?

Hold the Shift key while you draw a rectangle, and Paint will keep the four-sided figure a perfect square.

Answers for Hour 11

Quiz Answers

1. Where is the central Internet computer located?

No central Internet computer exists; the Internet is the composition of all computers networked using Web protocols.

2. What is a URL?

The URL is the uniform resource locator and specifies the exact location of a Web page or series of Web pages that comprise a Web site.

C

3. What is the purpose of the ISP?

The Internet service provider gives you access to the Internet.

4. How do hypertext links help you maneuver around the Web?

Hypertext links, also called hyperlinks or just links, enable you to jump back and forth between Web pages.

5. How does Internet Explorer 5.5 make searching for data familiar to you?

Internet Explorer uses the same search interface as Windows Me.

Answers for Hour 12

Quiz Answers

1. How do the windows in Windows Me mimic your Web browser?

The windows can all appear as though they were Web browsers, with toolbars and keys such as the Back key, so you can move back and forth among files.

2. What is the purpose of the Address bar on your Windows taskbar?

You can enter Web addresses and view those sites directly from your Windows Me desktop by typing those addresses in the taskbar's Address bar area.

3. *True or false*: You can only send text files, such as those that you create in Notepad, to your active desktop.

False. You can send HTML files to your active desktop meaning that you can place Web pages on your desktop.

4. What does HTML stand for?

HTML stands for Hypertext Markup Language, the language of Web pages.

5. What is the difference between wallpaper and an active component that you place on your desktop?

You can place as many components on your desktop as you have room for and resize them to fit the desktop. You can activate only one element to be used for your wallpaper at any given time.

Answers for Hour 13

Quiz Answers

1. What is the difference between a premium content online service and a regular Internet service provider?

The premium content providers offer special online services available only to their members.

2. Of the four services listed in your Online Services window, which ones are *not* a premium content online service?

   AT&T WorldNet does not provide premium content, although the service is perhaps the most accessible in the world. If you travel to other countries, you might need to use AT&T WorldNet service if you want to ensure that you have the same service both at home and abroad. Earthlink, like AT&T, also does not offer premium content, and is available in several countries. America Online and Prodigy, however, are available in numerous countries.

3. What if you don't want to provide your credit card online when you sign up for a service?

   Most online services allow you to phone in your credit card number if you prefer.

4. What is the difference between a portal and an online service?

   A portal is a Web page that provides content not unlike that of the premium content sites, but the portal's content is not subscription based; anyone with an Internet connection can access the Web page on a portal's site.

5. *True or false*: The online services allow you to create and store your own Web page on the site.

   True.

Answers for Hour 14

Quiz Answers

1. What is meant by push content?

   Push content is Internet content delivered to you, such as email or specific Web page information that appears on your desktop as active content.

2. Where does the selection of active desktop content reside?

   Microsoft has placed all active channel content on a Web page that you access through the Display dialog box.

3. Why do your Windows Me icons always appear, even when you display active desktop content?

   Without the icons, you would not be able to navigate Windows properly. Active desktop must take a back seat to Windows icons and the Start menu.

C

4. What folder can you place in a bar on your desktop for quick access to Web sites?

The Favorites folder can appear on the desktop in a bar that you use to view the pages and manage offline content.

5. When might you need offline content?

When you want to view a Web page or site without being connected to your Internet service provider while you view the page.

Answers for Hour 15

Quiz Answers

1. What is the difference between a local network and the Internet?

A network is a group of locally wired computers that share files and printers. The Internet is a loosely-connected set of computers worldwide that share files and access of a limited nature.

2. Which kind of physical network connection is easiest to install?

A wireless networking connection is by far the easiest to install.

3. Which network connection generally provides the fastest connection speed?

The Ethernet connection provides the fastest speed of the typical network connections.

4. *True or false*: If you have an Internet connection, all of the computers on the network can share the Internet connection.

True. Windows Me's Internet Connection Sharing system makes sharing a single PC's Internet connection simple.

5. What is a workgroup?

A workgroup, designated by a unique name, is a subset of computers on a network.

Answers for Hour 16

Quiz Answers

1. *True or false*: Outlook Express supports only a single email account.

False. You can set up multiple email accounts in Outlook Express.

2. What is the purpose for the Bcc field?

If you enter email addresses into the Bcc field, Outlook Express sends a copy of the email to everyone in the Bcc field, and the other recipients of your email will not know about the copy sent to the Bcc entries.

3. How do you attach files to an email letter?

Select Insert, Attachment, or click the Attachment tool on the Outlook Express toolbar to send an attached file (or files) along with your email.

4. Where does your incoming email reside?

Your incoming mail goes to the Inbox folder.

5. What is a newsgroup?

A newsgroup is a collection of recent messages sent by users interested in the newsgroup topic.

Answers for Hour 17

Quiz Answers

1. What is a legacy device?

A legacy device is a pre-Plug and Play hardware device that you must install.

2. What advantage does Plug and Play offer over legacy?

When you power-off your computer and install a Plug and Play device, your computer often recognizes that device and installs it automatically or with minimum intervention on your part.

3. What further advantage does a Plug and Play USB device provide you?

You do not need to power-off your computer to install a USB device.

4. What is a PC or PCMCIA card?

A PC or PCMCIA card is a wallet-sized circuit board that contains extra memory, a network card, a modem, a disk, or a combination of external devices.

5. What kind of port, serial or parallel, do you need to use for the Direct Cable Connection feature?

The Direct Cable Connection feature operates with either a serial or parallel cable.

C

Answers for Hour 18

Quiz Answers

1. Why would a laptop user need a docking station?

The docking station enables the laptop user to utilize full-size peripherals such as a monitor and keyboard.

2. What common upgrade method, outside of using a docking station, do laptop users use to expand their laptop's options?

Laptop users often update their systems with PC cards.

3. What utility program does Windows supply that helps you keep your laptop and desktop files in sync?

The My Briefcase application keeps your computer files in sync.

4. *True or false*: Users can use a floppy disk or a network to keep files up to date using My Briefcase.

True.

5. *True or false*: Infrared signals are visible, but can only transmit of distances of up to 1.2 miles.

False on both counts. Infrared signals are invisible and transmit only a few feet.

Answers for Hour 19

Quiz Answers

1. How does Windows know when an update is needed?

Assuming that you've turned on the automatic System Update option, Windows checks the Update Internet site every time you log onto the Internet, even if you are going to a completely different site. Windows Update checks in the background.

2. How can you keep Windows from updating automatically?

You can turn off the automatic update but you should manually check for updates regularly. People who have slow modem connections to the Internet often prefer to look for the updates manually when they can devote the entire connection time to the update download instead of sharing the connection with another Internet process.

3. What Windows program automatically runs programs for you?

The Maintenance Wizard runs programs at preset schedules.

4. How can the Maintenance Wizard help reclaim disk space for you?

The Maintenance Wizard can erase files you no longer need and defragment your disk drive.

5. *True or false*: The Maintenance Wizard runs the programs you set up as soon as you close the Maintenance Wizard window.

False. Maintenance Wizard runs the programs that you set up at the scheduled days and times you specify.

Answers for Hour 20

Quiz Answers

1. What is the difference between ScanDisk and Disk Defragmenter?

   ScanDisk checks your disk for errors and repairs simple problems while Disk Defragmenter collects fragments on your disk and gives you larger and contiguous chunks of free space.

2. *True or false*: ScanDisk can fix some disk errors.

   True. ScanDisk often finds disk problems and corrects them for you.

3. *True or false*: If you run ScanDisk regularly, you'll never have to defragment your disk.

   False. Run both ScanDisk and Disk Defragmenter to keep your disk in tip-top shape. ScanDisk cannot defragment your disk.

4. Why does your hard disk access speed improve when you regularly use Disk Defragmenter?

   When you regularly use Disk Defragmenter, your hard disk has fewer gaps between data within the same file and your PC can read and write that file much faster because the PC doesn't have to skip the holes.

5. What is a host drive?

   In DriveSpace terminology, the host drive is a virtual disk drive that does not actually exist but whose data area resides on one of your hard disks. The host disk keeps track of the bookkeeping necessary to track the compressed data on your disk.

Answers for Hour 21

Quiz Answers

1. Which program, System Monitor or Resource Meter, stays on your taskbar and monitors the memory, disk, and timing of your PC?

   The Resource Meter resides on your taskbar and keeps track of resources currently being used.

2. How can you use the System Monitor to determine if your PC needs more RAM?

   The System Monitor's graphs show you when you're running low on RAM.

3. Why does Dr. Watson provide the option of taking a system snapshot?

   If a system error occurs, Dr. Watson can compare the current state of the computer to the snapshot's and help you determine problems that might arise.

C

4. Which system program enables you to revert your computer back to a previous time?

The System Restore program enables you to restore your computer files back to a previous state.

5. What is the difference between Dr. Watson and System Restore?

Dr. Watson makes suggestions about problem sources, whereas System Restore completely restores your system to a previous state.

Answers for Hour 22

Quiz Answers

1. How can you insert an audio CD in your computer and keep the CD from playing automatically?

Hold the Shift key while your CD drive door shuts and spins up.

2. Where does the Windows Media Player get artist and track information for the CDs you insert?

The Windows Media Player gets its data from the Internet in most cases, although you can manually enter the information if you don't have Internet access or if you own a CD that doesn't happen to be found in the online database.

3. What is a skin?

A skin is a theme that controls the look of the Windows Media Player.

4. What is a playlist?

A playlist is a list of tracks that you collect and name.

5. What do you use to play video clips?

Use the Windows Media Player to play video clips.

Answers for Hour 23

Quiz Answers

1. Where does Windows Me initially send all printed output?

Windows sends all printed output to the printer subsystem's spool file before the output is actually printed.

2. If you plug in a new printer but Plug and Play does not properly detect the printer, what must you run to install the printer?

The Add Printer Wizard

3. If you have two or more printers attached to your computer, how can you direct output to a specific one?

   Select the target printer from the Print dialog box.

4. *True or false*: If you issue print commands to print ten documents in a row, you can change the order in which the documents print as long as you make the change to the documents that are still waiting to print.

   True

5. What fonts are considered to be the best Windows fonts?

   TrueType fonts

C

INDEX

SAMS
Teach Yourself
in 24 Hours

When you only have time for the answers™

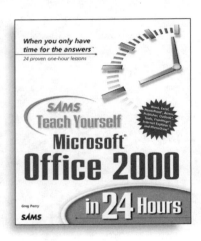

Sams Teach Yourself in 24 Hours *gets you the results you want—fast! Work through 24 proven one-hour lessons and learn everything you need to know to get up to speed quickly. It has the answers you need at a price you can afford.*

Sams Teach Yourself Microsoft Office 2000 in 24 Hours

Greg Perry
0-672-31439-8
$19.99 USA/$28.95 CAN

Other Sams Teach Yourself in 24 Hours Titles

Microsoft Excel 2000
Trudi Reisner
0-672-31445-2
$19.99 USA/$28.95 CAN

Microsoft PowerPoint 2000
Christopher Haddad
0-672-31432-0
$19.99 USA/$28.95 CAN

Microsoft Access 2000
Craig Eddy
0-672-31289-1
$19.99 USA/$28.95 CAN

Microsoft Outlook 2000
Herb Tyson
0-672-31449-5
$19.99 USA/$28.95 CAN

Microsoft FrontPage 2000
Rogers Cadenhead
0-672-31500-9
$19.99 USA/$28.95 CAN

Microsoft Word 2000
Heidi Steele
0-672-31442-8
$19.99 USA/$28.95 CAN

Microsoft Publisher 2000
Ned Snell
0-672-31572-6
$19.99 USA/$28.95 CAN

All prices are subject to change.

SAMS

www.samspublishing.com